What others are saying about this bo

"The next, possibly ultimate, plateau
- Burr Snider, **San Francisco Examin**

"The most comprehensive integrated guide to Eastern aɪ.ᴜ .... .ɴ
sexuality. Fills a major gap in sexological literature. An incredible
accomplishment. This book is destined to be a classic!"
- Bryce Britton, M.S., certified sex therapist, author, **The Love Muscle.**

"A pearl amongst the mud of the recent plethora of technical, medical
sex manuals. A virtual Aquarian age 'A to Z' compendium permeated
by awareness, sensitivity, conciseness and consciousness. The authors
have avoided goal-oriented sex, missed drowning the reader in medical-
anatomical details, and delicately escaped the hazard of engendering
performance anxiety - no mean feat! The gap for the new age reader
concerned with feeling and wholistic flow concepts of the esoteric
traditions has now unequivocally been filled by this book. I recommend
it without reservation."
- Dr. Jonn Mumford, author, **Sexual Occultism, Psychosomatic Yoga.**

"For couples who want to experience and expand their inner spiritual
awareness together and achieve a greater oneness and union, **this book
is the best available.** It not only offers a great deal of information on
the physical, spiritual and energy aspects of sexuality and lovemaking
as do other primary esoteric sexuality books, but offers much more
information on the building of intimacy, rapport and trust in the whole
relationship. With all the confusing information available today about
esoteric sexuality, sex and spirituality, tantra, sex magick, etc., **Sexual
Energy Ecstasy** clarifies the misconceptions along with offering usable
and practical suggestions. Many of these concepts I had not seen in
any book until now! It is a very good book, written in a very personal
and pragmatic style. I highly recommend it!"
- Steven Hanauer, Esoteric Sexuality columnist, **Llewellyn New Times.**

"This is **the most thorough and readable book** available on how to
improve your sex life. It brings together styles, skills and insights
from many cultures that will help loving couples maximize emotional
closeness, sensual ecstasy and personal development. It offers a
wealth of practical, detailed, easy to understand instructions. You will
journey to the dizzying heights of Tantra step by logical step."
- Elliot Tanzer, author, **Exercises for the Spiritual Body, Starviews.**

"I find this book to be well balanced, educating and instructing on the
potential of greater aliveness through conscious sexual rapport and not
exploitive of our cultural fascination with/aversion to sex. It will
teach many people how to live more fully in their bodies."
- Richard Moss, M.D., author, **The I That Is We.**

"Excellent. I love it! A practical guide to the finer arts of love-
making. I am recommending it to friends and other professionals."
- Barbara Roberts, L.C.S.W., sex therapist and sex surrogate trainer,
   Founder, Center for Social and Sensory Learning, Tarzana, CA.

SEXUAL
ENERGY
ECSTASY

A Guide to the Ultimate, Intimate Sexual Experience

By DAVID ALAN RAMSDALE
and ELLEN JO DORFMAN

PEAK SKILL

Published by Peak Skill Publishing
P.O. Box 5489
Playa Del Rey, California 90296

Edited by Lee Perry

Illustrated by Ellen Jo Dorfman and Terence Finley

Library of Congress Cataloging in Publication Data.
Ramsdale, David A.
    Sexual energy ecstasy.
    Bibliography: p.
    Includes index.
    1. Sex instruction. 2. Sexual intercourse.
3. Sensuality. I. Dorfman, Ellen J.
II. Title.
HQ31.R197   1985   613.9'6   84-60801
ISBN 0-917879-00-7 Softcover

Manufactured in the United States of America

FOREWORD

This book is a lovemaking guide of enormous practical value, and it properly belongs in the how to sex manual genre. But you will not find quick relief recipes or tables of survey statistics, as useful as such information is. Sexual Energy Ecstasy not only offers sexual knowledge, it offers sexual wisdom as well.

The authors assume that Westerners are ready to learn from tradition and other holistic sources. The skill with which they weave a tapestry of the old and new, of ancient Chinese Deer exercises and 1980's verbal affirmation techniques, may just make their assumption a reality. The authors have developed a pragmatic yet provocative holistic approach to enhancing the sexual experience for a culture that puts a higher premium on instant gratification than on well earned satisfaction.

Though many of the lovemaking styles and skills described herein will ask you to stop rushing after your "solitary crescendos," the authors are not advocates of deceleration per se. They would have us embrace the historical perspective embodied in the holistic lovemaking concept. They have presented us with a gracious gestalt of the sexual legacies of the world, including the little-known American holistic sexuality legacy, that we can understand and use and benefit from immediately.

Edmund Chein, M.D., J.D.

TABLE OF CONTENTS

LIST OF ILLUSTRATIONS

WARNING-DISCLAIMER

PROLOGUE

A SUGGESTION TO OUR READERS

This book is divided into nearly one hundred concentrated sections full of valuable practical information. While you can start here and read straight through, we also encourage you to skip to the sections that interest you most and immediately apply what you read. Do read the Prologue first, though.

HOW TO USE THIS SECTION

These concentrated messages are designed to awaken your intuitive right brain, liberating your deepest lovemaking potential. Exposure to these positive messages may also stimulate your thymus gland, making you more immune to disease and enhancing your personal energy. You may find that your ability to relate lovingly and peacefully to all aspects of life increases.

These messages are very effective and pleasing read aloud slowly just before making love or at any convenient time. Read them aloud to each other as well as to yourself. Soothing music creates an ideal background.

For maximum effect, apply the principle of linked repetition. Read your favorite messages once a day seven days in a row. Some of the messages are available on cassette with appropriate music.

These messages are ideal for private contemplation and for discussion with your consort and other friends.

You will find concentrated messages like the ones that follow here at the beginning of each section in this book.

BABY'S MIND

here is the secret:

forget everything
you ever learned about sex

from mom and dad
to Masters and Johnson
and everybody else
for
sexual maps are not the sexual territory

enjoy again
the baby's mind
not knowledgeable about sex
yet the body whole
one ecstatic organ

baby's mind
quiet and calm
yet full of life
like the meeting place
of
sand and sea
body and mind

set aside please
the familiar past
as much as you can

enjoy this adventure
of
baby's mind
in adult body

Sexual Energy Ecstasy

THE NEW SEXUAL REVOLUTION

there is a new "sexual revolution"
authentic
spontaneous
natural
free to all

not in conflict with morality
immorality
itself

unanticipated
by those
in favor of
sex without love
or
love without sex

this
new sexual revolution
is
happening now

this evolutionary revolution
simply helps make
making love
a statement of fact

enjoy now
the new intimacy
"sexualove"

a vibrant blending of sexual energy
and love
in a marriage of happy intelligence

SEXUAL ENERGY ECSTASY

making love is all about
people
becoming naked

the nakedness
begins with the body
but
it doesn't have to
end with the body
only

we can enjoy
emotional nakedness
mental nakedness
nakedness of
our innermost essence

some people rush
their lovemaking

they prefer just
physical nakedness
with maybe
a few flashes
of naked feeling
here and there

some people
feel burdened
by the flesh

they long to soar
as souls
through the sky

listen

our bodies
are not the baggage . . .
our bodies are the ticket

for example
men and women report that
while making love
their bodies seem to
contract
expand
liquefy
shake
burn
glow
melt
merge

they say
they feel like they are flying
they feel two people become one
they see brilliant colors
they feel like king and queen, noble and royal
they feel really "high"--naturally
some even say
they disappear for awhile

in other words
they experience that
making love
expands
their consciousness

these people were not on drugs
they were on sex

Sexual Energy Ecstasy
is a very safe
fantastic
natural high

sexual energy
is not a special or unique energy
in fact
sexual energy
is the energy of life
expressing itself
in sex

that's all

while you make love
you experience
this energy of life
quite intensely

while you make love
you feel more alive

while you make love
you ARE more alive

though we claim
our society is "sexually liberated"
sex and love
are still divorced

people feel a great sadness in their hearts

the revolutionary union
of sex and love
starts in your bedroom

it will be so beautiful

peace will smile
in the eyes of all of us

heaven and earth
will be in accord

MAKE LOVE, NOT WAR

SUPREME ULTIMATE (T'AI CHI)

here is the sexual secret
of the T'ai Chi symbol:

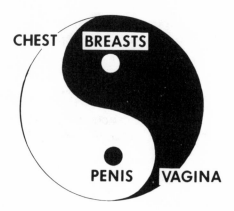

CHEST BREASTS

PENIS VAGINA

man juts out
or projects
from the bottom

woman juts out
or projects
from the top

a man's projection
is called
penis

a woman's projection
is called
breasts

a man draws in
or introjects
from the top

a woman draws in
or introjects
from the bottom

a man's introjection
has no official name
in our society

a woman's introjection
is called
vagina

T'ai Chi
reveals the complete secret
of ultimate sexual intimacy:

penis penetrates vagina
and
breasts penetrate chest

this is the mystery
of the second penetration

projection and introjection
must fuse
at both points of contact

two keys will enter
two locks
and open them

the first lock is well known
(vagina)
the second is not well known
(?)

the second lock
is the mysterious place
located
in the treasure chests
of both sexes
we call
the heart
or feeling center

I call this place
the Love spot

the key to the first lock
is well known: penis

what is the key to the second lock?

when the connections
above and below
are fused
a completed circuit
is created which takes the shape
of a luminous circle (or sphere)

I have felt and seen
this radiant circle (sphere)
and so have friends of mine

you may see and feel it too
there are many possible signs
such as an all-consuming joy

this great circle is T'ai Chi
the sexual super battery

the experience of
ultra-intimacy

relax
become the depth
you will be filled

you will be
T'ai Chi

SEXUALOVE

the slick way our society separates sex from love
sends chills down my back

this universal divorce
of the genitals and the heart
of the procreative and the creative
has left billions of
parentless children

until daddy and mommy
sex and love
get back together
the world will be unhappy

this is not a theoretical problem

have you noticed
that many short-term relationships
presume the failure of love?
that many long-term relationships
accept the failure of desire?

when adults have a sexual relationship
and choose to not share emotional intimacy
we call that a lust relationship

when adults have a love relationship
and choose to not share sexual activities
we call that a platonic relationship

when adults have a sexual relationship
and love relationship
and choose to explore and express both dimensions
as fully as possible
so that both potentials are fulfilled

what do we call that?

marriage comes to mind
but marriages in our society are
more about money and kids
than sex and love

so the label marriage
the theoretical favorite
is disqualified
by daily life

the words "in love" convey enjoyment
still
they imply a transient bond
a romantic vacation from everyday reality

this delightful peaceful harmony
of sex and love
is being lived today
by men and women around the world

since it cannot be sold
it is not advertised
it is a spontaneous fruit of human maturity

people sharing this joy
may not realize
how rare and priceless
their treasure is
it feels so natural and normal

we have no English word
that describes such a union

look in the dictionary
it is not there

your attention, please
where there was no word
there is now a word:
sexualove

CONSORT

god and goddess
play, or consort, together
in a realm made heavenly
by the harmony of their interpersonal relations

in English translations of many Eastern texts
the sexual partner lover wife husband
the intimate associate of a god or goddess
is called a consort

to consort is to unite

the dreariness of daytime duties is dissolved
by the ten thousand bodies and faces seen
in the twilight theater of uninhibiting loving

your most loving gift to each other
is to forget who you are
names faces ages beliefs histories
leave your driver's license identities
in your purse and wallet

husband and wife are often the worst offenders
love and ecstasy do not spring
from knowing another well
but from not knowing each other at all
from consorting
without constricting
from revealing nakedness
not from insulating
the soft feeling touching secret skin
in short-sighted certainties

sustain the enchantment
be forever mystified

slyly merge the thrill of meeting
the mysterious stranger
with depth of trust
developed over time

this is real sex magic

in the faces of the gods and goddesses
united beyond sadness
in the statues and pictures you will see
they are blissful with wise ignorance

when you look into the eyes of your sexualover
your consort
on some wonderful day
just after making love
or just before
say these or similar words
out loud or silently
with feeling in your heart

my sexualover
my consort
you are the mystery
you are the secrets
you are
the beginning and the end
and most important of all
you are me

even if our body-minds
never touch again
I have touched eternity
through you

by making use
of the friendly valuable gift of your body-mind
I have understood
that eternity is my only companion
my one true consort

so I insist
we are consorts
we are god and goddess
and nothing less

SOFT AND HARD

This idea
of soft and hard styles
is borrowed from the martial arts

there is soft and hard T'ai Chi Chuan
and soft and hard Kung Fu

the soft styles emphasize
circular movements
and internal
(energy-oriented)
development

the hard styles emphasize
linear movements
and external
(strength/coordination-oriented)
development

traditionally
it is taught
that both are necessary

below I give you some examples
of what I mean
by soft and hard lovemaking styles

RATING	EXAMPLE
Very Hard (VH)	*Bondage*
Hard (H)	*Studied by*
	Masters and Johnson
Hard/Soft (HS or SH)	*Tao Of Sex*
Soft (S)	*Imsak*
Very Soft (VS)	*Extrasensory Sex*

HOLISTIC LOVEMAKING

holistic, wholistic:
whole

the whole of lovemaking
includes both
hard and soft
ways
to make love

hard style lovemaking
is more familiar to most of us

it makes excellent use of abilities
like setting and achieving goals

soft style lovemaking
is new to many of us

it makes excellent use of abilities
like feeling and intuiting

information about hard style
is easy to get
in our time and place
(Masters and Johnson)

information about soft style
is not so easy to get

soft does not mean weak
soft is simply
the complement to
balance for
and opposite of
hard

this book is about soft style lovemaking
and
hard style lovemaking
with a soft touch

INTIMACY

Our word intimacy
has its roots
in a Latin word
that meant
"innermost"

people make love in order to

reproduce
relieve sexual tensions
experience pleasure
strengthen interpersonal bonds
enjoy a different state
of consciousness
(such as orgasm)
and so on

why do you make love?

what would the
ultimate experience
of sexual intimacy
be like for you?

this book describes
some great ways
to experience
intimacy
while making love

new ways
(soft ways)
to reach the
innermost place
the heart or core
of your consort
and
of yourself

life energy is simply that energy which, though invisible to the ordinary eye, makes the difference between a corpse and a living, breathing, animated person

life energy is that which vitalizes or gives life
life energy is not yet a fact of conventional science

as artists of sexualove, we don't have to wait for the scientific proof

as compassionate life-giving lovers, we can make love AS IF life energy were a fact of love (if not of life), and give and receive and share and otherwise fully feast upon a banquet of life energy over and over again with our consorts

this concept of a life energy dimension to lovemaking opens the door to a wonderful new world

life energy is a concept
that stimulates imagination, creativity, sensitivity
it is not necessary to believe in it

if life energy becomes a part of your direct experience, fine

if not, fine

to act or play AS IF is plenty good enough

change nothing . . . simply allow for the possibility of something flowing to and through and around and within and between you and your consort as you make love, something which has the essence of magic in it

. . . make room for miracles

RELAXATION-RELEASE VS. TENSION-RELIEF

relief is different from release

when I relieve myself
I am dumping
discarding
discharging
what I choose
not to contain

during lovemaking
a charge
is built up

it's not easy for me
to hold a lot of charge
when I'm very tense
because the increase in charge
increases the feeling of tension

release
on the other hand
is the letting go
of tension
without a loss of charge

I can choose to make love
in a relaxed way
or in a tense way

what I do when I make love
whether it's soft or hard
is not nearly as important
as how
I do what I do

there's a lot of emphasis nowadays
on building up sexual tension

just to get the rush of relief
that may follow

take the peak
quickly
then jump off
it's a fast ride down

today's hard styles
encourage this response

soft styles
on the other hand
encourage relaxation
and release

stay at the peak or in the valley
stay where I am and be filled by that

soft styles
are especially handy
for training
body-mind
to relax during lovemaking
and
to hold more charge

even so
one's not better
than the other

I find personally that
a balance is beautiful

I like
both hard and soft
tension and relaxation
relief and release

frankly
what I like
most of all
is having the choice

TOTAL RELAXATION ORGASM (TRO)

when somebody asked you
"Did you orgasm?"
after making love
how did you answer it?

you are an individual
orgasm
refers to quite a few
possible experiences
even for one person . . . you

for example
it is well known that
some men and women
who do not experience scientifically verifiable
physical orgasmic release
may still experience an exquisite release
of a different kind
an emotional climax

just as there are so many different ways
that people have the familiar kinds of orgasms
there are lots of wonderful things
that can happen during lovemaking
for which there are no names
in the English language

there is an enchanting uncharted world
in there (out there?)

where you go
what you see and feel
is unique to you
though you will share experiences in common
with others

here's the plan: relax totally
during lovemaking
(and I mean totally)
and see where that takes you

when you really relax
while making love
and don't make the standard orgasm your goal
you become available
to a grand new brand of
sexual peak experiences

experiences like these may happen
without making any special efforts to relax
there are many, many ways
but relaxation is a very reliable approach
the relaxation strategy enables you
to have these experiences
again and again

perhaps you have experienced such climaxes

if you have
you know
how elegant and beautiful
this whole new range of sexual opportunities is

in other words
there are other kinds of orgasms or climaxes
not yet the subject of scientific investigation

they are not just a head trip
or somebody's fantasy

they are as substantial and real as
the orgasms studied in laboratories today
only different, of course

their main features are the feeling of unity
between you and your lover
that lasts and lasts
the rushes of powerful energies and wonderful feelings
the expansion and elevation of awareness
some people describe it as "holy" or "sacred"

however
oneness can take many forms
and be of different degrees and qualities and duration

energy can flow in all directions
in many ways
with multiple effects

the good feelings can be of various kinds
and intensities and tones

the change in awareness will be drawn from the limitless
array of possiblities

these are the orgasms or climaxes of complete relaxation
these are forms of
Total Relaxation Orgasm (TRO)

Total Relaxation Orgasm (TRO)
is a new label

one form of the orgasm of complete relaxation
is described in The Joy of Sex

HONESTY

when our bodies make love
emotions and minds
and innermost we
make love too

ideally
all of me is naked
with my consort

emotions and mind
innermost me
as well as
this precious flesh

honesty in thought, word and action
apart from lovemaking
is lovemaking, too

GREED

greed is a guaranteed rip-off
greed dehumanizes

greed for bigger and better and more beautiful
sexual experiences

is still greed

greed craves for what is not
the true poverty is greed itself

the Chinese have a saying:
a man is rich who has enough

GARBAGE

during sexualove
emotional garbage will appear

it is a by-product of opening
the door
to the heart

my pain and anger and fear and doubt
will confront me
in my quest for the heart of gold

good
better sooner than later . . .
better now than then . . .
better from making love

SEX

sex
was not
is not
and never will be
the problem--
or the solution

the emphasis on sex
in our society
whether sex is put
in a negative light
or a positive light
is an attempt to fill a vast emptiness

in their heart of hearts
what people really want
is
unconditional love

unconditional love
is the
ultimate interpersonal gift

sex is a gift too
but the wrapping
makes all the difference

when the gift of sex
is wrapped in love
where is this problem of sex?

what can sex solve then?
the healing power of sex
is love in action

sex is
neither question nor answer
but magnificent gift
akin to the great gift of life itself

the emphasis on sex is by default
when the door to the heart is rusted shut
from lack of use
people are stuck in the basement

in spite of what people say
giving and receiving and being
unconditional love
is it

people look and look and look and look and
when they find themselves
they find unconditional love also
everywhere they look

the image of sex
which before was furtively molded
to meet their needs
they will now see
with clarity
is their own face

sex is beautiful
but its beauty is drawn
from the same source
as sunrise and sunset
flowers and fire
ocean and mountain
birth and death

sex can take me to that source
but I must forget to use sex
and let sex use me

I must forget to think sex
and let sex embody me

I must forget to hold onto sex
and let sex embrace me
for sex is none other than life itself

"having sex" with abandon is one thing

leaving the raft of thought
and diving into a pure ocean of sensation
swimming in a sea of self-loss
is quite another

many centuries ago
Western civilization took a wrong turn

sex was such a convenient scapegoat
it is considered so difficult to feel love
so easy to feel sex

perhaps it happened in this way:
thinking to drive out sin from the village of man
they heaped their guilts upon the goat
and drove him out
pelting him with stones and garbage

they were so proud of themselves

then the mother said
where is the goat that ate the refuse
and gave milk
and played with my son?

now is the time to get back on the road
that leads to happiness

by suppressing the sex urge
and denying its power to express love
violence is created

let us love the goat unconditionally

let us love the love that loves the goat
unconditionally

then all will be well in the village of man
and peace will prevail
once again

SEXUAL FREEDOM

one person's sexual freedom
is another person's
sexual prison

one person's sexual truth
is another person's
lie

puritan organizations sell "No On Sex!"
pornographer businesses sell "Yes On Sex!"
they would both like us to think
that we will discover our sexual integrity
by listening to them and buying their products

neither is right
only love is right

SEXSEXSEXSEXSEXSEXSEX
is
the primary creative urge at play

it cannot be legislated
it cannot be controlled
it cannot be sold

what is for sale
is only sadness

dreams die and their dead bodies are propped up
along the road and sold
to weary travelers blinded by hunger and thirst
the manicured husks of love, sex and freedom
sell the best

do not be fooled
true sexual freedom is not for sale anywhere
yet honest vulnerable consorts enjoy it for free

LOVE

We want love.   Fear is what we settle for.
Now we must face and defang fear.   Armor has served us
long enough.
Wake up!
We want love.   We push it away in order to test the
strength of it.
Love is infinitely strong and tender.
BE LOVE TO HAVE LOVE.

Cheryl Pappas, Psychotherapist
Brentwood, California

THE LOVE SPOT

In this society the focus is so great upon the genitals
that a balancing focus is needed, the Love spot.
The gland that corresponds to the Love spot is the
thymus, which is located a little higher than the Love spot
location at the center of the breastbone.   This gland can
be activated by thumping it with the fist (see Love Tap.)
The thymus plays a vital role in our body-mind's self-
defense system.   It helps maintain and distribute physical
energy.   It is the glandular equivalent of "I love myself."
To locate your Love spot precisely, draw a vertical line
with your imagination down the middle of your breastbone.
Draw another line, this one horizontal, through your
nipples.   Your Love spot lies at the intersection of these
two lines.
Draw the horizontal line a little higher if your breasts
sag.   Men as well as women may need to do this.
The Love spot corresponds to the danchu acupuncture
point (conception vessel meridian point number seventeen).
It also corresponds to the anahata heart center in yoga.
The Love spot is simply a door into a much larger room.
This door swings open easily.   Only a gentle push is
needed.

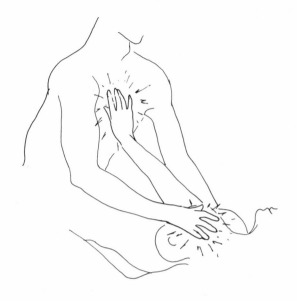

The Love Spot

The Love spot is connected to the spine. Have a friend place the palm of one hand over your Love spot and the palm of the other hand over the spine directly behind it. You may be able to feel the flow between these two special points.

This much larger room into which the Love spot opens is sometimes referred to as the heart space. Mystics who explored it thoroughly found it was so vast that they described it as being limitless. According to their reports, a brilliant light fills this vastness with warmth and joy.

Visualized, the Love spot is really more like a Love cave. Here is the core of our ability to deeply feel. On the surface are felt the more inconsequential emotions, whether they are positive, negative or neutral in content. Deep within the chest are somehow felt the soul emotions, the deep personal and interpersonal feelings that shake and move and bind sincere consorts.

Not everybody feels this place or core to this extent. Evidently, some people feel it hardly at all. You may be able to feel it extending back to the spine or, starting from the other end of the Love cave, from the spine to the chest.

The renowned Hindu sage Ramana Maharshi pointed out that when a person wants to identify themselves, they point to the center of their chest. This is, of course, where the Love spot is located. Try this as an experiment or just observe yourself in a social situation. You will find that you and others really do this.

During profound energy intimacy unusually sweet, noble, inspiring emotions may rise inward and upward from the chest. This is one sign that your Love spot has been activated through your lovemaking. There are many such signs. Positive changes in your life are the surest sign of Love spot activation.

It helps to have a specific area of the body-mind to refer to when talking about feelings of love. We talk about thinking from the head and desiring from the genitals. It seems equally sensible to talk about love from the heart and to give this love activity an equally specific location.

The ancient experts taught that to bring feeling and energy up to the Love spot and open the heart, or deep feeling center, is the big challenge. Once this is learned, energy can be directed throughout the body-mind.

What is the difference between making love and having sex? If your Love spot is stimulated, you are making love. If your Love spot is not stimulated, if your energy, feelings and attention stay below the belt, you are having sex.

You can send love energy from your Love spot to your consort at will. Try it. The more relaxed you are, the easier it will be. This skill is especially rewarding shared as a prelude to making love (see Pair Bonding.)

To feel, to breathe and to be in the present is enough to fully activate the Love spot. In fact, to just feel, just breathe and just be is more difficult than any of the styles and skills presented in this book. By working with these styles and skills, though, you will find it much easier to just feel, just breathe and just be while making love. Accomplishing this is a major act of power that will so clearly benefit your life as a whole you will be amazed.

PART 1
BODY–MIND

LIFESTYLE

lifestyle, lovestyle, mindstyle
are the same apple
viewed from different angles

slice the apple
you destroy the apple

an apple is a unity
you are a unity

eat wholesome food
exercise
take time to relax
and clear the mind

be aware of the possible side effects
of any drugs you are taking
prescription drugs included

if your personal energy
is not strong and clear
your sex life won't be
strong and clear either

if you're under lots of stress
this too may negatively affect
your sexual functioning

you can learn tricks
to attract the opposite sex

take the time instead
to learn to love

the opposite sex
will fall at your feet

you will be a natural sex magnet
of the finest kind

HOW TO BE A SEXY BODY-MIND

What is a sexy body-mind? A whole body-mind is a sexy body-mind.

A body-mind that is bursting with life and emotional warmth has an automatic sex appeal, a wholesome sex magnetism. Such a body-mind is not just a sex magnet. It is a life, love and happiness magnet, too.

Attitude is the mysterious catalyst that will bring it all together for you. How you feel about yourself in your heart of hearts, more than anything else, makes you a sexual dud or a sexy body that turns heads or, ideally, a fully magnetic body-mind that attracts life's blessings, including the sweetness of sexual contentment.

Frequently, the key obstacle to sexual fulfillment is physical and not mental at all. Sexual fulfillment is a synergy, a complex combination of many factors. A healthy, relaxed body-mind, a surplus of personal energy and a positive mental attitude are the most important ingredients.

COMPLETE BREATH

Human beings have a natural way to breathe that is complete, beautiful and instinctive. To see this natural breath in action watch a healthy naked baby.

People seem to fall into two categories: chest-breathers and belly-breathers. Chest-breathers are more self-assertive but less grounded. Belly-breathers are more grounded but need to assert self more. The balance, obviously, is found in breathing completely from both chest and belly. There are also upper lobes to the lungs which are utilized in the complete breath and other breath training methods.

Both men and women tend to hold their breath during lovemaking. When this is intentional, such as during semen stopping or in a tension position, it is rewarding. Holding the breath before or during orgasm can also be done on purpose, intensifying or otherwise altering the orgasm experience.

Unintentional holding of the breath is frequently an unwelcome expression of tension. The basic remedy is to remember to breathe completely and deeply. This may prove surprisingly difficult to do as the old habits are often very set.

Easy Complete Breath

sit erect but comfortable
in a chair
hands on your hips or in your lap

close your eyes
breathe through your nose
relax

now consciously draw the breath
deeply
so that it scrapes the back of your throat
and flows down against your spine

let it go all the way down
till it can't go any further
and it naturally flows upward
into your lower belly
and navel

when your belly is comfortably full
let the air rise
and expand your ribs
and let the chest rise

if your shoulders rise a little
that's OK. . . but only a little

you are now
full of air

you filled yourself
from bottom to top
from belly to chest

now empty yourself
from top to bottom
from chest to belly

compress the chest firmly
as if an invisible hand
pressed upon its center
(use your own hand at first
if this helps)

you may have been holding
the shoulders up
let them down if you were

exhale very slowly, very gently
no need to rush
you breathe 21,600 times a day

your belly deflates
automatically

you have just completed one complete breath

You can do the complete breath lying on your back, too. Practice this exercise just a few minutes a day. The above instructions can be read aloud to you by a friend.

The best time for breath training is early morning. You will avoid the bulk of the air pollution. Do complete breathing as soon as you get out of bed or even in bed before getting up if you prefer. If you become dizzy while doing this or any other breathing exercise, stop.

By practicing the complete breath just a few minutes a day for a few weeks, you will become aware of your current breathing habits. It would be useful for you to know, for example, that you tend to prevent the breath from being full and complete by tightening your belly during the inhale. Many people have this habit. A new awareness like this can enrich your lovemaking in unexpected ways.

Alternate nostril breathing from yoga is a good preparation for lovemaking. Swami Vivekananda of the Bihar School of Yoga in India states that five minutes of alternate nostril breathing balances the hemispheres of the brain, calming the emotions as well as improving mental functioning. Breathing through just the left nostril for five minutes or less creates a right brain dominant condition ideal for sensitive lovemaking. This has been verified, he reports, by brain wave tests.

Alternate nostril breathing is easy. Place the middle and index fingers of your right hand on the forehead. Close off the right nostril with the thumb. Inhale easily through the left nostril. Close both nostrils using the thumb and the fourth finger. Now lift the thumb but keep the left nostril closed with the fourth finger and exhale gently through the right nostril. Inhale serenely through the right nostril. Close off both nostrils. Now lift the fourth finger but keep the right nostril closed with the thumb and exhale calmly through the left nostril. You have completed one cycle. Repeat for not more than five minutes. To breathe through the left nostril continuously keep the right nostril closed off with the thumb.

Alternate nostril and left nostril only breathing are powerful. Start off with just a minute or two and gradually build up to five minutes. Yogis teach that this exercise purifies the nervous system. If you want to go more deeply into these techniques, get individualized instruction from an expert.

DEEP RELAXATION

The delights of deep relaxation just before, during or after lovemaking are so incredible that it is like entering another world. The combination of deep relaxation and lovemaking not only makes sex better, it liberates the hidden potential in lovemaking that consorts often sense but rarely tap.

It may be hard to believe that such a new wonder world is only twenty minutes away, the time it takes to go through a basic deep relaxation routine. But it is. How can such a simple act as a few minutes of strategic relaxation make such a difference?

There is an inner compulsive drive in most people that rushes them past the present in a whir of near-sighted concerns. They run through life's precious moments as if the reward for existence could only be found at the end of the race. Like a vacuum cleaner gone berserk, they swallow whatever is in their path without tasting it. Is it any wonder that the modern adult is referred to as a consumer?

The popularity of fast food restaurants testifies to this stampede for instant gratification. Food and sex habits are intimately linked and contemporary bedroom strategies reflect this connection. Modern lovers leap into bed and grab for the gusto as if their bedroom was a fast sex restaurant and their lover an instant orgasm burger in a plain white sack.

When you take the time to deeply relax, you effectively short-circuit this compulsive drive to rush through your experiences. As you do so again and again, the stranglehold on your senses loosens up more and more. Compulsion is replaced by appreciation. Your life, your love life included, is changed for the better forever.

There are many, many deep relaxation methods. These include yoga, the relaxation response, meditation, prayer, massage, self-hypnosis, biofeedback, progressive relaxation, autogenic training and floating in tanks. Find an approach that works for you and stick with it.

David has floated. Floating results in a state of deep physical relaxation and mental clarity that he finds ideal for lovemaking. Research at the Medical College of Ohio reveals that endorphins, the organic opiates in the brain, are released during floating creating a euphoric effect. Since no special training is required, you can make use of this holistic technology breakthrough right now. A practical hint: see your consort immediately after floating while your natural high is at its peak (see Appendix.)

Deep relaxation and deep meditation are not the same thing. Deep relaxation develops calmness, a prerequisite for deep meditation. This calmness makes it possible to see things more clearly. In deep meditation, this clarity is encouraged to develop as well.

This combination of calmness and clarity releases deep personal resources in a useful way. People who meditate regularly can experience an enormous acceleration in their personal growth. Just as there are many ways of achieving deep relaxation, there are many ways of approaching meditation.

Below we give three of our favorite methods. We have found cassette tapes very helpful. There's more information about cassette tapes in the Appendix.

Simple Deep Relaxation (20 Minutes)

lie on your back on a rug or blanket
with your eyes closed

your arms comfortably away from your body
your hands palms up

your legs spread comfortably apart
your feet angle outwards from the heels

if you can do so comfortably
keep the small of your back against the floor
if not
that's OK
(you can try placing some padding underneath
to see if you like the feeling of support there)

breathe through your nose
slowly and gently
do this for a few minutes

simply be aware of the passing
of air
in and out of the nostrils
nothing more

if thoughts distract you
allow them to be
and return to the breath

they will leave when they see
you are not interested in them

now
feel the weight of your body
feel the pull of gravity
surrender to it
give in to gravity

take plenty of time to do this
to surrender to gravity
it is a beautiful experience
it reconnects you with the earth

now
feel your contact with the ground
become aware of this contact exactly
between the ground and you

from the edge of your heels
to the back of your head
and every place in between
slowly discover

take plenty of time to do this
you may never have felt how the ground
supports you

feel the heaviness of your body
again

you are sinking
sinking
sinking
into the ground
it is a wonderful feeling

the ground
the earth
is caring for you
the great mother
holds you in the palm
of her loving hand

let go of your concerns
you have nothing to do
but lie here
nestled in her palm

let go
enjoy this
the feeling of being
totally and effortlessly supported

though your body is heavy
you may feel as if you are floating

this is normal
this is natural

now that you have let go
of your concerns
you are light

this ends
the simple deep relaxation

Another good way to achieve deep relaxation is to tense the muscles of the body to a count of three. Muscle groups can be tensed separately, starting with the muscles of the feet and going up to the neck or they can be tensed simultaneously. If you have time, do both and end by tensing the whole body at once.

Hold the breath while tensing and exhale while releasing. Take in a comfortable amount of breath, such as half your usual capacity. Avoid straining. This is not a contest.

After releasing the tension in each muscle group, reinforce the relaxation by affirming it. For example, after tensing and releasing your left foot, say "My left foot is relaxed, my left foot is relaxed, my left foot is relaxed. My left foot is now competely relaxed."

You can perform this total tension technique as soon as you lie down and then proceed with the above exercise for maximum results.

Whole body tensing by itself is a quick and convenient substitute. It can be very handy on those occasions when you need to relax and energize, but are unable to lie down or take the time to do the longer versions.

Simple Meditation (20 Minutes)

sit with your spine straight
in any way that is comfortable for you

if you sit in a chair
place your feet flat on the floor
do not cross them

place your hands on your thighs or knees
in a comfortable way

palms up
palms down
in a little cup
clasped together
interlaced
whatever is comfortable
will be right

the chin tends to float up
so tuck it down and in slightly
but only slightly

now begin to breathe through your nose
slowly and gently

simply be aware of the passing
of air
in and out of the nostrils
nothing more

if thoughts distract you
allow them to be
and return to the breath

they will leave when they see
you are not interested in them

simple be aware of the sensation
of air passing
in and out of the nostrils
nothing more

return gently
to this physical sensation
again

there is no need to change
the way you breathe

to be aware of the breath
as it is
is enough

there is nothing to interpret
or figure out
nothing is happening
except the breath
and it happens
by itself

there is only this physical sensation
of the air
passing in and out of your nostrils

in this moment
and this moment
and this moment

gently return to this physical sensation
as often as needed

be kind to yourself
when you stray from the breath

the breath doesn't mind

just return
come home
to the breath
you will be welcome

simply be aware of the sensation
of air passing
in and out of the nostrils
nothing more

return gently
to this physical sensation
again

there is no need to change
the way you breathe

to be aware of the breath
as it is
is enough

this ends
the simple meditation
on the breath

Come back to the everyday world slowly. Your senses
will be wide open. Enjoy the priceless private luxury of
relaxation. You earned it.

These exercises can be read out loud slowly by a friend
as you do them. You can put them on tape yourself. Or
just memorize the gist of the instructions, referring to
them before or after a relaxation or meditation session.

DRUGS THAT IMPAIR SEXUAL PERFORMANCE

A number of legal drugs that are prescribed for other needs are known to interfere with sexual functioning, including tranquilizers, sedatives, barbiturates and certain sleeping pills. Ironically, the Pill has been reported to lower sexual motivation in women. This may be a by-product of the depressive moods caused by oral contraceptive drugs. Drugs, Alcohol and Sex by Patricia Bush is an outstanding guide to the sexual side effects of drugs.

Drugs that lower high blood pressure are the most frequent culprits, followed by drugs used to treat psychological difficulties. Marijuana, alcohol, cocaine and heroin can negatively affect sexual motivation and the achievement of erection and ejaculation provided the dose is high enough and/or frequent enough. Even antihistamines can interfere with sexual capacity by blocking nerve impulses to the sex organs and glands.

Impotence is one of the most frequently reported symptoms but it is not the only possible undesirable side effect. Other reported side effects include decreased sexual desire, difficulty in sustaining erection, inability to ejaculate, painful ejaculation, uncontrolled ejaculation, retrograde (into the bladder) ejaculation, decreased sexual desire in men and women and delayed orgasm or difficulty in achieving orgasm in women.

Alcohol is one of the most flagrant offenders. It depresses the action of the central nervous system. The result can be an inability to achieve and/or maintain erection. Prolonged alcohol use is linked to male sex hormone imbalance. Caffeine and nicotine may also impair sexual function.

Women are far from exempt. Female sexual desire and performance is also negatively affected by many drugs, including those present in alcohol, tobacco, coffee, prescription drugs and illicit drugs. Because impairment of sexual performance in the female has been more difficult to demonstrate, studies have focused on other health risks.

For example, even moderate drinking during pregnancy can cause fetal alcohol syndrome resulting in facial abnormalities, low weight at birth and/or mental retardation. The caffeine present in coffee, tea, cola, chocolate and some over-the-counter headache remedies was implicated as a cause of benign breast lumps.

Women taking birth control pills are likely to be deficient in vitamin B-6, vitamin C, zinc and folic acid. Smoking and aging in combination with birth control pills increase these deficiencies.

Some drugs cause depression or mental confusion, which in turn hampers male sexual performance. Many of these drugs are also thought to reduce sexual desire or delay or make orgasm more difficult for women.

Know which drugs your consort is taking. This includes oral contraceptive drugs. Drug interactions, with alcohol especially, are yet another problem. Be sure to review in detail the possible sexual side effects of every drug you are taking with your physician. For a real eye-opening experience, go to your local public or college library and spend an hour reading about drug side effects in the **Physicians' Desk Reference (PDR)**.

If a prescribed drug is causing you trouble, ask to be placed on a different drug. Reactions are very individual. A drug that impairs sexual function in another person may not affect you and vice versa.

Some naturally occurring substances that have reputations as aphrodisiacs can exact a bitter price. Spanish fly, which is prepared from the dried wings of Cantharis vesicatoria beetles, is poisonous and has been known to kill. Yohimbine has been demonstrated in the laboratory to raise blood pressure dangerously. The danger increases when yohimbine is combined with alcohol. Jimson weed (Datura stramonium) can cause a coma lasting for days or death.

Of course, drugs are often only a contributing cause. Many of the conditions for which people take prescribed medications, such as diabetes, high blood pressure, hardening of the arteries and kidney disease, are also associated with sexual problems.

EXERCISE FOR SEXUAL WELL-BEING

No holistic approach to lovemaking would be complete that did not take exercise into account. Since we are each biochemically unique, there is no one set exercise plan for everybody. Each must work out his or her own optimum program for personal and sexual well-being. Be sure to consult with your physician regarding changes in your personal exercise habits, especially if you are just starting out on an exercise plan.

It is well established that regular moderate exercise improves health and sense of well-being. As a result, sexual health and well-being is also improved. However, it is not established that vigorous exercise programs, which do not appeal to everybody, are necessary for total sexual fulfillment.

On the other hand, sexual fulfillment is certainly less likely when some form of regular exercise is not being enjoyed. Since moderate exercise favorably alters the metabolism, exercise synergizes with food and nutritional supplements to maximize the benefits from both. Exercise has also been found to be a major factor in achieving weight loss. As an overweight condition can affect your sex life negatively, even down to the hormonal level, approximating your slim and trim ideal makes good sexual sense.

Moderate regular cardiovascular exercise such as aerobics or running may increase the sex drive in both men and women. However, heavy exercise may have the opposite effect and actually decrease sexual drive. We found that this is true for us. Men who are early ejaculators due to overexcitability, however, may benefit from frequent intensive exercise for this very reason. Other effects, such as loss of menses in female athletes, may occur. These effects are probably due to changes in sexual hormone levels and the redistribution of vital energy.

According to a July, 1982 Playboy article, lovemaking in the hard style is not a good way to get your cardiovascular exercise. Though the heart may beat 120 times a minute or more, this is the result of hormonal changes. That's the bad news. The good news is that European researchers have found that sexual arousal and activity elevate the testosterone level in the body-mind. Testosterone, of course, plays a major role in maintaining the sexual well-being of both sexes. Perhaps the best exercise for sex is sex!

There is another kind of exercise altogether. Neuroglandular exercise, which includes exercise styles such as hatha yoga and t'ai chi, is designed to balance and harmonize the human nervous system.

Neuroglandular exercise contributes to health and longevity by gently stimulating and tonifying the nervous and glandular systems of the body-mind. Many positions of hatha yoga, for example, are designed to benefit specific nerve centers or glands. Special attention to breathing further energizes and balances the whole system as well as specific parts.

The ideal exercise program includes both hard (cardiovascular) and soft (neuroglandular) exercising. The proportion of hard and soft activity, though, should be based on individual needs and preferences. There is no universal standard for you to conform with.

Exercise is holistic when the mind is concentrated in the movements of the body. It is much easier at first to focus the mind in the body during the slow, serene movements of soft style exercises. With enough training this same focus can be maintained during the fast, dynamic movements of hard style exercises.

A little holistic body-mind exercise goes a long way. It is better to exercise only as long as you can hold your concentration, even if this means exercising less. Exercising without concentration scatters the mind. Benefits are reduced. Injuries are more common.

Making love is a form of exercise. To experience holistic lovemaking, unite mind and body during this exercise, too, whatever your preferred style(s).

Bringing mind and body together in physical movement is a giant step towards total wholeness. You will begin to enjoy total health, a oneness of body and mind that leads to oneness with the universe. It is this experience of oneness that is the ultimate goal of holistic exercise.

FOOD FOR SEXUAL WELL-BEING

No holistic approach to lovemaking would be complete that did not take diet into account. Since we are each biochemically unique, there is no one set plan of diet and supplementation for everybody. Each must work out his or her own optimum nutritional program for personal and sexual well-being. Be sure to consult with your physician regarding any and all changes in sexual activities, diet and supplementation that you may want to make. If possible consult a nutritionally-oriented physician (see Appendix.) We recommend that you read **Sexual Nutrition** by Walker and Walker.

Garbage In, Garbage Out

Eat fresh wholesome foods. Eat to live. Don't live to eat. Sugar, salt, saturated fat and chemical food additives in the quantities found in the average American diet can impair your sexual performance and enjoyment. Minimize red meat, preserved meat and smoked meat consumption as these are known to contain toxic substances, stress the liver and contribute to high blood pressure, reducing sexual well-being.

Chronic sugar overindulgence can lead to hypoglycemia or diabetes, both of which can interfere with sexual functioning. A person with hypoglycemia (low blood sugar), for instance, may have a headache, experience mental confusion, feel depressed, lack energy or be subject to extreme mood swings. Due to a side effect of kidney dialysis, many diabetic men must take supplementary zinc in order to function normally sexually.

Regular indulgence in alcohol, tobacco or coffee has a price tag. For example, if you smoke you may need fifteen times as much vitamin C as somebody who doesn't in order to maintain your resistance to disease. These substances leech vitamins and minerals vital to your sexual well-being from your body-mind, making extra supplementation essential.

Ingredients in alcohol, tobacco and coffee irritate the prostate of the male. There is some evidence that sugar and salt in the large amounts consumed by many men today do also. This irritation of the prostate increases the need to ejaculate. If a man wants to try ejaculating less and recycling sexual energy, he should use these substances sparingly. Uric acid, found in red meat, may need to be avoided for the same reason. Some women who were subject to severe premenstrual stress symptoms found relief by going on a low-salt diet for ten days prior to the onset of menstruation. Eating lightly may reduce unpleasant menstrual symptoms.

Although it is not a widely accepted view, some holistic physicians believe that many of the sexual problems of both men and women suffer are the result of vicarious elimination of toxic substances in the diet via the sexual organs. Problems such as frigidity, lack of sensitivity in the breasts and vagina, non-orgasm and even the feeling of being only mechanically involved during sex may all be much more nutritionally based than most of us realize. Likewise, problems such as impotence, early ejaculation and low libidio may also be, in many cases, fundamentally nutritional. One well-known fact lends support to this theory: the taste of a man's ejaculate reflects his diet and his use of alcohol and coffee. Female vaginal secretions are also thought to reflect diet.

Many sexual problems stem from lack of energy. Orgasm, for instance, is a pleasurable release of energy. If the body-mind is struggling just to generate enough energy to survive, it will seek to avoid the energy discharge of genital orgasm. Many sexual problems which are thought to be psychological, and not just problems with orgasm, may be the result of low energy and little else. The so-called inhibited sexual desire syndrome that is common today may have a lot more to do with what's in the sex therapy candidate's kitchen than in his or her head.

The Society for Clinical Ecology (see Appendix) estimates that one out of every ten persons with a sexual dysfunction has their difficulty due to an allergy. Substances that can cause an allergic reaction range from the chlorine in drinking water to perfumes to oranges.

Supplements For Sex

You live in a toxic world. Supplement your diet with vitamins and minerals even if you are in good health now.

You need plenty of the vitamins A, the B group, C, E and P (bioflavonoids) for optimum sexual functioning. Vitamin E, for example, helps the blood carry enough oxygen to the sex organs to achieve and sustain arousal. Phosphorus, calcium and magnesium cooperate to maintain sexual desire and health. Maintaining the proper proportion of these factors as a woman approaches menopause can prevent unpleasant symptoms. Selenium helps maintain hormone response and is rarely adequate without supplementation. Manganese helps maintain normal blood flow essential to sexual performance and orgasm.

Zinc deficiency is a frequent cause of impotence in the male and a major contributing factor to prostatitis and prostate cancer. Premature ejaculation can be due to an undiagnosed case of prostatitis. Zinc deficiency in the female can result in inadequate vaginal lubrication. Unless you take a zinc supplement the likelihood that you are deficient in zinc is high since the average diet supplies only a third of the amount after assimilation recommended by the National Research Council.

Pollen and lecithin are also of great value. Pollen has helped men with prostate problems and women with menstrual problems. Cernitin flower pollen may be particularly potent. Lecithin assists in the production of sex hormones. The herbs ginseng, damiana, saw palmetto berries and kava kava reputedly help improve sexual ability. Damiana is available as a liquid tea concentrate from Herbal Kingdom. Just put 25 drops in your favorite drink. Damiana and saw palmetto together is even more potent and is said to be a reliable remedy for prostate problems. A report on a special way to prepare kava kava for maximum effect is available from us. Unlike ginseng and damiana, kava kava is not effective taken as a tea.

Many foods popularly believed to be aphrodisiacs do in fact contain vital sexual nutrients. Truffles and Chinese Bird's Nest Soup, for example, are extremely rich in phosphorous and oysters are by far the most concentrated natural source of zinc.

The nutritional factor in the achievement of orgasm by both men and women should not be overlooked. Pearson and Shaw report that taking niacin (vitamin B-6) fifteen to thirty minutes before the sex act stimulates histamine release in the body-mind. This can intensify orgasm and may help men and women achieve orgasm who could not do so before. Try 50 or 100 milligrams to start. Megadoses of magnesium orotate, potassium aspartate and bromelain have also brought success in the treatment of impotent men and preorgasmic women. The size of the doses required demand that they be administered by a holistic physician.

Vitamin B-5 (calcium pantothenate) is said to improve sexual stamina. Some sources assign vitamin B-15 (DMG) aphrodisiac properties and general sexual curative powers. Max EPA may significantly increase sexual energy and activity. SOD may also be a major sexual aid as well as an overall body booster. Aloe vera taken orally in capsules, as a liquid or gel is thought to be a sex stimulant and for some may supply quick aphrodisiac effects soon after ingestion. Pearson and Shaw report that reduced sex drive, enlarged prostate or prostatitis due to excessive prolactin in men may respond to 40 milligrams daily of GABA placed under the tongue. All of these substances are available at your local health food store.

Nutritional factors do not operate in a vacuum. They work together in complex ways to help bring about that condition we call optimum well-being, sexual and otherwise. To give an example, in order for your body to make use of supplemental vitamin C at least five other nutritional factors, including vitamin B-6, vitamin B-12 and zinc, must be present in sufficient quantities in the body. In order for so-called aphrodisiac substances and supplements to be effective, numerous other nutritional factors must also be present in your body.

Ellen's Tiger Tonic

Blend a cup of apple juice, a frozen banana, two tablespoons of protein powder, a tablespoon of lecithin and a tablespoon of honeybee pollen for a delicious protein drink. Peel the bananas and place them in an airtight container before freezing them. You can also add nuts or one tablespoon of nut butter, such as almond. Pineapple juice or milk can substitute for apple juice.

PELVIC EXPRESSION

Elvis Presley launched a musical career with his pelvis. Developing a loose yet dynamic pelvis can do the same for love lives. Pelvic awareness and freedom plays a big role in making orgasm voluntary for both men and women.

Below you will find three basic pelvic exercises. We have particularly enjoyed doing them to rock music. You can also take dance or movement classes, in fact, they are the most effective. Bioenergetics training and various bodyworking methods are also helpful. Total Orgasm by Jack Rosenberg is a valuable guide.

Wear either loose clothing or no clothing at all. Make sure you will be alone or that whoever is with you is as interested as you are. Release your self-consciousness. Play your favorite music and let it rip!

Pelvic Thrusts And Circles

pelvic thrusts
can be forward and back
with your hands on your hips
or circle to the right
then circle to the left

it works real good to
exhale as you thrust forward
or circle forward
and to inhale
as you pull backward
or circle backward

keep your weight low
really get into it. . .

do this for a bit
they're really fun to do to music

now for something even better

really cock your pelvis back
then snap it forward

combine this with an inhale
as you cock your pelvis
then exhale a sharp "Whooh"
from the mouth
as you release it forward

dispense with the hands on the hips
if you like

this coordination of
pelvis in with breath in
and pelvis out with breath out
is really valuable
especially for the guys

it may feel unnatural at first
but it isn't
this is the way the pelvis and the breath
work best together

you may find that you tend
to hold your breath
this is a common experience
when you discover this is happening
just let it go
and continue

Pelvic Bounces

Pelvic bounces are done on the bed or on the floor. Like pelvic thrusts and circles, they can evoke powerful sexual feelings. Bouncing face down may be the closest thing to being a man on top in the missionary position that a woman can experience. Bouncing face up may be the closest thing to being a woman on the bottom that a man can experience.

To bounce face down, lie on your stomach with your palms flat on either side of your chest. Breathing through your mouth, lift only your pelvis and then let it down, so that it bounces gently against the floor or bed. Breathe through the mouth, exhaling sharply with each downward impact. A standard joke in our workshops is to say to the guys "Don't do this one when you have an erection!"

To bounce face up, lie on your back with your palms flat on either side of your buttocks, knees bent. Breathing through your mouth, lift your pelvis and let it down, so that your lower back bounces gently against the floor or bed. Exhale sharply on each downward impact. You will naturally move your legs up with your pelvis, so you will feel more whole body movement with this variation.

In our experience, bouncing face up lends itself to improvisation. You can bounce without impacting the floor with your back, doing a kind of limbo dance with your back lifted from the floor.

Needless to say, don't do these exercises if you have a bad back or some problem with the pelvis. These movements are not intended to be therapeutic. They are adventures, not cures.

POMPOIR POWER

The voluntary control of the circumvaginal muscles during sexual intercourse is known as pompoir (pronounced "pahm-pour") in the Tamil language of Southern India. According to authors Herbert and Roberta Otto, a popular mythology developed around this ability in the United States between 1930 and 1950. Popular sexual literature made much of this ability under the name "snapping pussy," which in the South was called "snapping turtle."

The Arabic world had a word for a woman who had developed and mastered her circumvaginal muscles for the purpose of enhanced lovemaking. She was called kabbazah, "holder." If you've ever had the experience, from either side, then you know just how appropriate the label is. Women of Ethiopia and Southern India, in particular, enjoyed renown as kabbazahs. All in all, the skill was at one time more common the world over than it is now.

The erotic intensity of a pompoir-powered union in any style, hard or soft, should not be underestimated. Pompoir is a profound contribution to the entire spectrum of lovemaking that yields a new erotic universe. Dependence on male thrusting alone to reach the heights of erotic glory is like trying to win a foot race on one leg.

For women, this training can be a very rewarding experience. In pompoir the penis can be fondled, caressed, gripped, massaged, milked, licked, inundated and rippled as a whole or in sections. But don't think that the fun is all his. The experience is uniquely arousing and satisfying for you, too. You will be able to achieve genital orgasm more easily by clenching, especially when you combine it with breathing in or out (see Inspire Yourself.) Some women report the ability to achieve orgasm via clenching in a kind of "no hands" masturbation. Intense concentration is a major factor.

The gripping action of pompoir can be combined with thrusting, giving you the best of both worlds. Far from being an exotic trick, pompoir is the female counterpart to the male's thrusting ability. Men are born with penises but a certain amount of practice is usually needed to move a penis with real finesse. Likewise, women can train their vaginal muscles and develop the art of pompoir.

According to prominent sex therapist Bryce Britton, conditions that may be avoided or even eliminated by doing pompoir development exercises include vaginitis, cystitis, incontinence, constipation, failure to orgasm and infertility. On a personal health basis alone, do the exercises.

Using pompoir you may also experience many delights and psychological benefits as well as the health benefits mentioned above. You may become more orgasmic, experience more pleasure through your vagina, improve your sexual health, become more assertive sexually and even develop more self-confidence in daily life.

As your vaginal sensitivity increases, you may find soft style lovemaking more enjoyable. For example, lying motionless together after he has entered is more satisfying, especially with an impromptu squeeze now and then. When you do start moving, you can squeeze as he enters or leaves. As erotic intensity builds, movements of exquisite slowness bring intense pleasure (see Imsak.)

Develop the ability to mentally focus on the pleasurable feelings. Concentrate on the rich sensory details. Visualize the vaginal muscles in action. You can even relive the sensations in your imagination when you are alone. According to Britton, you are actually developing new nerve connections.

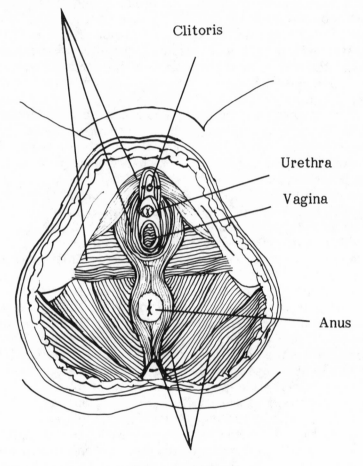

Front muscle group

Clitoris

Urethra

Vagina

Anus

Rear muscle group

The Muscles Around The Vagina

The book The G Spot gives a listing of gadgetry that may be of help, or at least make the training more interesting (see Bibliography.) The authors mention that training with a dildo (imitation rubber penis) may help.

The Love Muscle by Bryce Britton offers an outstanding pompoir training program. There is nothing mysterious about how to develop the pompoir skill. The Kegel exercises or other sexercises practiced daily for a few months will develop virtuoso ability in most women. Once the muscles have been trained, it doesn't take that much to keep them in shape.

In his smash best-seller, Everything You Always Wanted To Know About Sex But Were Afraid To Ask, David Reuben describes how the circumvaginal muscles work together to create the pompoir effect. The key to pompoir skill is there are two muscle groups involved. With all due respect to Dr. Reuben, this observation may not be a new one. Some of the ancient yoga sexercises were designed to develop these muscles groups separately first and then coordinate them.

The first group is the outer front muscles near the clitoris, which includes the bulbocavernosus, ischiocavernosus and urethral sphincter muscles. The second group is the inner rear muscles near the anus, which includes the pubococcygeus, iliococcygeus and levator ani muscles.

Together these muscle groups create the female pelvic floor. They are not so neatly separated as this analysis suggests. The pubococcygeus (pew-boh-cox-uh-jee-us), or PC, muscle stretches from the pubic bone to the coccyx. The point is that these muscle groups can be independently and voluntarily controlled.

The full pompoir action is a sequential or simultaneous contraction of the two muscle groups. The movement can be from front to back or from back to front or both at once. This action has most often been described as a milking or sucking or massaging motion.

The Ananga Ranga of Kalyana Malla describes a two-stage process that is based on the woman's ability to focus. The first stage is simple contraction and release so that a penis or other cylindrical object in the vagina will be firmly grasped. The second stage is the famed milking motion.

SEXERCISES

Sexercises is the title of a book by Edward O'Relly published almost twenty years ago. Sexercises, of course, is a combination of the words sexual and exercises. Sexercises are designed to maximize sex muscle strength and control.

Weak flabby muscles can't do their job well. Your arm muscles can do their job fairly well because you use them every day. Your sex muscles, though, are rarely used in your daily life. You use them to hold in urine or feces until you can get to the bathroom. That's about it.

The monarch of the sex muscles is the pubococcygeus (pew-boh-cox-uh-jee-us), or PC, muscle. This muscle contracts at the rate of one every .8 seconds in both sexes during orgasm. The anal muscles also contract.

The contemporary rediscovery of the value of these muscles for sexual health and pleasure is credited to a Los Angeles physician, Arnold Kegel. He developed the famed Kegel (kay-gill) exercises in the 1950's.

It may not be news that you can exercise your sex muscles. The popularity of Kegel exercises has seen to that. But do you know that the Kegel exercises are a rediscovery? Effective sexercises have been practiced in China and India for thousands of years.

The ancient experts viewed the human body-mind as a bucket full of energy with holes in the bottom where life energy leaked out. These holes are the urethral opening and anal opening and, in the woman, the vaginal opening also. It was believed that when the sex muscles were strengthened through exercise they sealed the bottom of the bucket.

The Eastern sexercises were developed in cultures that placed less emphasis on the genital orgasm. Currently, sex experts tout the development of the PC muscle and other sex muscles as a way to achieve, intensify, prolong and control genital orgasm in both sexes. Neither approach is better in itself. When less emphasis is placed on getting the orgasmic payoff, though, other personal gains, such as emotional growth or health benefits, may become more noticeable.

Whether or not you focus on having orgasms is not the real issue. That is a matter of personal style. Whatever your style, it simply makes sense to ask "How can doing sexercises contribute to my growth as a human being?"

Kegel Exercises

Before you start Kegel muscle squeezing, it is most important that you locate the exact muscle involved. The anatomical name of the so-called Kegel muscle is the pubococcygeus muscle. It's called the PC muscle by many people who work with it.

How do you find your PC muscle? It stretches between your legs, from your genitals and your anus. It is part of the pelvic floor in both sexes.

The standard way to find your PC muscle is to stop and start as you urinate. Do this several times. There--you've found it. Women need to keep the legs open wide so that the muscles in the buttocks don't add confusing signals.

Another way is to pretend you've got to hold back a bowel movement and tighten your anal muscles. Or you can try the direct approach. Insert a well-lubricated (use saliva, vegetable oil or KY jelly) finger into the anus and squeeze. You will feel the anal muscles as well as the PC.

Men should stand in front of a mirror and make their penis move up and down as they squeeze their PC muscle. Women can delicately place their index finger and/or middle finger in the vagina and squeeze. The vagina will grasp the finger(s), perhaps quite firmly. It may even push them out. The PC muscle itself can be felt in the vagina as a ribbed muscle about one and a half inches in.

Do not use any stomach muscles to do this. Once you get the hang of it, you can do "kegels" writing, reading, walking, sitting, working, watching TV, listening to music and so on.

You may find that a tightening of the muscles in the stomach and thighs happens no matter what you do at first. This is common. But after the first few days or weeks, when you've completely isolated the muscle, these extra contractions should be hardly noticeable.

Once you have definitely found the PC muscle, start with quick or short Kegel squeezes. Contract the muscle 20 times at about one a second or faster as one session. Do two sessions your first day. Gradually build up to 75 twice a day. When you can comfortably do 75 quickie Kegel contractions twice a day, add sustained or long Kegel movements.

Long Kegel squeezes are equally simple. Instead of holding the muscle contraction for a count of one, hold it for a count of three. Start with 20 of these per session, two sessions a day. Build up to 75 each session twice a day. Take your time. Avoid straining. The PC muscle is just like any other muscle. If you overdo it, it will become sore.

You will have built up to 300 reps a day. Make these focused, committed clenches. Concentrate on the physical sensations. You may find this easier if you close your eyes.

Learn to relax between contractions. Without this relaxation the muscles will not grow as quickly. Relaxation is as important to your control as contraction. If a man learns how to relax these muscles during sexual intercourse, he can last much longer.

It may help to breathe in time with your clenches or to count breaths. You may be holding your breath and not even realize it.

Some people include the bearing down maneuver in their daily work outs. The National Sex Forum's excellent SAR Guide can provide you with more details.

Men can add weight training to their Kegel practices. After achieving erection, place a small wet towel on your erect penis. Move this towel up and down. You can increase the size of the towel. Some men even use sandbag weights. A participant in one of our workshops told us that young men in his high school held locker room contests to see how many towels they could lift.

Women can work with cylindrical objects that provide resistance (see Pompoir Power.)

Use the power of visualization. The great bodybuilder Arnold Schwarzeneger worked out using precise mental images to guide the growth of his muscles. Women can see their vagina as a tunnel made up of several muscular bands that can contract or expand at will. These circular bands of muscle are seen growing in size and strength with each contraction. Men can imagine that the PC muscle is a steel cable running between their legs which they can tighten or loosen at will. The steel cable should be seen as growing thicker and stronger with each repetition.

You can affirm as you clench. With a quick Kegel clench say a short positive affirmation such as "Yes" or "Love." With a long Kegel clench you can say a longer affirmation. In the Ananga Ranga, Hindu women are advised to repeat "Kamadeva," the sacred name of the Hindu Cupid, with each clench.

Far from being the odd couple, a positive thought and a contraction pleasurably intensify each other. The experience is that you are saying the affirmation with your whole body, or that the contraction is awakening deep levels of feeling and sensitivity in your body and mind.

Don't be surprised if the exercises stimulate erotic feelings while you're doing them. This is part of the fun. Whatever your approach, develop your ability to focus your attention on your sensations and feelings for maximum results and enjoyment.

The benefits of the Kegel exercises are numerous. These include getting more in touch with your genitals and sexual feelings, improving the blood flow to these areas (which can be quite healing in itself) and making orgasm more voluntary.

Women can use it to firm up the muscles of the vagina after having a child. Kegel exercises have enabled many pre-orgasmic women to become orgasmic. Muscle control gained through Kegel contraction exercises makes genital orgasm during intercourse or masturbation more voluntary. Coordinate the Kegel clenches with breathing, visualization and concentration to maximize your control.

Men can use it to delay ejaculation. Intensely contract the PC muscle, then fully relax it. Contraction when on the verge of ejaculation or nearly so, however, is likely to bring it on.

After two months of dedicated practice, you will probably have achieved mastery over your PC muscle. If you have--you will know by the results in bed--you can maintain good muscle tone with occasional workouts. Virtuoso status, though, is achieved and maintained only by working out daily.

The Chinese Deer Exercise

In ancient Chinese health theory, the sex glands are the stove that heats the body-mind house. Feed the stove plenty of wood (keep the sex glands energized via lovemaking and/or sexercises) and the house will stay warm and full of life.

The Deer exercise is an ancient Chinese health practice. The muscles around the anus are contracted. This gives the sexual muscles a good workout. The anal contraction is coordinated with other techniques. These techniques help move the heat from the sexual stove to other parts of the body.

Actually, this distribution of energy takes place automatically. The overflow from the awakened sex glands goes up to the thymus gland. The thymus gland shunts the energy up to the thyroid, pituitary and pineal glands.

Depleted persons need to strengthen the sex glands first. After they have stoked the sexual stove by doing the Deer exercise consistently for several weeks or months, the heat will begin to spread. Energization and revitalization take place. A cold stove heats nothing, not even itself.

The Deer is part of a Chinese health system that includes two other basic exercises, the Crane and the Turtle, and a large number of other techniques. For more information about these valuable skills, refer to the Tao of Sex (Tao is pronounced "dow") section in this book and The Book of Internal Exercises by Dr. Stephen Chang.

Female Deer Exercise

First the Deer exercise is performed in two steps. Later these steps are combined. If possible, practice it right after waking up and just before going to sleep. If not, then do it once a day. Do NOT practice this exercise during menstruation or pregnancy.

Sit naked on a flat surface, such as your bedroom floor, with your legs stretched out before you. Bend either leg and place the heel in your vagina so that it presses firmly against your clitoris. If this is not comfortable, place a hard ball there instead. The pressure should be consistently firm.

Now bring your other leg close to your body. Raise the foot of this leg and rest it on the calf of the leg already in position. Insert the toes between the calf and thigh. If this is too difficult, place the other leg in front of you. Sit as erect as you can without straining. The most important thing is to be comfortable. A small pillow under the buttocks may help. If you practice yoga, you will know this position under the name siddha yoni asana.

Arousal may take place, which can be encouraged. This can be performed as an elaborate masturbation exercise, the self-stimulation caused by the heel being the first stage. But this is not at all necessary.

Rub your hands together quickly in order to create as much heat as possible. Put your hands on your breasts and feel the heat from the friction. From a central position, the Love spot, move your hands upward and outward and continue circling around gently massaging your breasts.

Maintain the pressure of the heel against your clitoris as you do a minimum of 36 circles and a maximum of 360 circles. A pleasant warm feeling may be experienced at the breasts or genitals. This is a good sign. You are accumulating energy.

This movement is said to have a healing effect on the breasts. According to Dr. Stephen Chang of San Francisco, lumps or cancer may be avoided or even eliminated. It may reduce the size of the breasts.

To perform the second part of the exercise, drop the hands to a comfortable position and maintain the gentle but firm clitoral pressure. The second part requires you to contract the vaginal and anal muscles. Hold this as long as you can without straining, then relax. Contract and relax these muscles as many times as you are can with ease. The correct feeling is that you are trying to suck air up into your vaginal and anal openings.

Take it easy. Don't overdo it. You may experience a delightful feeling that flows from the genitals to the top of the head. This indicates that your pituitary and pineal glands are being fed by the sexual glands.

After about a month, the muscle contractions will be easy to maintain. Begin combining them with the breast rubbing. The contractions can also be performed separately. Contractions may be easier to learn if the muscles involved are seen as fists which you are clenching.

Concentrate your mind on what your body is doing. You may be in the habit of letting your mind wander as you exercise. The importance of concentrating on these exercises to the limit of your ability cannot be emphasized enough.

There are many benefits claimed for this technique. Among these are the prevention or elimination of hemorrhoids, menstrual irregularities, vaginitis and infertility. It will improve sexual performance and may add healthy years to your life. You will develop pompoir power. It may increase your physical beauty and sexual and personal magnetism. However, you may first experience a cleansing phase as toxins in your system are released.

The Deer exercise is designed to naturally stimulate secretion of the hormones essential for personal and sexual well-being. As a result, you may find that you menstruate less heavily or even that your menstrual cycle ceases. According to Dr. Chang, this is a benefit as vital nutrients and energy that would otherwise be lost in the menstrual blood are reinvested.

If your menstruation stops or decreases and you want it to continue as before, simply discontinue the exercise. Missing even one day can be enough to return you to a menstruating condition.

The Male Deer Exercise

Benefical hormonal stimulation is also the goal of the male Deer exercise. Like the female Deer exercise, the male Deer exercise is first performed in two steps. Later these steps are combined. If possible, practice it right after waking up and just before going to sleep. If not, then do it once a day.

Perform this exercise naked sitting, lying down or standing. Choose the most relaxing position for you. If you practice yoga, the sitting pose siddhasana is ideal.

Rub the hands together so that friction and warmth are created. Then grasp the scrotum by itself or together with the penis with the right hand. Rest the scrotum in the center of the palm.

Circle the left palm just below the navel 81 times in either direction. A warm feeling will develop.

Then reverse the hands and the direction. If the left

hand moved in a clockwise direction before, now the right hand moves in a counter-clockwise direction. Do 81 repetitions in this direction also. You may imagine a fire building in the genitals if you like. This is step one.

To practice step two, you may remove your hands or keep them in place. Now contract your anal muscles. The correct feeling is that you are trying to suck air up into your anus. To tighten is not quite enough. Suck in with those muscles. This effectively contracts the PC muscle also.

Remember to relax completely between contractions. Hold each contraction as long as possible. Do as many of these long contractions as you comfortably can. This is step two.

After a month of practicing the anal contractions daily, if not sooner, you will have mastered the anal muscle contraction. Now combine the two exercises into one. You may feel a pleasant sensation rising up the spine or other pleasant sensations. This is the result of the anal muscles tenderly squeezing the prostate gland as they contract.

Concentrate your mind on what your body is doing. You may be in the habit of letting your mind wander as you exercise. The importance of concentrating on these exercises to the limit of your ability cannot be emphasized enough.

This exercise is said to prevent or eliminate prostate problems, hemorrhoids and infertility. It sensitizes the penis. It may even increase the size of the head of the penis. Regular performance of this exercise may improve or eliminate impotence or early ejaculation.

A man may bring himself to the verge of orgasm and then apply the exercise. Presumably, since more hormones have been rallied, this is more beneficial. But the discipline required may be prohibitive. Ejaculation is not part of the exercise. This version, however, is thought to be extremely effective in cases of impotence if performed faithfully every day for weeks or months.

Yoga Sexercises

These exercises provide the same health benefits to the genital and excretory organs. Like the Chinese exercises, they are part of a comprehensive system of body-mind exercise. They can be combined with a tranquilizing exercise like the Inverted Posture to draw the released energy up to important glands in the chest, neck and brain.

The yoga sexercises described below are the Horse Gesture, the Root Lock and the Thunderbolt Gesture. They combine controlled muscular tension with voluntary inhalation and exhalation of the breath, producing rapid results. Maximum efficiency and peak energization is achieved when the anal muscles become so strong that they can be locked in place as other more specialized exercises are performed. Unlike the Kegel and the Deer, they work the anal and urethral (urinary) sphincters separately.

Never do any yoga breathing exercise--these exercises included--to the point of discomfort, dizziness or light-headedness. Never do any yoga exercise while on drugs. Wear loose clothing or none. Practice early morning or late evening, especially if the air is bad where you live. Practice on an empty stomach. Yoga exercise on top of a natural-fiber blanket or a pad consisting of a layer of wool covered by a layer of cotton is believed to further enhance biomagnetism. For more information, please see Mumford, Janakananda Saraswati and Satyananda Saraswati in the Bibliography and Hatha Tantra Yoga in the Appendix.

The Secret Of Anal Locking

The secret of anal locking is knowing that the anal sphincter actually consists of not one but two sphincters or rings of muscle, an inner ring and an outer ring. Correct performance of the Horse Gesture and the Root Lock means that both rings are fully contracted at the same time.

The inner sphincter is located less than an inch up the rectal canal. To verify the two sphincters for yourself, begin by very slowly contracting the anus from the outside going in. You will feel some tension but not much. Continue tightening. At a place just a little higher you will suddenly experience a much more powerful contraction of the pelvic-anal floor. Now you have contracted the second inner ring. Contraction of the second inner ring is particularly important due to its multitude of nerve connections with other organs.

The Horse Gesture

The first yoga oldie but goodie we will explore is the Horse Gesture, so named because of the horse's control over the anal sphincter muscles. The Horse Gesture is step one in the yoga sexercise training program. It is practiced as a preparation for the Root Lock. During the Horse Gesture, we specifically contract and relax the anal sphincter muscles. Note the emphasis on concentration and conscious control.

Sit comfortably in a chair with your spine straight. The feeling of your buttocks against the seat of the chair provides feedback that will help you more rapidly identify and control the correct muscles. A thin pillow on the seat may also help. Place your feet flat on the floor, your hands at your thighs, palms skyward. Or lie on your back with your knees bent, your feet about a foot apart, the small of your back flat on the floor. Close your eyes and relax.

Variation One: Inhale deeply but comfortably and hold briefly. As you slowly exhale, contract the anal sphincter muscles, pulling the anus up and in.

Variation Two: Inhale deeply but comfortably and hold. Contract the anal sphincter muscles as rapidly as you can. Exhale.

Full concentration on the anal sphincters is what distinguishes the Horse Gesture from the other two exercises. Remember to focus on feeling these muscles relax after tensing them.

The Horse Gesture is said to prevent or eliminate hemorrhoids, enlarged prostate, fallen uterus and menstrual difficulties as well as develop penis thrusting power and vaginal holding power. Skill at isolated contraction of the anal sphincter rings increases control over ejaculation and enhances orgasm. Begin with five repetitions and increase as desired. Once you have clearly identified the two anal sphincter muscles for yourself, you may practice in any position as long as the spine is kept straight.

The Horse Gesture is a preparation for the Root Lock and the Thunderbolt Gesture. You may discontinue it once you have mastered the art of locking the anal sphincters. However, the tendency is to rush ahead to the Root Lock long before the Horse Gesture has been fully mastered. If you have mastered the Horse Gesture, you are able to feel a distinct locking sensation due to the increased strength of these muscles. You will have no difficulty sustaining a powerful contraction of both anal sphincters for the duration of these or similar exercises.

The Root Lock

The Root Lock also concentrates on the anal sphincters but goes on to spread the contraction through the pelvic floor. To get the feeling right, remember a time when you had to hold back feces or hold in an enema. The benefits of the Root Lock are reported to be similar to those of the Horse Geture.

Sit as before. Become aware of your anal area, first by feeling how the floor or chair below you is pushing up on your rear, then by focusing your awareness precisely at the anus. You may wish to close your eyes in order to feel the sensations more clearly.

Take in about one-half of your lung capacity. Swallow this air if it is comfortable for you to do so. As an alternative to the swallow or in combination with it, gently bend the chin down and in slightly. Concentrate on retaining the air deep within the body-mind. Now tighten your anal sphincter as much as you can. Tighten gradually. If these breath locking techniques are not comfortable for you, then just concentrate.

Now expand the contraction from the anus through the pelvic floor to the genitals. Women will feel a definite jerking or quiver in the lips of their vagina. Men will feel a definite tug on their testicles.

Still holding the breath, relax the anus, pelvic floor and genitals totally. The order is not important, but encouraging a feeling of letting go, as if the muscles were melting like butter in the sun, is important. Now sniff a small amount of fresh air and then exhale evenly and completely. You have completed one Root Lock. Follow the Root Lock with the Tunderbolt Gesture in the training program described below.

The Thunderbolt Gesture

Whereas the Horse Gesture works the anal sphincters

alone, and the Root Lock works the anal sphincters and the pelvic floor, the Thunderbolt Gesture works the urethral sphincter. To locate the urethral sphincter with accuracy, drink a quart of water. As you void the resulting flood of urine, stop and start the flow fifteen to twenty times. You have identified the urethral sphincter.

Sit as before. Place your attention at your urethral sphincter. Take in one-half of your lung capacity. Swallow this air or otherwise contain it. Now squeeze your urethral sphincter just as if you were stopping your urine flow while simultaneously drawing your "guts" (lower belly) up and in. Pretend you are trying to literally pull your sex organ up into your pelvis. Now relax the entire contraction completely.

Do as many urethral-lower abdominal contractions and relaxations as you can on a single breath. As you do so, encourage the sensations of sexual thrill to flow from the pelvis to the nerves in the spine to the brain, especially the pituitary gland region.

When you can contract no more on the one breath, relax the urethral sphincter, pelvis and lower belly completely, sniff a small amount of fresh air and then exhale evenly and completely. You have completed one Thunderbolt Gesture.

The Thunderbolt Gesture is said to benefit the urinary and genital organs as a whole. In particular, the ability to hold urine is improved. Women may find clitoral responsiveness heightened. Men may find the strength and rapidity of their erection increased.

The Thunderbolt Gesture self-check for women is as follows: Delicately put your index finger and/or your middle finger in your vagina. Do the Thunderbolt Gesture. The vagina will grasp your finger(s) lightly if not firmly.

The Thunderbolt Gesture self-check for men is as follows: Stand nude before a mirror. Do the Thunderbolt Gesture. The end of your penis will jerk or lift.

The Yoga Sexercise Training Program

Follow this training program after mastering the Horse Gesture.

Always do the Root Lock and the Thunderbolt Gesture together. Always do the Thunderbolt Gesture after the

Root Lock. Start with ten of each. Add five a week. After approximately three months time you will be doing the recommended maximum of sixty repetitions per day.

You may wish to experiment with the amount of air you take in. You may find the exercises easier to perform as well as more effective if you take in three-quarters of your lung capacity or even your maximum intake.

Relaxation is as important in these exercises as contraction. Be sure to completely relax the muscles involved at the time for release after each contraction. Relax them as completely as you tightened them before. Think "relax" at the areas involved. You will find that this not only increases your benefit but insures a stronger contraction following the relaxation phase.

These exercises are best performed as a relaxed meditation, a voyage of self-discovery, an adventure in self-love. These exercises are a form of personal creativity and self-created pleasuring that will add power and confidence to your personal life as well as your love life.

Another yoga exercise with notable sexual applications is the Stomach Lift. The Stomach Lift may alleviate constipation, menstrual problems and digestive difficulties. It is said to prevent or correct hemorrhoids, prostate enlargement, low libido, infertility, impotence and early ejaculation. Churning is the advanced form which may be performed during or after sexual intercourse to recycle sexual energy. These skills should be learned from a qualified instructor (see Appendix.)

Other Sexercises

There are many other exercises which benefit the genital and pelvic areas. These include kicks to the front, side and back and pelvic lifts, which are standard in aerobics classes. Swimming while kicking vigorously is also good. The Camel, the Locust, the Inverted Pose, the Cobra, the Forward Bend, the Shoulderstand and the Plough are taught in hatha yoga classes. Stretch and dance classes offer great pelvic-genital workouts.

SEXUAL ENERGY RECYCLING

When something is recycled, it is returned to its source. The wheel, or cycle, is turned back to the beginning of its circular path. There is some evidence that in human beings the sex energy cycle has two stages. The first stage begins in the brain, at the pituitary and pineal glands, and ends in the sex glands. The second stage of the cycle, the actual recycling step, returns energy to these master glands in the brain. This second step is often neglected.

Though health, diet, exercise, positive mental attitude and other holistic health factors play a major role, the most important single factor is your attitude towards sex energy in general and genital orgasm in particular. Positive results are achieved by developing a respectful, even reverent attitude towards this form of creative energy. Whether you are celibate or having intercourse with genital orgasm daily, your attitude will be the factor that decides if the reality of sex energy in your life will be a blessing and a blossoming. Allowing for the individual variations that must exist, your state of mind probably determines your benefit or loss via sexual thoughts, feelings and activities, orgasm especially.

Our belief is that each man and woman is a completely unique individual with his or her own sexual energy path to follow and his or her own unique orgasm needs. These change, too, as the man or woman changes. There is no right or wrong way to manage sexual energy. There is only the individual response which, ultimately, is valid precisely to the extent that it contributes to personal well-being.

It may be that how you have your sexual orgasm makes a greater difference to your personal energy than whether or not you have it. Do self-centered consorts who exploit orgasm for surface pleasure drain themselves of energy? Do ecstatically intimate vulnerable consorts gain energy via the orgasm?

Energy is spent via other kinds of sexual activity as well. It takes energy to think about sex, look for sex, worry about sex and so forth. Sexual energy can be channeled into art, business, religion, service. However you manage your sex energy, attitude is all-important.

The ancient sexercises were designed to return energy and biochemistries, including hormonal substances, from the sexual glands to the hypothalamic-pituitary region and pineal gland located in the brain. The hypothalamic-pituitary region is responsible for the stable functioning of the sex glands, adrenals and thyroid, all of which play essential roles in maintaining sexual well-being, and of the other glands as well. Although the role of the pineal gland is less clear, it is also known to play a vital role in the maintenance of sexual and emotional well-being. To return vital factors to the hypothalamic-pituitary region and the nearby pineal gland, is, in biological terms, sexual recycling.

The ancient experts believed that these sexercises contributed to healthful longevity. Is there any scientific evidence to support the belief that these practices may in fact promote healthful longevity?

Though the causes of aging and senility remain unclear, substantial evidence has accumulated indicating that it is precisely these parts of the body, the sex glands and the hypothalamic-pituitary region, which contain so-called aging clocks. Life extension researchers Pearson and Shaw, for example, report that male pattern balding is partially due to certain male hormonal activity that stays dormant until an internal clock gives the signal. The Leydig cells of the testes, which produce testosterone, are the prime suspect for the location of this particular aging clock. That male hormones must somehow be involved is shown by the fact that castration stops male pattern balding.

One prominent scientist, Dr. W. Donner Denckla, believes that the pituitary gland secretes an unidentified death hormone. It has been proven in the laboratory many times that removing the pituitary and/or hypothalamus from the brains of animals will extend their lives. Eels, mice, salmon and female octopuses have demonstrated an impressive longevity after having the pituitary or equivalent removed.

The ancient sexercises were traditionally practiced as part of a comprehensive body-mind rejuvenation program, such as the Chinese internal exercises or the Indian hatha yoga. These programs systematically stimulate the glandular and nervous systems from within.

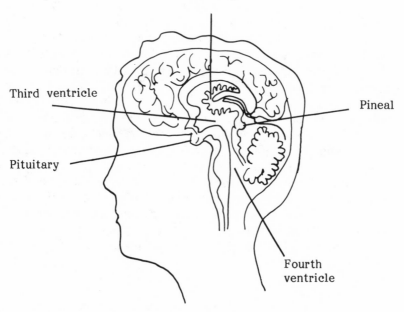

Choroid plexus

Third ventricle

Pituitary

Pineal

Fourth
ventricle

The Pituitary and Pineal Glands

Sexual stimulation releases hormonal factors that have a very positive effect. For example, rheumatologist Dr. George Ehrlich reports in an article in Forum magazine that many patients experience up to eight hours of relief from arthritic pain after sexual intercourse. To recycle sexual energy is to tune in to and purposefully take advantage of the wonderful benefits of sexual stimulation.

To experience the benefits of recycled sexual activity, be physically active. Cardiovascular exercise, such as aerobics, is recommended in lieu of these older methods if they are not practiced. Many sexual problems, especially in women, are the result of insufficient available energy. Regular exercise of any kind increases energy.

Successful sexual energy recycling is the result of self-awareness, sensitivity and positive mental attitudes. Your attitude towards orgasm is particularly important. Do you view orgasm as a convenient thrill with no purpose or value other than push-button pleasure? Or do you view the genital orgasm with a touch of awe, wonder, celebration, magic, even sacredness? Our experience has taught us that how we have orgasm largely determines aftereffects such as fatigue or energization, irritability or inner peace, dullness or inspiration.

One of the benefits of conserving the genital orgasm together can be that your desire for each other remains at a high pitch. You may enjoy a feeling of erotic intensity and intimacy unlike anything you've ever experienced before. You may feel the energy charge build up, intensifying your pleasure and sense of unity. When you do share genital orgasm, it is a special event. You can easily prove this to yourself by making love without genital release, then making love hours later or the next day. Hungry for each other, you share the erotic thrill at peak intensity.

SEXUAL ORGASM AND PERSONAL ENERGY

Modern sexologists and psychologists have performed a great service by debunking the deep negative programming associated with sexual pleasuring and orgasm. However, they may have gone too far the other way. Theories that tell us we are all the same arouse suspicion. Biochemical individuality is a fact. Why can't orgasmic individuality be a fact also?

Female Sexual Orgasm

According to some sources, such as the ancient Chinese sex experts, a woman does not ordinarily lose significant energy via her orgasm. On the contrary, she gains energy and experiences the beneficial release of healing power. However, by repeatedly making love to men with whom she is in disharmony, or by forcing the orgasm rather than allowing it, she was believed to waste her vital force. Female masturbation is consistently depicted in the erotica of the East, but male masturbation rarely is.

According to Dr. Stephen Chang, the ancient Taoists had a saying: "Man shoots to death. Woman bleeds to death." The Taoists believed that the female orgasmic energy loss is insignificant in comparison to her menstrual energy loss. In their view, female orgasm is light and dispersed, akin to vapor or mist or fine perspiration. It is an event of great natural beauty like sunset or moonrise.

When sexual orgasm is exploited for the pleasure that usually accompanies it, the law of diminishing returns sets in. Orgasms and intercourse as a whole may become less satisfying, a source of confusion, even meaningless. One solution is to abstain from sexual activity and/or sexual orgasm until physical, emotional and mental balance are regained.

Author Ashley Thirleby points out that in ancient belief there are two types of women. The first type is inclined towards and preferred multiple orgasms, although she enjoys single orgasms, too. The second type finds the achievement of multiple orgasms more challenging, even quite difficult. However, the women of the second type, even when achieving multiple orgasm, usually find that they prefer having one very intense orgasm.

Some women do find that they prefer to conserve the orgasm as well, that having an orgasm depletes them. Some women find that masturbation with orgasm seems to be accompanied by a noticeable energy loss. Possibly some women gain more when they withhold their own while taking in the energy of the male orgasm.

Consort chemistry can make a big difference. Orgasm with an incompatible consort may be fatiguing while orgasm with a harmonious consort is truly inspiring and energizing.

Several mystical schools teach the student to regard the female consort as a generator or open channel of life-giving forces. Rather than viewing the female ability to sustain arousal and repeat orgasms as a threat, males were taught that helping her build up to and sustain a state of ecstatic delirium brought both of them healing and inspiration.

The outer limits of female orgasmic ability remain uncharted. While some women are still struggling to have their first orgasm, there are women who have learned to have a genital orgasm through fantasy alone, to have orgasm when gently and rhythmically rubbed or patted on unlikely locations like the head, arm or foot, or to have genital orgasm easily during intercourse even with a hair-trigger lover who ejaculates in seconds.

What is orgasmically appropriate for women? Women should feel encouraged to find what is natural for them and do it, whether or not it conforms to a popular established norm.

Male Sexual Orgasm

In the ancient Chinese Taoist tradition (see Tao of Sex), it was believed that men experienced significant loss if they ejaculated more frequently than their age and overall state of health allowed. Books with detailed instructions were popular. Harmony between the sexes was thought to be possible only when a man was capable of prolonged, leisurely intercourse, enabling the woman to climax to her heart's desire.

For example, in **The Master of the Cave Profound** the ideal method is for a man to make love very frequently but to emit only two or three times for every ten coitions. By following this program, he is said to enjoy radiant health, long life and inner peace. In **The Secrets of the Jade Bedroom**, a less challenging plan is suggested. Vigorously healthy males at 15 can ejaculate twice a day, at 30 once a day, at 40 once in three days, at 50 once every five days, at 60 once each ten days and at 70 once in thirty days. Unhealthy males should wait twice as long between emissions, e.g., at 30 once every two days.

The ancient Chinese prescriptions, in spite of their differences, do agree on four important points: the effects of age, illness, seasons and frequent intercourse. A man fifty or older should ejaculate no more than twice per week. In times of sickness or extreme emotion a man should avoid emission. The spring/winter rule should be followed, so that during the spring the man is free to enjoy a maximum frequency of ejaculation, but during winter he should avoid ejaculating altogether, especially if it is very cold. A man should make love as often as possible.

Contemporary research does offer some support for Taoist ideas. Winnifred Berg Cutler, co-author of Menopause: A Guide for Women and the Men Who Love Them, cites several strong studies that indicate a man's sexual hormones and virility start dropping in his 20's and go downhill from there. Ms. Cutler's concern is that there are a lot of frisky fiftyish ladies out there who can't find men with enough perk to play.

The male ejaculate is high in zinc and lecithin. These substances are found in high concentration in the brain. The ejaculate may contain other valuable nutrients as well.

No less than Napoleon Hill devotes an entire chapter in his classic bestseller Think And Grow Rich to seminal conservation, praising it as one of the greatest success secrets a man has at his command.

Some contemporary men practice a kind of instinctive conservation. These men have no particular feeling for ejaculation conservation yet instinctively prefer to avoid ejaculation when they are under a great deal of stress or simply are working hard. They reserve ejaculation for the weekend and for vacations.

Perhaps each man experiences an individualized cycle of true ejaculatory need. This need would vary a great deal from man to man. Many factors could determine a man's natural cycle of ejaculatory release, including heredity, age, vitality, stress level and lifestyle.

Irritability, low self-esteem, loss of self-confidence, sensations of loss or regret, depression, resentment towards or contempt for the woman or for himself and notable energy loss are some of the signs that may follow a very inappropriate ejaculation. Less dramatic and probably much more common is a subtle but noticeable flatness in emotional tone or energy level following a forced ejaculation that may last for hours or even a day or two.

Any program of voluntary ejaculation conservation must be tailor-made. A man must listen closely to his body-mind. For example, a man on a severely toxic diet should improve his diet first (see Food For Sexual Well-Being.)

Leisurely intercourse is better for conservation. A man should usually ejaculate after vigorous lovemaking to avoid overstressing his prostate gland, especially if he approached the point of no return several times.

A man who ejaculates according to his personal cycle of ejaculatory need experiences an invigorating renewal with ejaculation. To this fully celebratory ejaculation which is based on a man being very much in touch with his body-mind we have given a different name, ejac-elation.

ULTRA-INTIMACY AND EMOTIONAL MATURITY

The advice of the Greek philosophers--know thyself--applies just as much to lovemaking as it does to work, money, food, relationships and the pursuit of personal truth and happiness.

With the increase in personal power and creativity that Sexual Energy Ecstasy lovemaking produces goes the responsibility, or response-ability, of emotional maturity. What you say and do will have a noticeably greater impact on others, especially your consort(s). You will find that you are more deeply affected by your consort(s), due to the intense bonding that takes place via Sexual Energy Ecstasy practices. Ups and downs and game playing that may have been acceptable to you before will not be acceptable to you now.

You will need to identify your key motivation(s) for participating in the sexual act. Can you be honest with yourself? Identify your motives, your emotional motives especially. Sex is very much an acting out of your most typical emotional states.

It does not matter what the motivations are, really. Just know what it is that you are after. Simply be very, very honest with yourself. Do what you like to do without harming others in the process.

Well before making love, say at a meal, air out your anxieties, frustrations, doubts, fears. Talk about your emotional garbage. Don't take it to bed with you. Emotional states are contagious and can be transmitted during sexual communication. Not only that, what you hold in when you are with your consort in the living room will hold you back from ultra-intimacy (see Glossary) in the bedroom, and perhaps hold your consort back as well.

Your attitudes and beliefs about lovemaking, the opposite sex, the same sex and orgasm also play a major role in what you will experience while making love. Ultra-intimacy and sexual relationship satisfaction in the fullest sense is a direct by-product of knowing yourself.

PART 2
FOR PLAY

COMPATIBILITY

*I will be specific
compatibility is describable
here are some of the signs*

first, and most important, peace

*when you are together
do you at times
rest in a pool
of stillness
of quiet clarity?*

*do you at times
feel a great peace
a sigh of whole-body relief?*

*do you at times
feel at home
as with your ideal
father or mother?*

*you will know
with effortless certainty*

*drink deeply that kiss
red dragons dancing
release the healing juice
quaff it well
lick your lips
roll the tongue, dragon bold
within the oral cavern*

*like a wine taster vastly experienced
you will know if the wine of that lover
is the answer to the questions
asked by your body day and night
in their saliva
the essence of their chemistry
an answer beyond the brain's devices
of fantasy and fear*

the taste of his or her skin
is like reading a life diary
written with invisible ink
electromagnetic effigy
personality is spread
like oil on a canvas
there for the discerning

a man's armpits
the nape of a woman's neck
everywhere are lighted shrines
open to worshippers whose key
they will unlock
(truly, the nose knows)

smell is the mystery
master of the brain
so direct is its message
so subtle its caress
you will be lost at once

emotional chemistry
beyond the body
revealed by the natural odor
of man and woman
a good whiff is enough
to tell bad from good
discover your destiny together
or apart
with your nose
(not your head)

never force the union
of earth and sky
dawn and dusk

the magic of the twilight
where all is possible
including happiness
and perfect balance of the sun and moon
is only found
eyes wide open

soixante-neuf, 69
completes the great circle
energy is freed
by your eagerness
take the time to taste
the lap of your lover
the code of your communion
is written in the flowing juices

electricity is king
in the land of lovers

some couples who pursue peace
sacrifice chemistry
they avoid conflict and no longer attract each other

some couples have chemistry
but no peace

better to have both

peace is the father-mother of love
chemistry is the glue of ecstasy

if you two would last
listen to the song of your secretions
your biological messengers
answer the royal request

force not the form

friend or lover
both or neither
it makes no ultimate difference

you are your true lover
you are your best friend

close your eyes and listen
with your whole body-mind

your heart is a radio
is he or she playing your tune?

IT'S THE THOUGHT THAT COUNTERS

The supreme discipline is to live in the present, even under such appealing circumstances as making love. In particular, we are distracted from the present by our thoughts as they regurgitate the past and fictionalize the future.

Beyond the curtain of everyday thinking mind lies a fabulously rich realm.

"Yum. That ice cream was good!"

Did you really experience the ice cream? The ice cream was there, were you there?

What was the texture of the ice cream? How soft or hard was it? Could you sense the coldness and crispness of the ice cream? What was the color of the ice cream? How did this color vary? How did you hold the spoon? Did you see the spoon dig into the ice cream? What kind of sound did the spoon make as it penetrated the ice cream? What did the very first bite of ice cream taste like? The second bite? The last bite? As the last bite of ice cream taste faded away, what taste replaced it?

Everyday thinking mind creates mirages. We think that we are eating the ice cream. In fact, we are eating our thoughts about it. Go back to the last time you ate ice cream. Chances are you missed the ice cream's uniqueness. What you experienced was mostly replays of your ice cream memories and displays of your ice cream expectations.

We usually experience our experiences through the screen of our thoughts. Unless we pay very close attention, the artificiality of experiencing through a screen of thoughts goes unnoticed.

We think thousands of thoughts in the time it takes to consume a bowl of ice cream. Most of them have nothing at all to do with ice cream. Our minds wander in the nowhere lands of annihilated past and fantasized future. The purity of ice cream experience, of sense experience in general, is polluted by irrelevant, irreverent thoughts.

Exactly the same problem is encountered in lovemaking. For most people, though, lovemaking is more important than eating ice cream.

How to make love in the sensory present?

How to make love in the realm beyond the curtain of thought?

Don't eliminate thought. Shift the mind into neutral gear. Just like a few fluffy white clouds drifting in the brilliant blue of the summer sky, occasional thoughts float in and out. This tranquillity is most easily developed through deep relaxation before or during lovemaking.

Thoughts are a natural phenomenon, like clouds. The clouds in the sky of mind are no more a problem for us than the clouds in the sky of earth are a problem for the sun.

Sometimes, the clouds of thought mass together, creating a thought storm. What did you do that last time you were caught in a thunderstorm? You probably sat down and waited it out.

A thought about impotence or about not having an orgasm is not a problem. Only when impotence thoughts or no orgasm thoughts mass together and make a thought storm do they seem to become a problem. Then the sky of the mind looks troubled and dark. The thunder of anger, the cold wind of fear, the snow of loneliness, the hail of doubt make their appearance.

Sometimes, in spite of our best efforts, thought storms appear. This is fine. A thunderstorm viewed from a good vantage point is a beautiful, awe-inspiring show. Thought storms are no different. All it takes is a good seat a safe distance away. Then we will enjoy the free show.

When a thought wants to come in, don't argue with it. Let it in. If a thought wants to stay awhile, let it stay. If it wants to leave, let it leave. Thoughts appear, persist and disappear. Thought storms appear, persist and disappear. That is their nature.

MAKING LOVE IS A TOUCHING EXPERIENCE

To stay in the sensory present as you make love, remain aware of change.

Totally be at the points of contact between skin and skin. Be one, literally, with the sensations themselves. Stay at the intersections of sensory greeting.

Sensory moments begin, grow, peak, fade and end, only to be replaced by new sensory moments. Make love in the shadow zone of endless physical transition. Make love in the raw reality of mindless bodyfullness. Leave the sensation of self behind.

Drink the unfiltered sense experience. Add nothing to the raw sense data. Be sensitive to the kaleidoscope of changing details at the interception of flesh by flesh. Allow the smouldering sea of sense activity to sweep interpreting thought and self-consciousness away.

When touching or being touched, make that touch fill all awareness in that moment. That touch, or, more precisely, the field of sensitivity where toucher and touched intercept to create touching, is the total universe. There is found an infinity of sensory nuance. When the curtain of thought is drawn aside, this is the natural way of experiencing the senses.

At the cutting edge of sensation lies a realm of indescribable beauty that has no equivalent in the mind. Words cannot describe it. The everyday thinking mind cannot comprehend it. It is a mystery beyond belief. It is the miracle of direct experience. Reach out. Be all that you can be by being only what is. Be the sensory present reality itself. Go beyond touching and being touched. Go beyond confining labels. Be the touching itself.

Just touch.

Here are the instructions in their entirety for discovering the ultimate fulfillment of making love: Making love is a touching experience.

FOR PLAY

The act of making love has a beginning, a middle and an end. For Play is about the beginning, Awakening the middle and Climax the end. These correspond roughly to the phases in the Masters and Johnson model of sexual intercourse, excitation, plateau and orgasm/resolution.

You have seen "for play" spelled foreplay. In that spelling, it refers to erotic stimulation with a very definite goal: genital union. Playing with each other with that goal in mind is fine, but it is not the only way to play.

Instead of playing for orgasmic payoff, play for play.

Duplicate the mood and energy of happy children at play in your lovemaking.

If genital union didn't exist at all, how would you behave? Touch itself would be the climax.

Instead of you deciding when it is time for foreplay to end and genital intercourse to begin, let your genitals decide. Act as if the penis and vagina have minds and wills of their own. Rest penis on vagina. Let them make their own introductions. If they decide to go ahead, then you will. But if they don't, you won't. This "as if" game can inject a startling zest and freshness into your lovemaking, but you must stick to the rules.

There are simple skills that smooth out the rough spots in your relating, ways to set up your lovemaking environment, strategies to draw out the best in a person without taking advantage of them. This is relaxed, intelligent, skillful effort. This, too, is for play.

When you were a teenager, did just a touch or a look from the object of your desire drive you crazy? To return to this whole-body total eroticism that starts with a glance and builds and builds and builds is for play, too.

You are not giving up anything, you see. You are taking in everything, and giving yourself the time and place and space in which to enjoy it.

You are just having fun--right now--playing for the play of it.

ACULOVING MASSAGE

Acupressure or shiatsu massage before lovemaking is one of the most precious secrets of the Oriental lovecraft. Oriental courtesans have offered this service with great success for many centuries. These women were trained in the art of giving a whole body acupressure massage. Before his massage, the man was completely bathed and scrubbed by the courtesan. Some of the most prized courtesans were also trained in pompoir (see Kabbazah.)

The arms and hands are extensions of the heart. You can send love through your hands at will (see Love Spot.)

Here is a technique to use before making love that is very effective. According to acupuncture theory, healing energy is stimulated throughout the body-mind, and deep relaxation is created. The internal organs are also massaged; the person feels relaxed and renewed inside and out.

Acupressure expert Michael Blate, director of the G-Jo Institute in Florida (see Appendix), suggests massage of both hands or both feet. This takes about twenty minutes. Now allow your consort just to be in that relaxation, even if they seem lost to the world. Within thirty minutes they return, refreshed, revitalized and, more than likely, wonderfully ready to make love.

If your consort is tense or unresponsive, try this massage. Also, the first time you make love to a new person, try this massage. Remember, you are giving a deeply relaxing, healing experience, not just trying to seduce someone. It will be obvious whether you are doing it from your heart, as a gift, or from your head, as a strategy. Odds are that if he/she does want to make love to you, this approach will bring that, and with the best possible results.

If you are massaging the hands, massage both hands entirely, including the wrist. Do one entirely, then do the other. Do the palm, the back of the hand, the fingers, between the fingers, everything. If you are massaging the feet, massage both feet entirely, including the heel, the area just below the ankle and the Achilles tendon. Urinary-genital organ stimulation points are located at these spots.

For optimum results, use this method. Press as deeply and firmly as you can without causing pain. Knead each tiny bit of surface area, penetrating deep below the skin. The first few times you do this it may be helpful to imagine a grid of tiny squares over the hand or foot, creating a multitude of minute massage areas. Take ten minutes or more on each hand or foot. Knead each zone thoroughly.

The face, ears and sexual organs are also rich with nerve reflex points. Massage of these areas benefits the entire body. Ear massage is a technical skill beyond the scope of this book. However, many people find a gentle massage of the upper inside halves of the ears invigorating. Avoid the ear canal, of course. Genital acupressure massage is discussed in Tao of Sex.

Facial massage releases the mask of facial tension that tends to develop in tense social interactions. Dropping this facial mask may noticeably increase social and sexual responsiveness. Men who tend to ejaculate early and women who have difficulty reaching orgasm during intercourse especially benefit from letting go of the facial tension mask.

Before beginning the facial massage, ask him/her to clench their teeth and scrunch their face towards the tip of their nose in a tight ball. Concentrating with eyes closed on the tip of the nose, they hold for a count of five, then release. Rub the cheeks, nose and forehead gently up and out to the side with the fingers or palm. Upward motion counters the downward pull of gravity, aging and negative emotions. The temples respond well to a gentle circular motion. Knead the scalp and the base of the skull to release additional easefulness and energy.

Conclude by firmly but very gently pressing the depression at the top and towards the rear of the skull (the fontanelle) for a count of three. This powerful acupressure point releases the face, head and neck at the same time. Caution is advised when stimulating this last point. Please review the cautions regarding the use of acupressure points given below in the Aculoving Massage mini-guide.

A quick way to evoke a calm energy in your consort is the big toe massage. This can be performed by using the mouth as if the big toe were a man's penis. We call this big toe fellatio. Acting out the fantasy that the big toe is a penis is part of the fun, especially when a man fellates a woman's big toes.

The sensations may be felt all through the body, right to the top of the head. The stimulation may feel incredibly good, so good, in fact, that the sensations could be compared to a continuous low-grade orgasm.

Special stimulation points for the pituitary and pineal glands are located in the big toe. The pituitary stimulation point will be found in the middle of the big toe pad. The pineal stimulation point is slightly up and to the right of the pituitary point. The location of these points varies from one individual to another. Massage these points gently with a circular movement with your thumbs. Positive identification is found by pressing firmly in the general location. You may use the eraser end of a pencil. The precise locations will feel tender to the recipient.

Pituitary stimulation harmonizes the physical dimension of sexual response; pineal stimulation harmonizes the emotional dimension. A thorough big toe massage evokes a subtle aliveness in the whole body. Five minutes on each big toe is a complete massage in itself. Be sure to do both big toes.

Of course, you can suck on and massage all ten toes. Tired of oral genital sex, i.e., 69? Suck on each other's toes at the same time and enjoy "20."

We like to use oil for manual massage of the hands, feet, big toes or the whole body. Our favorite oils are almond, coconut, jojoba and avocado oils. We avoid petroleum-based oils. Jojoba and other natural vegetable oils are handy genital lubrication aids. We prefer vitamin E cream or aloe vera cream for facial massage.

An ancient tradition that we would like to see revived is washing feet. Most of us would like a full body massage before lovemaking but that takes a lot of time. Or it may feel like too much work. Washing feet requires very little effort and can be performed fully clothed (minus shoes and socks, of course) as a preliminary to lovemaking or as a caring gesture that is complete by itself.

Bathe the feet first in warm water. After drying them off thoroughly, anoint the feet with oil or cream. There are special foot oils, though. Our favorite for the feet is

Sunshine Herbal Foot Lotion with wintergreen oil. Gently rub the oil or lotion in. Allow the warm feelings that you have for this person to flow out through your hands. Exchange roles if convenient.

Also very relaxing is a warm towel over the face, as any man who has had a shave the old way knows. A warm wet towel over the lower back (the kidney area) may stir the libido as well as relax. You can follow up the foot washing with a foot massage.

The psychological implications for some people of washing the feet of another person may include respect, humility and service. Washing the feet can be a part of a ceremonial preparation for making love (see Doing It Rite.)

But these implications don't have to be explored. The tender sensuousness of the experience makes it one not to be missed. Next time, instead of or along with giving them a bath or massage, wash their feet. Washing feet is relaxing and energizing for both the giver and the receiver, which makes it an ideal preparation for making love.

Everybody has personalized tension stash areas. They may not be located near a standard erotic zone. For example, people stash tension in the jaw, neck, shoulder, upper and lower back, thigh and calf. Find the secret tension hideaways and you may not only guarantee a great time together, you may have made a friend for life. It's better to be a little too gentle than too firm when dealing with potentially painful areas of the body like these tension stash spots. You can find these areas out by asking them where they store tension and/or by gentle probing as you massage them.

Below we describe more massage movements that make use of quite a few sexual acupressure points. Acupressure to some of these points can be self-administered. Therapeutic applications, such as dealing with persistent impotence or frigidity, are beyond the scope of this book.

For a practical guide to acupressure self-help, see J.V. Cerney's Acupuncture Without Needles. Also useful are Shiatsu by Tokujiro Namikoshi, The G-Jo Institute Sexual Pleasure Enhancement Program and Sexual Secrets by Douglas and Slinger. An excellent guide to friendly massage is The Massage Book by George Downing, which includes good anatomy illustrations.

Some aculoving areas are effective for just men or women, but most are effective for both. Some, like the buttocks, the nipple tips, anal and kidney areas, can be conveniently stimulated while making love (see Oriental Arousal.) Remember, you are giving a friendly erotic massage, not a therapeutic treatment. The ideal style is gentle and playful. Just the same, you may achieve some startling results. The person receiving the massage can inhale deeply just before their consort begins a technique, then exhale as the pressure is applied.

Repeat each technique several times before moving on to another one. It is better to do fewer with more sensitivity. Unless you are incorporating these aculoving areas into a leisurely whole-body massage, stimulate just a few areas thoroughly.

The back or feet are good places to start. Being touched there feels safe to most people. Finish with the medulla oblongata point. Since the effects of aculoving massage may take a few hours to reach their peak, experiment with timing the massage for maximum benefit.

A regular massage is erotically effective because it relaxes your consort. An erotic massage, which arouses your consort, is effective because it stimulates your consort. Match your massage style to your consort's needs at that moment.

Acupressure is a powerful tool to be used with discretion. Do NOT press on an area that is healing or scarred. If you have any of the following conditions you should NOT receive acupressure stimulation. (1) If you are pregnant. (2) If you have a chronic heart problem, particularly if you have a Pacemaker. (3) If you are heavily intoxicated with alcohol or other drug(s), including any powerful prescription drug you may be taking.

This mini-guide starts with a point at the base of the skull and ends with the soles of the feet. The location, a massage technique, the benefit and whether the technique is designed for men, women or both are described for each aculoving area. Here is an example.

ACUPLACE: medulla oblongata
LOCATION: hollow in the base of the skull
TECHNIQUE: press with thumbs or rotate middle fingers
BENEFIT: energizes entire body   SEX: (M/F)

medulla oblongata (see above)

thyroid gland
in front of neck above clavicle on either side
firm pressure with ball of thumb
increases sexual response   (F)

wrists
entire wrist, especially down from the thumb
gentle massaging motion
improves sexual response   (M/F)

thymus gland
valley between the breasts on either side
above and below Love spot
gentle massaging motion
emotionally and sexually warming   (F)

breastbone
bony region between breasts
gentle massaging motion
improves sexual ability   (M)

nipple tips
delicate feathery touch
increases sexual desires   (M/F)

adrenal glands
just above kidneys (between thoracic vertabrae 11 & 12)
press gently but firmly with your fists on both sides
right above where the adrenal glands are located
under the lowest ribs
increases sexual stamina   (F)   uplifts emotions   (M)

liver
under right rib cage
press fingertips of both hands under edge of right rib cage
liver, anger, sex connection improves sexual function   (M)

solar plexus
pit of stomach right below breastbone
press with fingertips of both hands
delays ejaculation   (M); boosts & balances sex drive   (F)

navel
press with fingertip
relieves loss of sex drive due to congestion (M/F)

lower back area
kidney region
create friction by moving palms in circles, then go up
both sides of spine--repeat as you intensify friction
increases sexual desire and relaxes (M/F)

lumbar
the five lumbar vertabrae just above the sacrum
press thumbs in space on each side of spinal column
between each lumbar vertabrae
stimulates internal organs and sexual drive (M/F)

sea of energy
about two inches below navel on midline
press with fingers
directly stimulates sex glands, increases energy (M/F)

pubic
along top edge of pubic hair line
gentle massaging motion
stimulates sex drive (M/F)

symphysis pubic
a little below pubic hair line where pubic bones meet
five points, one midline with the navel and two on each side
one and two inches from midline to left and right
rotate finger or thumb or gently rub
relieves constipation, stimulates bladder and sex drive
increases testicle sensitivity (M)

sacrum
inverted triangle of bone at base of spine
fingertip or thumb pressure
delays ejaculation (M) boosts & balances sex drive (F)

gluteal fold
where the buttocks and legs meet
gentle massaging motion
increases sexual vitality (M/F)

cleavage of buttocks
between cheeks near the end of the tailbone
gentle massaging motion
increases sexual vitality   (M/F)

buttocks
gentle and penetrating massage motion
relaxing and arousing   (M/F)

valleys of buttocks
valleys in cheeks close to hips
penetrating kneading motion
rapid erection following ejaculation   (M)

inguinal region
high inner thighs
press palms with heels of palms in towards genitals
gently arousing, especially for female   (M/F)

penis control
beneath pubic bone just above penis
press with third finger
delays ejaculation   (M)

governing vessel one
between anus and tip of tailbone in the middle
gentle massaging motion
stimulates sexual heat & performance   (M/F)

anus
around rim and just inside rectum
gentle massaging motion
warms up inhibited consort; may stimulate orgasm   (M/F)

perineum
nickel-sized area midway between rectum and genitals
gentle circular rubbing motion or stationary pressure
stimulates sexual heat & performance   (M/F)

kidney one
middle of foot soles just below ball of each foot
firm pressure with thumb or finger
overall energizer, including sexual vigor   (M/F)

AURAL SEX

"If music be the food of love, play on," wrote the Bard of Avon in his play Twelfth Night. Like Shakespeare, many people enjoy making love to music. As a background, music generates mood, stimulates fantasy and suggests rhythms and kinds of movement.

Rock and roll is one obvious choice because of the explicit sexual themes and hard driving rhythms. Rhythm and speed vary enormously from song to song. The connoisseur will create a customized cassette. Here is a sample sequence with the same beat throughout: "Don't Stop Till You Get Enough" (Michael Jackson), "Heart of Glass" (Blondie), "Urgent" (Foreigner), "Gimme All Your Loving" (ZZ Top) and "Hit Me With Your Best Shot" (Pat Benatar). You can design your tape to begin serenely with a sweethearts soft pop sound and build up to a hard rock crescendo. Funky dance music and Jamaican reggae offer some delicious sounds. Instead of making your own tape you may want to buy workout music, e.g., aerobics records. These collections provide a strong consistent beat. Make sure you get the music without an instructor's voice.

Some of our favorites from the classics include the Strauss waltzs, "Bolero" (Ravel), "Afternoon of A Faun" (Debussy), "Scheherazade" (Rimsky-Korsakoff), "Rite of Spring" (Stravinsky) and "The Four Seasons" (Vivaldi). If you are looking for intensity, try Wagner. We also like Ravi Shankar's sitar music, African drum music and calypso music.

Put on a recording of the ocean and get swept away. We recommend "Psychologically Ultimate Seashore" on Atlantic Records. Equally spellbinding are "Slow Ocean" and "Ultimate Thunderstorm," available from Syntonic Research, Inc., 175 Fifth Ave., New York, N.Y. 10010. Many record stores carry these. Perfumes can be coordinated with the natural setting depicted by the sounds. For instance, the perfume called "Rain Forest" would add to the effect of listening to "Ultimate Thunderstorm."

Light headphones can be worn while you make love. Even if you are not such audiophiles, wearing headphones is delightful when you are on the receiving end, such as during fellatio, cunnilingus or a massage.

Listen to relaxing, inspiring music before or during making love. We find that "Tantra-La" (David Casper), "Eastern Peace" (Steve Halpern), "Wave #1: Inter-Dimensional Music" (Iasos), "Lemurian Sunrise" (Steve Kindler and Paul Warner), "Ambient 1: Music For Airports" (Brian Eno) and "Music For Zen Meditation and Other Joys" (Tony Scott, Shinichi Yuize, Hozan Yamamoto) are ideal for this purpose. More energetic but quite enthralling are "Oxygene" (Jean Michel Jarre) and "Rainbow On Curved Air" (Terry Riley). The modern classical composition "The Photographer" (Philip Glass) concludes with, as one of us (David) describes it, the best musical description of sexual orgasm on vinyl. We offer a cassette of selected readings from the Prologue with a suitable musical background.

Certain music is ideal for Extrasensory Sex (see Style). Though the selections just mentioned would be fine, our choices of music for Extrasensory Sex include "Angels of Comfort" (Iasos), "Himalayan Bells II" (Karma Moffett) and "Tibetan Bells II" (Henry Wolff and Nancy Hennings). These pieces are uniquely cosmic in effect. Some people have found Extrasensory Sex to be "boring" due to the low stimulation level. Listening to evocative exotic mood music counteracts this tendency.

Record your albums on one side of a 90-minute cassette tape, so that you can enjoy 45 minutes of continuous sound. You won't have to get up to flip the record over. We prefer Maxell UDXL II High.

Place your stereo speakers on stands in the far corners of your bedroom. If the head of your bed is against one wall, your speakers go in the corners of the opposite wall.

An inexpensive setup designed by composer Brian Eno may add to your bedroom pleasure. A third small speaker is placed behind the bed to create a quadrophonic-type musical environment in which the sounds seem to surround you. This speaker should be connected to the red (positive) junctures on your amplifier. If this speaker is too loud, add a potentiometer of 6-12 ohms and 10 or more watts. For more information, see the back cover of Eno's album "Ambient #4: On Land."

BOUDOIR BASICS

Here we suggest some inexpensive additions to your bedroom. These holistic boudoir bonuses recreate the psychological and electromagnetic conditions that prevail under more idyllic circumstances, such as making love in the forest or on a tropical beach. Subtle environmental cues and stimuli play an enormous role in sexual response. Without much expense or effort, you can fine tune your bedroom and enjoy the benefits of a personalized boudoir that radiates vitality and relaxation.

An abundance of negative ions is thought to be relaxing and may improve many aspects of sexual functioning, including potency, reproduction, breast milk production, menstruation and sexual performance and enjoyment. The Zestron product line is said to be reliable. Excessive positive ions may be associated with increased stress and may have a negative effect on sexual functioning in some people. Negative ion generators produce billions of negative ions, restoring the ion balance to that found in healthful natural settings.

If you have sexual health or performance problems, place a negative ion generator close to the genitals so that the negative ions stream directly on them. Try this in daily twenty minute sessions for two weeks. Research in Italy and Russia suggests this procedure may help, but by law no claims can be made for it, of course.

Keep your television somewhere other than at the foot of your bed. According to pyramid power expert Dee Jay Nelson, the pyramidal shape of the television picture tube produces a mildly debilitating radiation. Nelson used a copper sheet to cover the screen in his laboratory. A thick piece of wood may do the job.

Orient your bed so that the head faces magnetic north. Place a wool blanket under cotton sheets on your bed. Both steps should enhance your available bioelectromagnetism.

Use natural fabrics on your bed. You will help the

pores of your skin breathe. You can avoid possible skin irritation and/or allergic reactions.

Far better than a bed pillow for support under your consort's buttocks while making love is a crescent-shaped pillow. Beautifully embroidered crescent pillows can be found in stores that carry Indian imports. Don't ask for these pillows as accessories for making love. They probably won't know what you're talking about.

Some scents are traditionally thought to be reliable in the bedroom. These include musk, patchouli, sandalwood, jasmine, rose, ylang-ylang, and juniper as an essential perfume oil or an incense. If you want to explore the more subtle effects of oils, be willing to pay a little more for "first quality" essential oils (see Appendix.)

Fresh flowers in the boudoir do a lot more than decorate. The red rose not only offers its special fragrance; under its outer lips the vagina resembles nothing so much as a partly opened rose. The color of the hibiscus flower as well as the flower itself has long symbolized ultimate sexual fulfillment in the Orient.

A robe the color of hibiscus (scarlet) is considered ideal for the female consort to wear before lovemaking. This is one inexpensive way to incorporate the power of color in your love life. What about the bedroom itself? You will not have to repaint your bedroom walls and redecorate. Thanks to the miracle of lighting, virtually any bedroom can be quickly transformed into a seductive, eductive cove of comfort and sensuous communion.

When Edison and Swan developed the incandescent lamp in 1880, they changed the way people would make love in the twentieth century. The household electric light bulb sends out a pallid yellow light with just a dash of orange in it. This type of lighting tinges human flesh with grey, white and yellow tones that are, to say the least, unflattering. Since, scientists tell us, the brain gets 75 percent of its sense data via the eyes, a change in the way you light your boudoir may light up your lovemaking as well. Light is known to affect the pineal gland, which plays a major though as yet unclear role in our sexual lives.

One option is to go primitive, that is, pre-Edison. Candles are reliable. Small and large colored glass containers, available from religious and occult supply shops, offer some of the advantages of colored lighting. Their intensity is less but candlelight flatters the human body by making it look more fluid and smooth. Some people prefer the illumination of a beeswax candle or kerosene lantern. Coals in a brazier are another option. A brazier has the advantage of also being an incense burner. Frankincense and myrrh can be bought as little chunks and tossed on the coals. The fireplace is another popular sensuous light source. Your natural light sources may give off a slightly eerie blue light which adds surprisingly to the erotic mood.

Pre-electric light sources are not the only way to brighten up your bedroom activities. A swinging San Francisco hostess recently consulted with a color expert on how to perk up her parties. He suggested magenta, a blend of red and purple. The expert advised magenta lighting in every socket and beneath the furnishings as well. He also made her promise that for the first couple of hours of the party only non-alcoholic refreshments would be served. In the orgy that followed nobody bothered to break out the booze.

The magenta tone can be approximated by blending the light from a red bulb and a purple bulb. You may be able to find a magenta plastic light filter or achieve a magenta tone by combining red and purple filters. However, other color tones are also very effective.

If you purchase only one colored bulb, your best choice is probably amber. Keep the watts low. Orange adds a vibrant glow to the skin, but amber does this and adds a luxurious softness to the appearance of the skin. Cool tones, such as green and blue, are erotically effective. This goes contrary to conventional thinking which assigns red the sexy color status, but you will see for yourself if you experiment with the cool tones. Actually, red is too much of a good thing. Under a red light skin tones have an artificial appearance and glands and emotions are said to become overstimulated, resulting in unstable arousal and unprovoked angry conflicts.

Purple and ultraviolet lighting offer a uniquely enthralling effect. Hindu sexual yoga texts claim that certain shades of purple or violet are the color of the female sex energy. In some rituals, a rich violet light is shone upon the female consort's genitals before intercourse begins. The shade of red unique to hibiscus flowers is also used.

You may want to experiment with several lights. You

may want to combine cool lights, warm lights or a cool light and a warm light. You are also able to vary their brightness by choosing light bulbs of different wattage. Author Howard E. Smith, Jr. suggests blending a bright green light with a dim red light.

The psychological illusions created by colored lighting are impressive. Under blue and green lighting, men reported that their consort's breasts not only appeared larger but seemed larger when touched. Under the same lighting women saw men's penises larger than life. Tests conducted on college students revealed that red illumination hastened erection while green illumination slowed it down.

Oils and powders are yet another way to play with the effects of lighting. Oils increase contrass. Powders soften and smooth out the visual drama.

One excellent source of colored light bulbs is GE Party Bulbs. These inexpensive all-purpose bulbs are available in a wide variety of hues and wattages. Floodlights are available in a variety of colors. Plastic light filters may enable you to obtain subtle coloring effects, such as magenta. Ultra-violet lamps are easily purchased. However, don't look into the U-V light. This shouldn't be a problem, as you will be looking at each other instead. Full-spectrum lighting is now available also (see Appendix.)

Your basic boudoir is complete with a short table for food and drink. Fruits, bread, a flask of light red wine, vials of damiana and saw palmetto berry liquid essences and some fresh spring water will nourish and invigorate without weighing down.

CHARGE UP

One very effective way to charge up with energy before making love is this method developed by practical mystic Betty Bethards of the Inner Light Foundation (see Appendix.) It combines alternate co-breathing and positive images. Don't be concerned about how clear or vivid your mental image is. You may not see anything. You may just have an impression or feeling of it. That's enough.

Achieve genital union.

Sit in YabYum on the bed, floor or in a chair (see Peaceful Positions.) Put your attention at the point of genital connection.

Visualize a sphere of golden light the size of a beach ball there. Take a moment to build and enjoy this beautiful image.

Either consort may begin the breathing. Let's say the man begins. As he exhales, he imagines that he is thrusting this light from the genitals up her spine to the top of her head. As he is exhaling she is inhaling. As she inhales, she imagines that she is drawing that same light from the genitals up her spine to the top of her head at the same time.

Now, when she exhales, he inhales. She sees the light going down her spine, through the genital juncture, and up his spine to the top of his head. She thrusts the light with her exhalation as he draws the light with his inhalation. When he finally thrusts the light back through her, he will send it from the top of his head, down his spine, through their genitals and up her spine to the top of her head.

You may want to make a gentle noise as you inhale and exhale so your partner can be sure of where you are in the exchange. Or you can hold hands and squeeze as you exhale. Remember to breathe as fully and as completely as is comfortable for you. Take 5 minutes or less to charge up.

The charge up is ideal preparation for Extrasensory Sex. When charge up is complete lie back into the Seesaw (see Peaceful Positions.) We suggest YabYum first because you can hear each other breathe.

DO IT RITE

The basic premise of ritual is to increase available energy, increase available emotion.

The words rite and right are semantic cousins. The

basic purpose of a ritual is to help you feel and be right with the world and right with yourself. Back when ritual was big, it was believed that if you did not do each required rite (ritual), or if you did not do each rite right, then life might do you wrong. In the old, old days, doing it right meant doing it rite as well.

The chief value of ritual for us moderns is that it can penetrate our cultivated cool. In the face of nuclear threats, pollution and turmoil, we turn off. We can watch only so many depressing TV news programs and read only so many violent newspaper headlines before we submit with relief to a mild self-administered emotional lobotomy.

It takes courage to recognize this desensitization. To not just have sex, but to make love, to meet heart core to heart core, is the very opposite of self-insulation. Making love requires that most precious and rare yet uniquely human response, deep and sincere feeling. But to feel or not to feel is not the question. Men and women who can no longer feel are somehow no longer human.

What is needed is a way to cut through these emotional straitjackets and get to you and me where we really live. But how?

Direct confrontation, as you might find in an encounter group, is one way. But sexual intercourse already tends to be tense and confrontative. A sly method is needed, one that get's to the guts through the back door.

Is there a strategy that is pretty, friendly, fun, entertaining, enchanting, clever and sly all at once? Is there a way to sneak in through the basement of the human psyche and take control of its gas, water and power? There is. The name of this time-honored strategy is ritual.

Of course, sexual ritual isn't for everybody. But before you dismiss the idea, think about contemporary sexual rituals like candlelight dinners and romantic vacations. Sexual ritual in the privacy of your own home as a prelude to sexual intercourse is just as much fun. There's no way of knowing in advance if you will like it.

The key is to feel a blend of wonder, reverence for life and carefree playfulness. Some consorts worship each other as god and goddess to get in this mood.

Here is an easy ritual. Doing an easy sexual ritual together is a great way to get to know each other. It can

114

put new life in an old relationship, as can playing other games for lovers. This ritual is easy but it is very powerful. It combines the most powerful elements of several effective rituals (see Boudoir Basics, Appendix.)

Choose a time and a place.

Prepare the environment sensually, sensitively and colorfully. Keep romance foremost in your mind as you decorate. Include flowers, especially roses or hibiscus. If possible, place a powerful negative ion generator in the room and turn it on before beginning. Natural settings generally have the right negative ion balance, especially if near water.

Bathe or shower separately. Cold water bathing or showering can be surprisingly invigorating. Anoint the body with natural essential oils. An expensive French fragrance is also acceptable.

Prepare a table with flowers and fruits, bread and wine or a favorite light beverage. The table should be a height that is suitable for eating while sitting on cushions.

Candlelight or kerosene lantern light is preferred. No standard light bulbs allowed.

Have no music unless at the very beginning.

Assure no interruptions: no telephone calls, no appointments, no kids, no other things to do for the next three to four hours.

The man enters the boudoir first. Dressed only in an elegant robe, he sits at the table contemplating the delights of the goddess he will soon be enjoying.

Eventually, she also enters. She is also dressed in a stunning robe, one which he has never seen before.

Silently, they may share a light meal together along with a few glasses of wine. Sharing a peach with sincere sensuality would work great, too.

She slips her robe off first, **very** slowly. He admires her several minutes. Do not rush this stage. He should savor every detail of her flesh as it is revealed inch by inch as if he had never seen her before. Then he takes his robe off, also **very** slowly. She admires him, in turn.

Now, finally, they touch. Still no words are spoken. They may massage each other. They may worship each other's sexual organs, manually or orally. This stage prepares the sexual organs for intercourse. Do not over-stimulate here.

Sexual union takes place, preferably with the woman on the man's lap. The man can sit on a pillow or have his back supported or both. He can half-recline. But she is on top. These are all variations of the classic YabYum position (see Peaceful Positions.)

You might want to read love poetry or make a verbal declaration (confession) of affection and good will before beginning. Make your declaration sitting facing each other as you hold hands and look in each other's eyes.

One ritual step which can be very effective is to do the Root Lock exercise together as part of the ceremony any time before the ritual meal (see Sexercises--Yoga and Elevate Energy.)

You may also wish to limber up with some hatha yoga stretches or other relaxing, energizing movements. You may want to go through a stress reduction or whole-body relaxation routine or listen to an inspiring cassette tape (see Aural Sex.)

In the Orient, the female consort may dance for the man. She may dance so beautifully that he is lifted above his tensions and anxieties. She takes on the appearance of a goddess to him. Far from being a coarse seduction, this kind of dancing leads both lovers to an elevated plane long before the transcendental delicacies of intercourse are tasted.

Be creative, be yourself and, above all, be light and easy. It is good to take preparing for the ritual seriously, but once you have started be playful and have fun. You may find that the best ritual is one you design yourself. Completely personalized, it caters you with your preferred stimuli.

The ideal ritual mood is that you are already there. You are already in a fabulous heaven world where the two of you reign supreme as god and goddess. Free of cares, fears and doubts, all of which are the fare of mere mortals, you have chosen to meet together in this elegant way as an expression of the richness which you already possess in great abundance.

EDUCE EACH OTHER

Educe means "to draw out." Eduction is the act of drawing out. Eduction and seduction are not the same. Seduction is a maneuver. Eduction is a giving.

You want to find the deep rich valley of the sensory present when you make love. You want to stay in it as long you can. You want to be there together. Learn the fine art of eduction. Educe each other.

Create a transition from the day-to-day struggle to survive to the love of lovemaking. The transition is a bridge. Rely mainly on non-verbal means--food, drink, herbs, massage, tender gestures, cuddling, games--to cross that bridge. Words may work, but touch, a universal language, is more reliable and direct.

This transition is absolutely necessary. This is why lovemaking can be so much better on a vacation. You are both relaxed.

Allow the desire for sexual union to appear spontaneously. But first create the atmosphere of peace and relaxation. Enjoy the shape of your togetherness as it is in that moment. How would you describe the shape of your togetherness? Its color? Its texture? If it was music, what would that music be?

If lovemaking arises, fine. If not, fine. This is the attitude that works best of all. This attitude keeps you in the here and now with your consort. You are finding love and peace together. You are fulfilling the vision of hope for love and peace in your hearts.

There will be times, though, that talking first thing is necessary. Do this in the very beginning. Later on, though, as you both relax, as you both begin melting in your mutual touching, you may have something you need to say. Say it. Don't suppress it. Talking is a way of touching another person using sound vibrations. Sexual intercourse is a touching of very sensitive organs.

If you don't force the format, everything will work out beautifully. Simply being together is itself the total fulfillment. You are already fulfilled. Everything that follows after your first meeting is discoveries of that fulfillment. But you will never be more fulfilled together than you are right now.

You may feel that your desire is spontaneous and completely natural. But this society teaches the forcing of sex. The modern world swims in an ocean of exploitative sex stimulation.

Where is anything different taught? Where is the allowing of sex allowed?

Go for it. Grab it. Get it. Take it. Dedicate yourself to the pursuit of happiness, sexual and otherwise. These are the slogans of industrialized countries. But have you noticed that what is pursued runs away? When does the pursuit end and the enjoyment of the happiness begin?

Relax, release, relish. It is good, so good, to just hold hands. It is glorious to be free to just breathe your consort's scent, to laugh and accomplish nothing whatsoever. To not have to do or prove or be anything, to be a carefree explorer of the unknown instead. The best way to guarantee that your lovemaking will be special is to share some relaxation and peace together first.

Men and women are different.

The woman can assume the soft role of peacemaker, if she likes. This puts the power of the feminine, of the nurturing mother, to work. Like a knight returning from the battlefield, the man willingly surrenders to the peaceful balm of her gentle touch, of the bath she has prepared, of the bed in her boudoir. Not a word is needed. This sounds so archaic. For many couples it is exactly what is wanted. In other couples, the man is the peacemaker. He is more able to express that peace than her. She is the knight seeking refuge.

Women work in a battlefield, too. Now women tend to become hard in their struggle to survive and win as well. Neither man nor woman may have softness in reserve. But softness, roundness, is essential. Love makes the world round. Two hardnesses, two angularities, will fight.

Perhaps you can do this for each other. But understand what you are doing. You are not just massaging, you are not just serving dinner. You are enabling the critical transition from fighting to loving. If the transition is not made, then lovemaking tends to be the same daily struggle to survive in another form. Lovers win or lose; score or fail to score orgasms.

To create the peace and security mentioned earlier, talking about it can be the least effective approach. Caring deeply can be shown without using words. In an atmosphere of peace and caring, anyone will melt. There will be no conflict because nothing is being demanded. Then, as your consort falls into the sensuous valley of deep relaxation, you will be regarded very positively because you are giving what is really wanted.

Don't do this just as a strategy or it will backfire. Nobody really wants to be manipulated. You may have to be very patient. When the two of you find the place where just being together is enough, you have opened the door. Give and do not expect or demand anything in return. The results may astound you.

Prepare yourself for this role by taking the time to find more relaxation and peace in your own life. You cannot give to another what you do not have yourself. Take time out just before making the transition from fighting to loving. Take time out in your daily life for your own happiness.

Women often ask us what they can do to bring out the gentler, more sensitive side of their man in bed. Realize, first of all, that he is different from you. He looks at life differently. He probably views himself as a warrior, even if he is an accountant or gas station attendant. To him, life is war, and he wants to emerge the victor.

Men's bodies are different. They are harder and tougher. A man tends to relate to his body as if it were a suit of medieval armor. He wants a tough, strong, durable body that can handle any kind of punishment. This relationship to the body may be helpful in the business world, but it is a hindrance in the lovemaking world.

It is very likely that he himself does not know how to let out his sensitive side and take off his suit of armor. Therefore, you must give him a little push in that direction. He may not know where to start. He probably lacks experience in this. His training as a child and young man emphasized other things.

Assert yourself sensuously. Be sensually inventive. Make creative use of the sense of touch. If you would like to have him stroke your face, stroke his face first. Then gently bring his hands to your face. If you want to use words, use them to reinforce your sensuous message. Tell him how good it feels with your eyes, your body, verbally, too. We know one fully sensuous woman who claims this approach works like magic virtually every time.

"I give my men an exotic bath. I rub their backs as we watch TV. I show them how much fun it is to be sensual with me. I don't put the responsibility for being sensual on them. I am the woman. I lead them into the delights of love. After all, where can they learn about this? Who is there to teach them? So I assume they don't know anything about playful sensuous lovemaking but are eager to learn and they absolutely love me for it. It's very stressful being a man and having all those performance expectations on your head. I make it clear I don't care about orgasms. What do orgasms matter when you're having so much fun? Of course, this defuses the situation so that orgasms are more likely for both of us. The mere act of one human being touching another is a miracle that by itself just overwhelms me. They are grateful to me for taking an active role."

So relax first. The joy will soon follow.

ENERGIZE YOUR HANDS

The most powerful life energy center in the hands is right in the center of the palms. To energize the hands, Bernard Gunther suggests that you clap them for about 30 seconds and then rest them (palms skyward) on your knees. You can also play an energetic game of "patty cake" with your consort and then rest your palms on their knees or your own knees.

Another way to energize the hands is to pack an imaginary snowball between your palms, moving your hands slowly together and then apart. A sensation of heat or energy density or tingling may occur.

Once you have the sensation going, you can move your hands more creatively while still playing against the feeling of density that is building up.

EXTENDED FOR PLAY

Your biggest and most important sex organ is your brain. Lovemaking usually begins in your mind long before the clothes come off and the physical act takes place. Your imagination plays a major role in creating what you will experience. The physical act is partly a performance of the movies that play in your mind. This is why people can become so aroused via fantasy. The mind is a powerful tool that can work for you or against you.

The very meaning of "foreplay" can be redefined and expanded. Your pattern may be to go out for dinner or a movie, return home and eventually get into bed. Reframe this entire experience and call the entire time you spend together your foreplay. How you touch his or her hand, the tone of your voice, your choice of food, are now seen as forms of "foreplay," that is, play before intercourse.

You will make better use of your "social intercourse," which relies heavily on words, as a preparation for sexual intercourse, which is chiefly non-verbal. As your understanding of foreplay/for play is expanded and refined, you may arrive at the conclusion that even one brief thought about your consort is a kind of foreplay or afterplay.

This fact can be put to advantage. One way to virtually guarantee a memorable lovemaking session is to delay satisfaction and build up anticipation. Elevate the powerful strategy of teasing and tantalization to a new level of effectiveness. Spend one to seven days flirting with each other but don't allow sexual orgasmic release. Then, at the day and time you chose in advance, make love with wild abandon. Set aside plenty of time. Add to the special occasion by enhancing your boudoir in new ways (see Boudoir Basics.)

You can also build up anticipation by spending a few minutes each day visualizing your successful union. You may want to have special dinners, give gifts or dance together for the purpose of blending your energies in a graceful way. The more you put into it, the more you will probably get out of it.

The totality of foreplay as it usually occurs breaks down like this. Imagine in your mind that you are going to be meeting your consort after an absence. This might be after being at work, the first date, whatever appeals to you. First, you think about them and about making love to them. Then you see and/or hear them. You make eye and verbal contact. You may touch or smell each other, e.g., shake hands or hug or smell their cologne or perfume. If you begin kissing them, you taste them. Eventually, your encounter may lead to a full embrace. Your encounter may conclude with sexual intercourse.

This sequence can be observed in an experiment. Set up a time for a meeting at your home. At the chosen time, the consort at home is already in a separate room. They cannot be seen. When the other consort arrives, both remain quiet.

Spend a few minutes in silence, observing your thoughts of anticipation. Now you both make some sounds. Then, a little later, one of you enters the living room. You look at each other from a distance but say nothing. You experience this for a few minutes. Eventually, you make eye contact, and experience this fully also. Then you make verbal contact, tactile contact and so on, pausing after each step in order to fully experience each stage of increased physical intimacy. Concluding the experiment in sexual intercourse is optional. You may find that you are getting so much out of the stages that you usually skim over that you delay intercourse for another time.

GOOD TIMES, BAD TIMES

The best time to make love is when you are feeling calm, relaxed and full of energy. Be in neutral gear emotionally. This contradicts what today's romantic novels, movies and songs tell us. But you will notice that the supersexed heros and heroines depicted in these products argue violently, seesaw from one emotional extreme to another and live in a world of deception, anger, confusion and unhappiness. Such characters, real or imagined, are too preoccupied with their personal dramas to understand the subtleties and value of good sexual timing.

People think long and hard about when to buy a house, get married, change jobs or even go to the store. Surely it makes sense to consider when to make love as well.

Some couples are in the habit of arguing bitterly, then making up by making love. This is not a good idea. Wait until your system is completely calmed down before making love after an argument. Otherwise, you will only feed the negative cycle you have gotten into. According to ancient Chinese medicine, you may damage your heart, kidneys or liver by doing this repeatedly.

In fact, the Taoist sex experts advised against making love when either of you are extremely happy, depressed, angry or tired. Extremes of emotion were not considered healthy by the Taoists. Balance should be achieved as quickly as possible. Then, with the mind clear, a smart decision is made as to the next course of action, including whether to make love or not at that time.

The Taoist sex experts believed that times of natural disturbance were bad times for lovemaking. This includes eclipses, heavy sunspots, earthquakes, tornadoes and fierce thunderstorms. Since it is now known that the electromagnetic field of the earth can be disturbed at such times, this theory has some scientific foundation.

Matching biorhythms is a useful strategy. Choose times when biorhythms are at their highest point and their lowest point. Biorhythm valleys as well as peaks represent times of superior response. You may find that maximum sex responsiveness is indicated by emotional (sensitivity) cycle peaks and valleys, followed by physical and mental. Double and triple peaks and valleys indicate that even more intensity can be expected (see Appendix.)

Astrological timing is also a valuable tool. The simplest guideline is to make love on the day or night of the full moon. Astrologically speaking, a solar or lunar eclipse is a powerful energy moment and may represent a good time for ritual lovemaking or some other sexual power awakening event. The summer and winter solstice (June 22 and December 22) are recommended because of the huge influxes of energy that occur at these times.

With very little effort, you can learn enough astrology to take advantage of many other heavenly opportunities. These include Jupiter or Venus in the sky trine or conjunct one of your natal planets or vice versa. The Sun, Mars, Uranus, Neptune and Pluto may also release hidden sexual potentials, but the effects tend to be more subtle and, with the exception of the Sun, more unstable, too. The Moon offers special sexual timing options almost daily because it goes around your entire chart in about two and a half days. For more information about astrological sexual timing and astrological relationship consultations, see Appendix.

According to ancient Hindu sexual traditions, the best times are between 7 p.m. and 12 midnight, and again between 12 midnight and 2 a.m. The fifth or eighth day after her menstrual period ends is recommended. The eighth or fourteenth days of the dark of the moon are also suggested.

Another good time is when she is menstruating. She will be more sensitive and sexual activity, especially with genital orgasm, may help relieve menstrual tensions. Use woman above postures so that the blood is able to continue flowing freely.

PAIR BONDING AND TUNING

As you may have already noticed, every person "feels" different from every other person. Each of us has his or her own unique and very personalized vibration.

This vibration is often felt without even trying. You may not realize that this is what you are tuning into. It may all be subconscious. Yet you make important decisions about other people based on these "feelings."

This vibration factor takes on real importance when choosing a consort to make love to or live with. Can you tune into someone else and get behind their personality mask? Can you harmonize and strengthen your bond when it seems to be weakening? Can you deepen your bond when it is already secure?

Yes, you can do all this and much more, with very little effort.

We have tried many techniques for tuning into each other's vibrations. Those included here worked the best for us. They do not rely on some far out theory to be effective. They directly enhance the feeling of being bonded and being in harmony with each other. They are very powerful.

These can be done with clothes on or off. Do them apart from lovemaking as well as just before making love. Some people refuse to do them because the reward is too subtle. This is understandable, but love can be rather subtle. Perhaps it is in the willingness itself to share little celebrations of closeness such as these that "true love" distinguishes itself.

The state of "being in love" is glorified and imitated in our society. The pop and rock music stations blare the message that "being in love" is the most exhilarating state of mind possible. With these techniques you can create and share this state of mind whenever you want to.

When "in love," it is natural to gaze into each other's eyes, to hold hands as if never to let go, to hold each other close for hours, to sit together in silence content just with the feeling of closeness. For every couple, apparently, the initial magnetic merger of bodies and minds comes to an end, for some much more quickly than for others.

By gazing and holding and adoring any object, you can fall in love with it again and again. You are focusing your emotional energy. You can do this with animals, seashells, flowers, rocks (remember "the Pet Rock"?) and, of course, people. This is the principle that is behind the exercises.

The Triple Tuner consists of Solar Plexus Peace, Heart To Pulse (or Heart To Heart) and Two Heads Are Better As One (see illustrations). This is the preferred order in which to do them. These exercises performed in this order naturally and gently bring the energy up. In other words, you will first enjoy instinctive feeling (the solar plexus), then emotional feeling (the heart) and inspirational feeling (the head). It is a good idea to bring the energy back down to the belly after an exercise like this (see Ground And Store Energy.)

In the Heart To Heart exercise you sit across from each other as in the Heart To Pulse. To do the Heart To Heart, extend your arm and place your right palm on the Love spot of your consort. Place your left palm over the back of their right hand which is gently resting on your chest.

You can breathe together, make harmonious sounds together or just look into each other's eyes. Strive to feel the other person from your heart. The longer you do one of these exercises, the more you will get out of it. Try to allow at least twenty minutes for the Triple Tuner series.

We also recommend doing Spine Wine, so called because of the intoxicating effect it can have. Sit back to back. To make your contact more sensual, interlock elbows. The Spine Wine exercise can build up lots of heat energy, which you may be able to feel even when your bodies are separated. This is a good one for energizing the two of you. You can try it when you both need something to pep you up. Some consorts meditate together this way.

Trespasso is a very old exercise which gets its name from the fact that sustained eye contact is a trespass into the other person's identity. Take off any glasses or take out contact lenses. Take a few minutes to relax first. Imagine that your eyes are becoming soft like jelly. Then gently stare into each other's eyes or at the center of your consort's forehead for at least five or ten minutes.

Sometimes it is just too challenging to make the heart-felt contact during sexual intercourse. This is one of the chief advantages of these techniques. They are actually diluted intercourse, sex without the genital bonding. Sexual intercourse is a matter of degree and of physical convenience. Naked with genitals united just isn't the only way to make love.

David made love in this way to a woman friend while standing on a quiet moonlit street corner. They kept their clothes on. They did not kiss or fondle an erotic zone. The energy of their polarity was enough to lift them into ecstasy. Genital intercourse would have been a letdown compared to the energy climax (TRO) that they shared.

The solar plexus exercise was developed by Betty Bethards. The heart and head exercises are taught in the Sufi spiritual tradition (see Bethards, Dass and Aparna, and Gold and Cybele in Bibliography.)

Solar Plexus Peace

Heart To Pulse

Two Heads Are Better As One

SPREADING

Spreading is a fun way to relax and get energized at the same time. It is also good training for all the Sexual Energy Ecstasy lovestyles (see Style.) Spreading practice helps you hold bigger and better sexual energy charges, enhancing lovemaking in any style, hard or soft.

The main advantage of spreading is that you are free to focus completely on spreading your sexual energy and feeling the enlivening arousal throughout your entire body-mind. You don't have to perform or exert effort or succeed.

If you are the physically passive partner, you are internally active. Sense, feel, breathe, direct, imagine, send the sex energy. Gently encourage it to move from the genital locale to other parts of your body-mind.

Remember to breathe deeply and completely throughout the exercise. Unconscious breath holding is very common and the active partner can point this out when it happens. Gently return to your complete breathing.

In fact, if a certain part of your body-mind is in need of healing or is starving for energy, direct some surplus to that area. Naturally, this very same skill can be applied during intercourse for personal and interpersonal healing. The results may surprise you.

Partner A is active. Partner B is passive.

B lies down with his or her back on the bed, genitals exposed. Motionless, B relaxes as much as possible. To insure maximum relaxation, B's hands are palms up. The arms are at about a 45 degree angle to the trunk. The feet are slightly apart. The toes naturally fall outward. Relax the jaw so that the teeth are separated slightly. This position will be familiar to those who have taken hatha yoga classes. It is the pose for the "final relaxation" (see Deep Relaxation.)

A sits to the side of B and smoothly strokes B's body-mind all over. The touch is always gentle. When A's hands leave B's body-mind at the end of the stroke, it is done with a gradual lessening of pressure. This "helicopter" stroke is continued throughout the spreading. The "helicopter" stroke moves the hands half an inch to two inches above the passive partner's body.

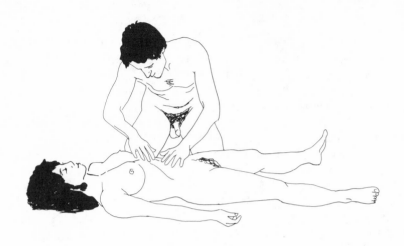

Spreading

A stimulates B's genitals until he/she is clearly aroused, then "spreads" the arousal to the rest of B's body-mind. Concentrate on the genitals for only a minute or so, or even for just a few seconds. The emphasis is on spreading.

Once B is aroused, A slowly sweeps the hands three to five times down B's legs ending near their feet. A uses a feathery touch and gradually lessens the pressure before leaving B's body briefly but completely.

Next A repeats the spreading stroke, moving up the body from the genitals three to five times.

Do this for ten to fifteen minutes, then switch roles. However, even a few minutes for each partner is valuable.

Once you get the hang of this simple exercise modify it to suit your individual needs. Be sure to include the "helicopter" stroke as you taper off each caress.

Sexual activity, especially of the non-orgasm variety, may leave a residue of tension. A similar technique passed on to us at our workshop by a sex surrogate training graduate is quite effective. Wipe tension off the body-mind upward and downward from the abdomen. You can do this yourself or your consort can do it for you.

PART 3
AWAKENING

CONSCIOUS CONFLICT

man and woman is a dream
in essence there is no difference between them
alike they are in fact
still, fire and water
the difference is necessary
to keep the world spinning

conscious conflict
created out of love
in a context of peace
is the secret
of everlasting love
be it for a night
a year
a life

for in all life
variety
is inevitable
and necessary
uninvited
conflict destroys
invited
conflict invigorates

the conflict of fire and water
is a delicious play
that boils away fear, guilt and anger
in the bold honest
heroes of the heart

to open to the opposite
is the only possible path
you are already what you are
your transformation is complete
but you cannot see it
from where you stand

your opposite has eyes
where you have doubts

THE ART OF EROTIC AWAKENING

You arouse your consort; you awaken him or her. You rouse their senses from the deep dullness fostered by daily living into vivid expanded vibrating aliveness. You penetrate self-protective layers with your caring life-giving touch. Now he or she is in the present. Now he or she is more able to appreciate and celebrate the gift of life.

Go beyond conventional notions of "foreplay" and "arousal" completely. Act as if giving the awakening touch is the climax, that genital union does not exist at all. Maximum fulfillment during genital intercourse will result.

Consorts who are gifted in awakening may take hours worshipping and adoring their flesh cosmos. Transported to an ecstatic plane long before genitals are joined, mutual ecstasy during genital intercourse is virtually assured.

Quite a variety of skills are described in this section. You may find some of them very useful. Even so, the most valuable and most authentic lovemaking skill is to feel. This skill, like any other, can be developed.

When the human heart aspires to total wholeness and consumes the entire body, so that the whole body is given over to living love now, even for but a moment, then a touch or glance conveys the entire potency of the erotic promise. In order to make love and not merely to have sex, tender heart-felt caring, identity with the consort and/or other self-forgetful moods are sustained while moving through the physical act. This can be achieved with practice.

Without deep feeling, without the participation of the heart, the thousand and one techniques of the ancient and modern lovecraft will never lead to total satisfaction. Total satisfaction requires total participation.

Love, or maximum feeling response ability, is the only method. But love is not a method. In order to feel with your whole being, the whole mind, the whole heart, the whole body must be awakened. These skills will help you do just that while you enjoy lighthearted pleasures.

To understand and expand sexual awakening, try this. At a time when you feel sexual desire or arousal and the situation is convenient for contemplation, take twenty minutes to explore the sensations. Place all of your attention in your body-mind there. Then penetrate it, become it, allow it to unfurl like a rose. Contemplate how this emanation of energy is part of the life energy that sustains you and the rest of the universe every day.

If you continue the contemplation long enough, the usual feelings of arousal will change. You will feel a tingling and a brightness that spreads through your whole body-mind.

Ironically, one of the best ways to prepare for lovemaking is to contemplate or meditate upon the reality of change in general and of physical death in particular. Do this for half an hour or so privately. You will awaken to the preciousness of this moment and of your consort.

CO-INSPIRATION

Inspiration is a beautiful word that means both the act of breathing in and the act of enlivening and uplifting. Co-inspiration is the act of enlivening and uplifting each other by breathing in each other's vitality and personality, as well as relaxing and energizing your own body-mind in the process.

Have you tried breathing together during lovemaking? It often happens spontaneously. Rhythmic deep breathing together as you are approaching climax can help create a truly mind-blowing experience. Rhythmic deep breathing together at any stage of intercourse will intensify the feelings and energy level. (See also Complete Breath, Inspire Yourself, Oriental Arousal.)

You do not have to be in motion, though. During a full stop (see Full Stop) you can co-inspire each other.

Breathing is a beautiful way to communicate non-verbally. Breathing together is an adventure in itself. Generally speaking, fast breathing is associated with excitedness and slow breathing is associated with calmness.

Breathe according to the effect you want to have on each other.

People talk about flowing together or being in rhythm. There is no better way to do this than with the breath. However, this does not have to be a rigid one-two one-two. By giving yourselves an opportunity to fall into a rhythm, it can happen automatically.

Logically, two people can breathe together in two ways. Two consorts can breathe in and out as one, or they can alternate like two pistons, with one breathing in as the other breathes out and vice versa. Kegel contractions can be combined with in or out breaths when genitally united. Concentrate on pulling the anus up and in when you do this. You may want to intentionally hold your inhalations or exhalations together, perhaps in time with music.

Facing each other sitting up or lying on your sides you can place your faces so that your nostrils are side by side. Or you can hold a passionate kiss on the mouth as you breathe in and out the nose together or alternately. Face to face you feel your consort's breath on your skin and hear them breathe. You are giving each other life energy by breathing on them. A tranquil alternative is "spoon breathing." Lie on your sides belly to back.

Knowing something about the subtleties of the breath in lovemaking may come in handy when making love to a new consort. Breath harmonization leads quickly to interpersonal harmony. You set the breathing pace. If your consort is new to soft style lovemaking, they will pick up your lead without realizing it and soon be comfortable with this approach. If they are breathing too quickly, first match breathing patterns with them. Once you are on their wavelength, you can then begin to change your rate ever so slightly. They will then follow you into a your more serene rhythm.

Just simply being aware of the drama of breathing as it unfolds in your world of two can be quite a treat in itself. Be aware of your breathing as it is for at least several minutes and then go where that takes you. In this way you will experience the effects of breathing variations firsthand and develop your own ways to co-inspire each other.

COMPLETE BIOMAGNETIC CIRCUITS

There are biomagnetic circuits within the body-mind and there are biomagnetic circuits that can be created between two body-minds. These circuits correspond to acupuncture energy flows. When completing biomagnetic circuits with your consort think of it as completing circuits within one whole bigger body-mind (see Elevate Energy, Pair Bonding and Tuning.)

Completing biomagnetic circuits brings you closer together emotionally. You may share moments of bliss as your energies joyfully merge into oneness. You may improve your health and sense of well-being. You don't have to know that you are completing biomagnetic circuits during your lovemaking to enjoy the benefit. Just the act of the penis entering and resting in the vagina completes many biomagnetic circuits (see Tao of Sex.)

Biomagnetic circuit closure can be solo or duo, simple or fancy, in any comfortable position. One simple solo way is to put the palms together in a prayer position or make a cup out of them and interlock the feet at the ankles or press the soles of the feet together.

Fancier solo methods include the ring of calm and the tongue press. To do the ring of calm, press the thumb and index finger or middle finger of either hand or both hands together in an "OK" sign. The gesture helps circulate sexual energy throughout the body. We find it encourages a calm, contemplative state of body and mind.

The tongue press seems more unnatural, but it may be the most powerful biomagnetic closure technique that a person can do solo. Among other things, it may balance the activity of the brain hemispheres, complete the major energy circuit in the body (the Functional and Governor vessels of acupuncture) and increase the flow of saliva (increasing saliva may have cooling, calming, healing benefit). It is also said to directly stimulate the pituitary gland. The ring of calm and the tongue press can be performed during daily activities.

Place the tip of your tongue against the soft palate in the back of the roof of the mouth. If this is too uncomfortable, place the tongue just behind the first ridge of the gum in the indentation where your palate has a soft spot. The rough area of the hard palate is not recommended as this tends to dry out the mouth. Keep your jaw loose. If either of these approaches is uncomfortable, just keep the tip of the tongue behind the two front teeth where the gum begins, your upper and lower teeth slightly apart. When the mouth and jaw are relaxed, this alignment happens automatically. A tight or clenched jaw is often a sign of pelvic or genital tension, which is reduced by releasing the jaw in a big pretend yawn.

Perhaps the ideal time to practice circuit closure solo is when you are in a passive, receiving role during your lovemaking (see Stairway To Heaven.) In this role you are free to go within and feel the subtleties of your experience. A unique combination of effects is achieved by performing the tongue press while covering the eyes with the fingers and the ears with the thumbs. You can stimulate a private phospheme light show by pressing firmly but gently on the eyeballs. Various breathing patterns can be used to further deepen the sensitivity these techniques foster (see Inspire Yourself.) Try this as your consort takes you into orgasm (see Climax.)

Biomagnetic closure between consorts can be as simple as matching same body-mind parts. This happens to some extent during lovemaking (including for play) but the effect can be enhanced by making this a chosen activity. You can match forehead to forehead, palm to palm, stomach to stomach, chest to chest, back to back, sole of foot to sole of foot and, of course, mouth to mouth and tongue to tongue.

Connections can also be made between different body parts. These connections include hands to feet, hands or feet to chest, and hands or feet to head. Other examples are mouth to hands or feet, and mouth or hands to genitals. Some positions, e.g. sixty-nine, make this completion of circuits feasible for both consorts at the same time, increasing the effect.

There is no right length of time for maintaining a connection. You will be able to feel the soothing effect of the life energy as it flows through a completed circuit. Disengage when this sensation goes away or you feel moved to create a new match between body-mind parts. You may find that you are performing a joyous biomagnetic dance as you hold one arrangement for awhile, then move on to the

Complete Circuits

next. If you find that your tendency is to hold con-
figurations for only five or ten seconds, try holding a few
for a minute or two each. You may be delighted by the
new sensations you experience.

The eyes are also a powerful way of connecting.
Looking in each other's eyes while making love can be
challenging as well as inviting. Eye contact for more than
a few seconds is interpreted as a fully intimate act. It is
so intimate that some consorts who are willing to join
genitals with you will not want to join glances. If you
have ever locked eyes with someone of the opposite sex at,
say, a party or a restaurant, then you know how eloquent
the eyes can be. Multiply this by the intensity of
lovemaking and you have a very powerful tool for creating
ecstasy and also personal and interpersonal encounter and
understanding. Breath from the nostrils or mouth also
carries biomagnetism (see Pair Bonding and Tuning--
Trespasso and Creative Sexual Orgasm.)

ELEVATE ENERGY

This is quite potent. Do it together and double your fun (see Complete Biomagnetic Circuits, Inspire Yourself.)

First, the easy version. Inhale gently, clench your PC muscle and pull your anal muscles up and in. Close your eyes direct your attention upwards, such as to the top of your head. Don't strain. Just relax and float away.

Now the more challenging version. Inhale through your nose deep into your belly, scraping the air deep against the back of your throat. As you do this, slowly roll your eyes upward and inward. Tighten your PC/anal muscles as you do this. Press your tongue against your soft palate, at the roof of your mouth towards the back. Your head may want to lean back. If so, let it.

A convenient time to do this is during a full stop (see Full Stop.) Don't be surprised if you experience a natural drugless high. In theory, you are also stimulating your pituitary and pineal glands for longer life, more vitality and personal growth. Because this technique involves holding the breath, it is not recommended for persons with high blood pressure.

FOCUS

Your most valuable sex organ is between your ears, not your legs. The ability to concentrate, to focus the mind on what is happening in the body or on positive features in your experience, is universally agreed to be a major factor in sexual success of any kind. The power of concentration can enhance lovemaking to an extraordinary extent. The love elixir that many people are looking for is the ability to totally concentrate, to fully focus. This ability is acquired through practice. A simple concentration training exercise is watching the second hand of a clock.

Just touching (see pages 96-97) can be practiced as a training exercise or while actually making love. Just touching can be practiced by touching your own body, or oranges and apples, cloths of different textures and so on. Just touching for tactile sensitivity training can also be in the form of very slow, barefoot walking. Practice in being more in the sensory present will benefit your entire life as well as your love life.

There is another kind of focus which is rarely spoken of in relationship to lovemaking. This is, in the words of philosopher Franklin Merrell-Wolff, the state of "high indifference." This is not a heartless, cold state of mind but rather a delightful detachment, a spacious ultra-involvement, that takes you out of your head and into the present. Try making love at a time when you are a bit indifferent to sex, when you can take or leave the genital orgasm. This mood of detachment may lead to some of your best experiences.

FULL STOP

The full stop is taking the time to take stock, to just feel, to appreciate. You step off the elevator of arousal and explore the floor you have reached, be it the 9th or the 49th. You take this time to reestablish the reality that it is you two, and only you two, here now together.

Look into each other's eyes. Feel each other from deep in the belly and chest. Caress each other, breathe on each other. Acknowledge that the fact of your being together is itself a miracle. Take at least a minute or two for this. Take five minutes, fifteen minutes or more. If it ends in sleep, that's fine. You will feel completed afterwards, not frustrated.

You may want to squeeze, really squeeze, each other to say "I really care." It is sometimes difficult to remember to do this as you rush past each other in pursuit of solitary crescendos. Stop and squeeze each other in an enthusiastic bear hug. Make it a long one.

Resist the temptation to pull back if deeper feelings come up. You are making love.

We like to full stop in YabYum. We will sit upright in each others arms, silently, and direct the attention within.

These peaceful moments are some of the moments together we treasure the most. Seconds before we were a raging fire. Now we are a cool mountain breeze scented with pine. The contrast is not a problem, it is the source of delight. We also prefer the Seesaw for full stops (see Peaceful Positions.)

A playful version of the full stop is the freeze or alarm clock game. There are two ways to go about it. The first is to set a timer, or several timers, in advance. The second is to assign one of the partners the role of alarm clock. Switch roles at some point, either halfway through that session or during an entirely separate lovemaking session.

When the timer goes off, both freeze. Stop completely. Do not move. Simply lie still and be aware of the continued motion of your sensations, thoughts and emotions. The main thing is to not move in the slightest. Do not move for at least one minute, if not longer.

What is the benefit of this game? It is extremely difficult to make love without a driven, compulsive, edgy feeling. This exercise will give you some valuable distance from that compulsive feeling.

You may want to breathe in unison, very informally, as you tenderly return to the peak of passion. You can be like a two person steam engine, breathing slowly at first, then more and more quickly.

Without the valley, the peak is meaningless. Without the peak, the valley is fruitless. Take time to enjoy both.

The ups and downs of lovemaking are inevitable. Somehow when you make rising to the peaks of excitement and descending to the valleys of peace a choice, the cyclical, ebb and flow quality of ecstasy and intimacy in lovemaking is more acceptable. This is true of relationships on a day-to-day basis, too. Like surfers on the ocean, sooner or later you learn to ride the waves.

Since taking a break short-circuits male arousal, intercourse can be prolonged indefinitely in this way. Lovemaking with frequent full stops takes on a rhythmic, flowing dance-like quality (see War and Peace style.)

GROUND AND STORE ENERGY

Techniques for personal grounding are widely taught today. Lovemaking can generate huge amounts of energy. You may open and expand so much that you will want a way to collect and insulate yourself before facing the world again. Grounding techniques help you manage and keep the energy you generate. They help reestablish in you a feeling of groundedness, of having both feet on the ground. In general, grounding centers you physically and psychologically.

The first technique, developed by Betty Bethards, has the effect of sealing your personal energy field. Sitting in a comfortable position, place your hands on your thighs and make fists out of them. Visualize yourself immersed in an enormous globe made of brilliant white light. Do this for a minute or until you feel noticeably more settled and collected.

Another technique uses the earth itself, or a convenient floor, as your ground. Bending from the waist, press the palms of the hands and the soles of the feet firmly into the ground. Breathe deeply and rhythmically from the belly. If this breathing makes you dizzy, don't do it. Take your time. This exercise is best done barefoot. Sunrise on dewey grass is said to be the best time and place of all.

The squat brings you down close to mother earth, too. Begin with your legs wide apart and your feet angled out slightly. As you squat down, put your hands together in a prayer position and extend them in front of you. Use your hands as a counterweight to keep your balance. When this is easy, bring the palms closer and closer to your chest. This can be combined with breathing in and out of the genitals in the imagination.

A method taught in psychic development classes is to stand in a relaxed fashion and imagine that there is a cord of light extending from each of your feet down to the very center of the earth. Allow yourself to feel totally rooted as you do this.

Some people are concerned that they will accumulate more energy with prolonged lovemaking than they can handle. Taoist Chinese yoga teaches that the way to manage big energy loads is to store the charge in the belly.

One way to accomplish this is extremely simple. Place your attention on your navel. Move your right fist in a circular motion 36 times in one direction, then 24 in the other. Make the circles bigger gradually but not more than half a foot wide.

If you are a man, move your fist clockwise first, then counterclockwise. If you are a woman, move your fist counterclockwise first, then clockwise. In other words, if you are a man you first spiral into the navel, then spiral away from the navel. Do the opposite if you are a woman. Hold your watch at your navel to make this simpler for you.

In fact, this is only one of many techniques for gathering and storing energy in the navel region. The spiraling can be done completely in the imagination as if it were being done deep within the navel.

In all seriousness, we would like to recommend a simpler version of this ancient Chinese exercise which we call the yummy tummy exercise. As you know, kids rub their hands in a circular motion around their tummy as they say "Yummy." Try it. If you can, watch a kid do it.

The lower belly region is the life force storage battery for the human body, at least according to Eastern thought. The Taoists believed that energy ascended up the back and descended down the front. To encourage upward energy flow without also encouraging downward energy flow was considered by them to be downright foolhardy.

You may experience a heady, spaced out feeling from energy-oriented lovemaking. If you are feeling uncomfortable or if you feel the need to be more down-to-earth, take a few minutes after making love to ease your transition with one of these grounding techniques.

Finally, to be fully grounded is to fully participate in the sensory present. Anything that will help you come to your senses, such as a shower and a rubdown after a prolonged lovemaking session, also helps to ground you.

INSPIRE YOURSELF

Below we describe a variety of special ways to breathe while making love. They are ways of either heating up or cooling down the system. Heating breaths tend to increase arousal and may be used to bring on or intensify orgasm. Cooling breaths tend to diffuse arousal and may be used to delay or rarify orgasm. The skills described below are all solo skills, though two people can certainly perform them together. (See Charge Up, Co-Inspiration, Complete Biomagnetic Circuits, Complete Breath.)

Deep breathing is far more useful than most people realize. Strive to breathe deeply and completely throughout your lovemaking.

Pelvic breathing coordinates the thrust, be it male or female, with the breath. When you thrust out from your body and to your partner, breathe out (exhale). When you pull in to your body and away from your partner, breathe in (inhale). This rhythm may feel uncomfortable at first, but it is definitely the way the pelvis and breath naturally move together. This is a basic and very powerful skill. It is not just a way to delay ejaculation for the man, though it will certainly do that. (See Pelvic Expression, Voluntary Orgasm--Men, Imsak.)

To heat yourself up breathe with your mouth. Pant on purpose if you want to heat up rapidly. Breathe rapidly from your belly (not your throat) with your mouth open. You can extend your tongue a little. Panting helps bring orgasm on if you are close, but if you are not it relaxes the belly and pelvis and delays orgasm.

Another way to increase arousal and bring on orgasm is to coordinate PC muscle clenching and deep breathing. Clench on the rhythmic exhale or on breath retention. Pull up and in with the anal muscles for maximum effect. Add affirmations and/or visualizations if they work for you.

To cool yourself down breathe slowly and rhythmically through your nose. Since ancient times, the application of breathing skills to lovemaking has been of great interest to the man. Since his tendency is to rapidly heat up and then explode, not unlike a volcano, he has searched for ways to stay cool under pressure. There are also women who are too "hot" and need to cool down and enjoy more peace and harmony while making love. The ability to calmly experience and appreciate sexual arousal is a benefit of this technique.

Even more effective may be the cooling breath. Open your mouth slightly and part your teeth a little. Press the tip of your tongue to the back of your teeth or out between your teeth. If you can curl your tongue, then roll your tongue up to form a tunnel and protrude it slightly out your mouth. Inhale long and deeply through your mouth. Exhale lightly and serenely through your nose. Encourage the calm, cool feelings. You may want to close your eyes.

Also having a cooling effect is inhalation through the teeth. A hiss is created as you inhale. This breathing technique is called sitkara in the Kama Sutra. You may find the hissing sound that it creates quite sensual. You can also exhale through closed teeth, though this is not thought to have a cooling effect.

Air can be sucked or slurped or sipped in between pursed lips, which aids concentration. The sounds created in this way are considered quite erotic by some consorts. You will sometimes see inhalation between closed teeth and through pursed lips in porno movies for dramatic effect. They are ways to have control over arousal, too. You may also want to experiment with breathing in and out of the nose and mouth at the same time.

The genital air lock technique effectively delays orgasm by relaxing the entire pelvic and genital region. At the same time it prepares you for a deeper and fuller orgasm later. Fill up your lower belly with air, then pull up and in with your anus and penis (anal and urethral sphincters). It will feel as if you are trying to suck them right up into your pelvis, never to come out again. Then let the contraction go and press down and out with your pelvic muscles. Then release the air. Relish the relaxed feeling that follows. Do not do this when you are teetering on the edge unless you want to encourage orgasm. At that point, go limp with your whole body or relax in some other way without tensing first. This technique helps the man delay his orgasm and helps the woman speed up hers, making mutual orgasm more likely (see Sexercises.)

Potbelly breath is keeping the abdomen enlarged at both inhale and exhale. It will enable both of you to contain more sex energy charge longer.

The lion breath is a fun variation. This is best performed when you are on top. When you exhale open your mouth wide and loll your tongue forward. Roll your eyes up into the top of your head and roll your head back. You may want to exhale quietly and gently, making a slight rasping sound. You may want to roar like a lion. You may roar mentally if you want to roar but not out loud. After exhaling, stay in the exhaled position and enjoy the expanded feeling.

The muscles of the body can be tensed or relaxed in time with the breath. Here is a technique that brings strength to the lower abdomen and genitals and increases vitality and endurance. Breathing through the nose, the muscles of the stomach are drawn in firmly during the exhale, forcing a maximum amount of air out. After the exhale is complete, allow the inhale to happen on its own. The PC and anal muscles may also be tightened during the exhale.

Another approach is to make the belly and pelvic region as soft and relaxed as possible, like cotton or jelly. The whole body can be made relaxed or tensed in rhythm with the inhale or exhale. Imagine that the erotic energy is spreading through your entire body.

A kind of breath that quickly leads to a heightened sensitivity is connected breathing. Ordinarily, people pause briefly after each inhale and each exhale. In connected breathing this pause is eliminated. Connected breathing can be performed via the nose or mouth. Breathe deeply from the belly. Stop if you experience discomfort.

Try just holding the inhalation or the exhalation on purpose without breathing in any special way. People tend to do this unconsciously. Doing it consciously during lovemaking will lead you to insights on how to use the breath to creatively color and shape the sensual joy you are experiencing.

Locking in the breath is a way of increasing energy. This is done by inhaling and then holding the breath while tightening the PC muscle and pulling up and in with the anus. The lock is released before the breath is released. (See Sexercises: Yoga--Root Lock.) This is not recommended for people with high blood pressure.

The breath of fire is another valuable energizing breathing technique. It should be learned from a qualified teacher.

Positive creative images can be coordinated with breathing. Imagine that you are breathing light if you want to feel inspired. Imagine a fire with its red flames leaping high around you if you want to heat up. Your inhalations and exhalations fan the flames. If you want to cool down, imagine a cold wind.

Genital breathing uses the imagination to feel air or water flowing in and out of the genitals. The feeling of arousal can be encouraged to spread through the body as a whole by imagining that your exhalation is going out in all directions from your pelvic region.

Other variations of whole-body breathing include pore breathing and bone breathing. Imagine that you are breathing in and out simultaneously through all the pores of your body at the same time. In bone breathing you imagine that the air is entering your body through the soles of your feet and going out through the top of your head on the inhale, then entering back through the top of your head and going out through the soles of your feet on the exhale. Imagine that the breath flows up the bones in the legs, through the pelvis, up the spine and through the skull. Try to feel the breath moving through the very marrow of your bones.

A related technique is to place your attention at the soles of your feet. The precise point is in the center of each sole towards the toes just below the ball of the foot. Located here is a major energy focal point known as bubbling spring in Chinese acupuncture (Kidney-1). You may feel the gentle ebb and flow of your breath at the soles of your feet. You may want to enjoy the fantasy of a bubbling spring bathing the soles of your feet. This is the same point that is pressed as part of an aculoving foot massage. You can press it while making love, too.

LOVE TAP

The valley between the breasts is frequently neglected in lovemaking. The entire valley is an erotic zone for men as well as women. At the upper end of this valley is the thymus gland, which is easily stimulated by forceful tapping, pressing, rubbing and so on (see Love Spot, Aculoving Massage.)

According to John Diamond, M.D., an expert on the role of the thymus gland in optimum health, invigorating the thymus by thumping the chest with the fist--he calls this the "thymus thump"--instantly enhances your ability to handle stress, balances your left and right brain hemispheres and increases your available life energy. He reports that the tongue press has the same beneficial effects (see Complete Circuits.) Jacquelyn McCandless, M.D., a psychiatrist and sex therapist, emphasizes in her practice that opening the heart and loving yourself and others improves the health of the thymus and vice versa. A healthy thymus gland is crucial to good health because the thymus manages your body-mind's self-defense.

Ninety-five percent of the people tested by Dr. Diamond had underactive thymus glands. Arousing your thymus gland may be a strong preventative health step and may enhance your ability to love self and others. What better time to arouse the thymus than while making love?

In the Kama Sutra, an intercourse technique is described which stimulates the thymus in this way. After entering his consort, the man begins striking the valley between her breasts with the back of his hand, at first very slowly and gently, then more rapidly and more forcefully.

The Kama Sutra also suggests a technique for the woman. When she senses that the man is approaching ejaculation, she should slap his buttocks and his chest with her open palm. If she slaps with enough force, his ejaculation will be delayed. She should repeat the technique until she achieves sexual orgasm. The Ananga Ranga advises that gently patting his chest with her closed fist will add to his pleasure. Caressing or rubbing the Love spot just plain feels good anyway. Caring feelings are transferred heart to heart with a tender touch.

Music, spoken rhythmic poetry, singing and gazing at a painting of a beautiful natural scene are also thought to stimulate the thymus gland. In his book Your Body Doesn't Lie, Diamond also recommends the "thymus gesture," a maternal gesture seen in some medieval paintings of the Madonna with both arms reaching out.

MAKE LOVE WITH YOUR MIND

Many people have sex from the viewpoint of body alone. But making love must be a joint creation of body and mind. Here we focus on some ways to enhance your mental involvement by using your thoughts and your imagination creatively.

Many experience an abundance of distracting thoughts while making love. Our favorite way of dealing with these freeloaders is to focus on staying in the sensory present (see Making Love Is A Touching Experience.)

One approach is to substitute positive thoughts for negative thoughts. If you are thinking "I feel tense," you substitute "I feel relaxed." A simple positive thought such as "I feel peaceful" or "Yes" can be substituted for undesired thoughts as they appear. Another approach is to insert a thought which has no meaning to you, such as "Mmmmm" or "Ooohhh." These counter thoughts can be coordinated with the breath. These are some strategies you can use in the privacy of your own mind (or out loud if you wish).

An affirmation is a short positive statement that is repeated over and over again. Negative or undesired thoughts are kept at bay. Unity of body and mind is encouraged.

Affirmations are quite popular with some people. You can make up your own or try a standard one like "God Is Love" or "We Are One" or "I Am You" or "You Are Me" or "Love Is All Around Us" or "We Are Love." Affirmations can be coordinated with breathing and PC and anal muscle clenches. You can also use them with harmonious images of your choice. Affirmations are natural during love-making. Why not make a good thing better? Do affirmations privately or together, silently or aloud.

The best affirmation is one that is personally meaningful to you. Experiment with one of these: "Yes," "Oh God," "Fire," "Mygasm," "Come," "Yummy," "Mama," "Papa," or "One." Or try these favorites, "You Love Me," which is the other and often neglected side of "I Love You," and "Thank You."

Affirmations can be explored in at least two different ways. One is to use the literal meaning. Another way is to play with the sound it creates. For example, "We Are One" is a potent statement in the English language. The sound "Weeee Ahhrr Wuuhnn" has its own potency independent of the dictionary definition. If you use an affirmation from another language, contact an authority in your area who can instruct you in the subtleties of the correct pronunciation or attend group chanting sessions led by an expert.

Above all, do not engage in a struggle with any unwanted thoughts. If a thought insists on sticking around, then simply allow it. This may make you uncomfortable for awhile, but sooner or later it will leave due to your lack of interest.

As you approach the deeper level of lovemaking participation, you may find that your thoughts are like the skin on an orange: the skin must be peeled away in order to enjoy the delicious fruit beneath. Even the thoughts "I am a man" or "I am a woman" are discarded as consorts pierce deeper and deeper into the mystery at the heart of making love.

Though thoughts may distract or trouble you, the thoughts themselves are not the problem. It is good to understand that every thought we entertain is there because we claimed it and let it in. At the same time, we are free to dismiss any unwanted thoughts any time we wish, for our mind is our home.

Fantasy imaging is very effective for some people. How would you like to make love to a living breathing god or goddess of love? How would you like to be that god or goddess? Well, you can--with your imagination. You can imagine blood, energy and arousal rushing to your sex organs, too. Make the image vivid, colorful, detailed and full of action for best results.

A very practical suggestion is to use breath with the fantasy, or visualization, you have created. Allow the image to expand and contract, appear and disappear as your breath flows in and out.

The possibilities available in the world of imagination are infinite. You can surround yourself with golden mist, transport to another planet, fly through the air, make love in the heart of the sun. There are suggestions below. These can be done solo in the privacy of your own mind or together. If you decide to share a fantasy, you may want to choose one of you to act as guide or coach to pace the scenario. You may want to co-create, enhancing a set fantasy model or improvising new ones. Co-created fantasies can be enjoyed silently or verbally, with music and other props and without props.

The Bubble: Imagine you are a bubble floating on the ocean. Wave after wave carries you higher and higher. At orgasm or another right moment, you burst--into . . . .

The Effulgence: As you breathe in, draw radiant energy from an effulgent source above your head.   Inhale this breath energy down the front of your body into your perineum (area between the genitals and anus).   As you exhale, you release this breath back up your spine to the infinite, nameless source of effulgence above your head.

The Firecracker: You are a firecracker lit at the genitals.   Your spine is the fuse.   When it reaches your head, you explode.   Or vice versa, you are lit at your head and when it reaches your genitals or feet, you explode.

The Garden: You are making love in a tropical garden. You can hear the waterfall nearby and the distant surf, too.   Lush tropical vegetation, exotic birds and a perfect temperature add to the delight of this tropical island for two (see Aural Sex.)

The Golden Fog: A golden circle of misty light surrounds you.   The light turns into a golden glowing fog which spreads all through and around your body. You melt into this fog until you are the fog itself.

The Blue Lotus Flower: There is a blue lotus flower in the center of your chest.   As you make love, it expands and radiates a beautiful blue light.   It expands and contracts in rhythm with your breathing.   As you reach a climax in your lovemaking (which may or may not include sexual orgasm), this blue light expands to penetrate and enclose both you and your consort in blue bubble of peace, love and happiness.   You may prefer visualizing a brilliant blue jewel shining in your chest.

The Ruby Laser: Iridescent ruby red laser beams shine from your navel, Love spot, throat and forehead, bonding and branding the two of you in some unexplainable yet glorious way.   Or they shine from your nipples.

The Super Penis and Super Vagina: His penis is a mountain or a thunderbolt or simply of enormous size.   It is made of hard beautiful rock such as diamond or jade.

Her vagina is the mouth of the volcano or a lagoon that opens to the boundless sea. It is made of bands of gold that grow in size and strength, so that they have tremendous gripping power (see Pompoir.) Or she is taking him in and being penetrated deeper and deeper, impossibly deep. Do this privately if you wish. Use an image that appeals to you.

In addition to the techniques described above and many fine books and seminars, cassette tapes are available that will help you handle impotence or other specifically sexual performance problems. Some tapes enhance already positive experiences and make them even better (see Appendix.)

ORIENTAL AROUSAL

Although no part of the world has a monopoly on subtle arousal techniques, the Oriental sexologists suggest sexual stimulation points that many consorts are not aware of. Some of these points become effective only after the receiver is already aroused. Others require sensitive methodical stimulation for a much longer time than the pace of quick genital relief sex allows (see Aculoving, Love Tap.)

Actually, the entire body-mind from toe to top, including the emotions, mind and spirit, is one unified erotic zone. This is the feeling when erotic arousal is directly experienced without cultural programming and other preconceptions. Erotic zone boundaries exist mainly in the mind. When everyday thinking mind is set aside, even very briefly, you perceive the flesh as a perfect whole with no divisions at all. Though the ingredients of a chocolate chip cookie can be identified by analyzing it, its "cookieness" must be experienced directly by eating it as a cookie unity.

On the other hand, this is not a standard of arousability against which you need to measure yourself. Everybody has a different pattern of physical sensitivity. What is very arousing for you may do nothing for them and vice versa. Have a good time discovering the individualized hot spots of your body-minds. Whole-body massage, erotic or relaxing, is a great way to find these spots.

Oriental sexology stresses the value of personal cleanliness. The anus, for example, is a fabulously erotic locale--but only when it is completely hygienic. In the Oriental ideal, a consort should be able to probe, lick, squeeze and rub every square inch of their companion's flesh without the slightest concern. The thought that you cannot explore your consort entirely for hygienic reasons inhibits lovemaking before it even starts.

On at least one occasion take two hours to explore these secondary erotic areas before connecting genitals. You will probably discover that you are naturally a great sexual artist. All it takes for most consorts is some time, a little knowledge and a sprinkle of sensitivity.

We've included some of the standard erotic zones because we suggest an unusual method of stimulation. If nothing follows an item, we do not suggest any method of stimulation in particular or a special technique was described under Aculoving. Some of this information came from the sources listed at the end of the Aculoving section.

Along The Spine On Either Side: rub and knead
Ankles: caress and nibble
Armpits: gently bite; insert penis here
Anus: penetrate with finger at peak of genital orgasm
Back of Neck: long deep sniffs/breathe on from deep in throat
Behind the Elbows
Behind the Knees
Big Toes and Little Toes
Buttocks and Valleys of Buttocks: probe deeply
Centers and Mounds of the Palms
Earlobes: tug, bite, chew or suck
Eyelids: gently brush with fingertips or tongue
Finger Tips
Forehead Between Eyebrows: gently rub or lick
Front of the Forearm
Head: rub scalp vigorously, hands curled into claws, with tips of fingers
Hindu Sequence: repeated stimulation of female nose tip, armpits and navel in order before attending to genitals

Incense Heater: move stick of lit incense up centerline of front of body two fingers width distance away

Just Under Bottom Lip: press hard for count of three to increase lip sensitivity

Kidneys: rub vigorously with palms of hands then move palms all the way of spine on both sides and repeat several times

Lips: male gently chews female upper lip as female does same to male lower lip

Nasal Kiss: faces close inhale each other's exhalation through nose; may rub noses as you exchange breaths

Navel: circle around navel with flat of palm

Nipple Tips: freely stimulate tips manually and orally, including breathing on them, without any stimulation to rest of breasts

Nose Tip: nibble and bite gently or rub noses (suprisingly effective)

Penis Tip: man squeezes just before going in vagina to delay ejaculation

Perineum

Pubic Hair Line And Just Above

Pubic Mound

Roof of the Mouth (Hard Palate):   use tip of tongue

Sacrum

Shoulders At Bony Part Where Arms Are Joined: bite

Soles of the Feet

Tailbone (Coccyx):   rub gently and repeat until warm

Thumbs and Little Fingers

Upper Inner Thighs

Valley Between Breasts

PEACEFUL POSITIONS

   Lovemaking can be made more fulfilling by taking time out to appreciate what it is that the two of you are doing. Stop moving and just hang out together.   Take in all the sight, sound, smell, taste and touch sensations.   Relax and allow your tender feelings to take root and blossom.   It is good to have some alternatives to the standard missionary position in your repertoire. Side-by-side and woman above positions suggest physical and psychological equality as well as being comfortable for long periods of time.

These positions are suitable for soft style lovemaking (see Style.) They can be transition poses between more active or tension producing poses. They can be enjoyed as a passive way to warm up to each other or as a way to share the afterglow that follows climax.

These peaceful positions are outward symbols of an inner peace and contentment. What you are looking for, be it in sex or success or self-knowledge, you already have. By outwardly assuming a peaceful position, you encourage an inward peaceful position or attitude. Motionlessness has the psychological effect of slowing down the mind, reducing anxiety, thought activity and stress.

Each position is a sophisticated form of frozen body language, an hieroglyph of flesh. If you spend enough time with different positions, you will experience how each one has its own unique effect on the two of you and may even serve as a doorway to the mysteries of the subconscious (see Full Stop, Stay Together, Tension Positions.)

Peaceful positions encourage mutual surrender. Surrender is perhaps a controversial, even scary word. But there is a joy to surrender that must not be missed. Surrender means the fighting is over. Peace prevails. You give in. You implode (rather than explode). You make room for a new fullness. You become the empty cup. Now you can be completely full-filled.

The key peaceful positions are the YabYum, Scissors, Carriage and Seesaw (or "X" position). Also illustrated are the exotic Serenity and Statues postures.

To achieve Scissors, man lies on his side and woman raises inner leg. For example, if he is on his left side, she raises her right leg. Easy way to achieve Seesaw is to get into YabYum and fall back away from each other. One way to achieve YabYum is to start out in missionary, then, embracing each other, he pulls both up into a sitting position. YabYum is easy to reach from woman above positions provided she is facing him. To do the Carriage, she lies on her back and lifts both legs as he enters.

You will find illustrations of other peaceful positions in these sections: Complete Circuits, Stay Together, Creative Sex, Extrasensory Sex and Kabbazah Sex.

Scissors

Carriage

YabYum

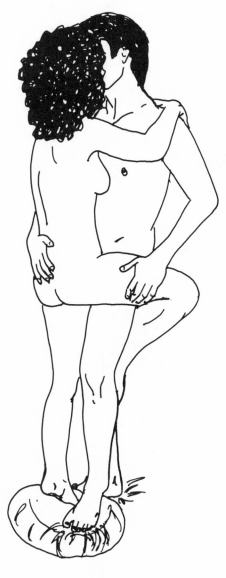

Statues

Seesaw

Serenity

160

SLOW MOTION

Slow motion is exactly what its name implies. As you make love, move as slowly as possible. Whatever you think is slow, move even more slowly still. At times, you may become absolutely motionless. Allow this. The next impulse to move will originate from deep within you. You will discover a greater depth in your lovemaking, perhaps much greater than you had imagined, because you will be moving from a deeper part of yourself.

You may find that doing this is more difficult than you thought. It is a good idea to agree ahead of time to make love in slow motion for a specific time period. Do slow motion for at least five minutes. Twenty to forty minutes is ideal.

Slow motion can be incorporated into your regular lovemaking as a prelude to sensitize you or as an interlude to slow things down. Slow motion is both an exercise and a way to make love.

One of the benefits of this technique is that it tends to increase awareness of detail. You may notice literally hundreds of new things about them--the pulsing of blood in their throat, the softness of their belly, a fleck of green in their otherwise blue iris--and about yourself. You may discover that the usual quiet current of non-verbal signals that flows between you when you make love has suddenly become a torrent of meanings.

Slow motion can begin even before you touch each other. Lie side by side on your bed. Only when you are moved from deep within to reach out to the other should you do so, and then with supreme slowness. You may feel awkward at first, but this won't last long.

Do several slow motion lovemaking sessions in a row so that the impact accumulates. Doing it every now and then after that is good. You will see the positive effects spill over into your love life, and perhaps your personal life as well. Alan Watts describes the slow motion experience beautifully in his classic Nature, Man and Woman.

SOUND SEX

Sounds help to vibrate the body and spread energy, helping to make sexual orgasm more voluntary. Getting into sound making with the whole body awakens and relocates arousal and energy so effectively that it can make male ejaculation completely and effortlessly voluntary (see Make Love With Your Mind.)

Feel what you are doing and then allow that feeling to become a sound. Allow whatever comes out--a moan, a groan, a grunt, a growl, a sigh, a cry, a laugh. Use sound to send energy to your consort as well.

If you overlay a technique of making sounds onto your making love experience you may miss the point. Some people are noisy in bed. Some are quiet. The quality of the sounds, rather than the quantity, makes them sounds of the whole body.

The impulse of whole-body sounds come from deep inside. The sounds seem to originate as much from your toes and your hair as from your vocal cords. The sounds may seem to appear independent of your will. The kinds of sounds you hear yourself make or kinds of emotions you feel may astonish you. Your experience of the act of making love may change to a startling degree.

The whole body is the human sex instrument. To make beautiful music with that instrument, encourage sounds without forcing them. Perhaps making love, with its sounds, rhythms, full stops, slows, quickenings, crescendos, emotional tones and vibrations is, at some level, literally making music.

You may want to make the loudest, most primal sounds you can as a kind of therapy. It may feel artificial. But it can help you get over some of your inhibitions about making sounds during sex, and so it may be beneficial to you.

Make sounds that express your total feeling of being with your consort, sounds that come from your deeper feelings as well as your genital thrills. Use your voice to express your desire for oneness with them.

Animal Sounds: Animal sounds are fun. Animals generally lack the self-consciousness that so often gets in our way. To feel like a tiger or tigress, sound like one.

Laughter: Good-natured laughter before, after or even during lovemaking really loosens things up. Of course, nervous laughter or snotty laughter will only make matters worse. People do take sex a bit too seriously, don't you think?

Power Sounds: Power sounds are grunts, growls, howls and hollers, and emotion-laden percussive words like fuck. Their key feature is gut level response. Two sounds that are noted for their ability to release power from the solar plexus (the storehouse of vital energy) are "Gah" and "Kiyai." Power sounds build arousal and can be used to trigger or intensify orgasm.

Release Sounds: Lovemaking can create a very emotional, very intimate place. You may discover many feelings coming up that you ordinarily sit on. These may be feelings of need from as long ago as infancy, feelings of loneliness and neglect, feelings of fear. Allow them to surface and give them a voice. You may discover that doing this improves your ability to feel release in stressful situations, such as working or dropping an undesirable habit.

"Ah" is a sound used since ancient times to encourage deep emotional, pleasurable whole body release. Sex therapists Kline-Graber and Graber suggest making the "Ah" sound deep in your throat. Just let it come out. "Ah" is an incredible sound that contains an entire symphony of release in it. Stay with "Ah" for several lovemaking sessions and explore its many subtle variations.

The simple hum of two lips together and then making an expressive sound--a moan, a groan, a sigh--is also special. Let this kind of hum express many different feelings. It may surprise you by spreading over your entire body-mind, creating pleasant tingles in your toes and scalp. The hum can be combined with the tongue press, vibrating the brain and skull.

Wholeness Sounds: You can do affirmations as if you are talking or you can do them as pure sound. "We Are One," for example, can become "Weeeeeeeeehhh Aaahhhhhhrrrrrerrr Wuuuhhhnnnnnngg." Note the extra sounds at the end of each syllable to make them vibrate more.

Eastern holy (wholly) sounds, or mantras, are now popular. The mutually created harmonious vibrations of the mantra creates harmony in your union. An excellent way to do mantras together is facing each other, hands to the chest in a prayer position. This positions vibrates the chest, opening the deeper feelings of the Love spot and stimulating the thymus gland. Further resonance is a-chieved by adding a slight nasalness to your tone.

Mantras can be done before lovemaking begins, as part of for play or during a full stop. Chant twenty minutes or longer if convenient, but as few as five minutes is enough to open up feelings and harmonize your emotions. In order to keep the sound going, creating a "surround sound" effect, alternate your breathing so that while one of you is inhaling the other is exhaling and making sound. On the other hand, sounding together and then silence together as you inhale is great, too.

Some of the best mantras are also the simplest. In this category are "Om Mani Padme Hum," "Om Ah Hum" and "Yum."

The Tibetan mantra "Om Mani Padme Hum" is correctly pronounced in a variety of ways. These sounds are very old and variations have developed. Here is one version you can get started on: "Ohhmmm Muhnee Pahdmay Ho-um." A breath is taken between "Muhnee" and "Pahdmay" and the sounds are, of course, prolonged. However, it can also be performed very rapidly. If possible, attend a group chanting session where this mantra is being per-formed to expose yourself to the nuances of pronunciation and creative sound blending. Also, there are records and tapes.

The "Om Ah Hum" is is a sequence of sounds that occurs in everyday life. For example, you run into someone after some years of being out of touch. You say "Oh" in surprise. As you tell the person what you are doing, he says "Ah" in agreement. Pleased with seeing you again, he utters a sound of contentment, "Hmmm." These sounds express feelings, needs and affirmations that are natural and universal as well as religious. Intellectual comprehension is not needed to benefit.

Another favorite is "Yum." This is a mantra for opening the deep feeling center at the heart, the Love spot. What is interesting about it is that when you get going fast with it "Yum" turns into "Yummy," the familiar sound of contentment. "Yum" is an example of a well-known spontaneous sound that was turned into a technique.

STAIRWAY TO HEAVEN

Conventionally, the active role is assumed by the male partner, the passive role by the female partner. Not only can this be reversed, it can be exchanged. The effect of going back and forth from active to passive can result in what we like to call the stairway to heaven (see Creative Sexual Orgasm.)

The key to this technique is that the passive partner is stimulated to near-orgasm by the active partner, then the roles are reversed. Male ejaculation orgasm brings an end to the ascending cycle but female orgasm does not. Stimulation is achieved via your preferred means.

The final climax allows for simultaneous male and female orgasms. Of course, this is only one of several possibilities.

You can incorporate this give and take into your lovemaking without a particular format or goal in mind. The man may find the experience of being the passive receptive partner a welcome relief, or he may find it threatening. The advantage here is that not only does the female get a chance to be dominant and aggressive, but the male is less threatened by the role reversal by knowing that his turn is next.

STAY TOGETHER

After you have made love, stay together. This is a precious time. Even if one or both of you fall asleep, you are strengthening the bonds of your intimacy (see Peaceful Positions, Tension Positions.)

Making love is like everything else in life. It takes time to get into it and time to get out of it.

The entree of a gourmet meal is heralded by a great

variety of lesser dishes. Following the entree is dessert, coffee and perhaps a liqueur. To arrive just in time for the entree, then bolt it down and leave immediately is simply not proper. But this is precisely what people do at fast food restaurants.

This time that you spend together after making love, still genitally joined, is the dessert, coffee and liqueur. You may argue that the orgasm is the dessert. That may be, but the sweetest part of lovemaking is the sweetness of the hearts that have melted.

We find that peaceful position Surrender, with her on top and him on his back, is ideal for this tapering off time. His legs may be extended or bent at the knees. She lies on his stomach and chest, her knees bent.

Surrender

Next time you make love, try this cycle. Start with a man above position, switch to a side or YabYum or Seesaw position, and finish with a woman above position.

Allow at least ten or fifteen minutes, if not twenty or thirty. If ejaculation has occurred, keeping genitals connected may be more difficult, especially in a woman above position. If you have had an exceptionally moving or profound experience, this cool-down time is needed so that your system has time to digest what just happened.

Unless the woman is heavier, a woman above or side-by-side position will probably offer the most comfort.

Staying together is the ideal time to expand and prolong your genital orgasm. After the initial intense phase, direct the waves of enlivening pleasure throughout your body-mind. These waves will respond to your will, multiplying your pleasure and enhancing the benefits of sexual orgasm.

TENSION POSITIONS

Tension positions offer a thrill that neither serene peaceful positions nor dynamic thrusting positions can offer. You may want to hold the position or you may want to move with tantalizing slowness. Tension positions are stimulating. After resting in a peaceful position, they can be used to build up arousal while maintaining feelings of closeness and calmness (see Peaceful Positions.)

Here are some examples. (1) The Cobra: the female arches back as far as she can (woman above facing man). (2) The Penetrator: male superior with the man pressing powerfully into the woman by pushing against the wall behind him with his feet. (3) The Lover's Rack: man or woman above with all four arms and legs stretched out to the maximum. (4) Rear Entry: both consorts on knees. Some women report rear entry stimulates the G spot more.

Some of the peaceful positions have arousing variations. The Seesaw, for example, offers a delightful active version in which lovers lock hands and wrists and slowly frictionate each other to genital orgasm by seesawing back and forth. It can also be held as a stationary tension position.

The Seesaw is the YabYum unfurled and the transition is smooth (see Stay Together.) In YabYum you can create

Female Cobra

a feeling of intensity by maintaining eye contact for five to twenty minutes (see Pair Bonding And Tuning.)

If you are fairly limber, you will enjoy going into and holding stretches. Illustrated here is the Cobra. This may stimulate her clitoris. The male can do the Cobra stretch also. She can push on his chest to increase the stretch. The feeling that goes with doing the Cobra is that you are stretching yourself open wide. The Cobra can be combined with the elevate energy technique.

Other yoga-type stretches can be incorporated into lovemaking, combining the sheer physical delight of elegant movement with the erotic fire of your merger. In fact, many of the postures that make up these routines can be transferred whole to the bedroom. An example of an advanced position would be woman above and facing away from him as she performs the splits on his prone body. This is only briefly held, of course.

PART 4
CLIMAX

When you come, where do you go?

It is now scientifically established that orgasm is an altered state of consciousness.

In other words, orgasm really is a natural high.

Some people have reported that at the Peak Of the Peak of an orgasm (POP) that their thoughts stopped completely or that their ego sense of self disappeared.

When you are having an orgasm, especially such an intense orgasm, who are you? What are you? Where are you?

During a moment of no thought, what sex are you? Do you exist?

The moment is, of course, very brief.

But being brief makes it no less real.

We could say that anybody who is having such an intense orgasm, so intense that they really lose themselves in the experience and reach the POP, is a momentary mystic.

Even the crudest sexual relations offer such a possibility for mystical experience, of this mystical moment.

Naturally, most people cover it over as quickly as possible. A moment of no mind can be quite unnerving, especially when you weren't looking for it and haven't been preparing for it.

On the other hand, some people, people who seek this mystical freedom beyond the mind, do cultivate this potential of sexual intercourse in general and of sexual orgasm in particular. Of course, just because people have sex doesn't make them mystics.

Sex is one of the few activities in life which more or less automatically draws us into uninhibited yet fully focused participation. So, the next time you orgasm, ask yourself where you went.

CREATIVE SEX AND PROCREATIVE SEX

when you want to make a baby:
procreative sex

when you want to make love:
creative sex

the function of procreative sex is to create babies

the function of creative sex is to create
whatever you want
with the energy that becomes available to you
such as
more harmony and wholeness
better health and better life
or just more fulfilling lovemaking

use the tools in this book to be
a creative couple
not just a couple
choosing
or avoiding
procreation

physical creation
through sexual union
can take many forms
of which a baby
is only one

sexualove healing
of bodies and hearts
can happen too
especially
when you invite the Power of Life
by whatever name you call it
or with wordless feeling
into your union

remember
results can be yours

without doing or believing anything
that runs contrary to
your present understanding
no matter what that is

at the time of orgasm
or just before
see in your mind's eye
whatever it is
that your heart desires

this is a powerful moment
this orgasmic pulsation
pleasure is just part of
what it has to offer

during lovemaking
see the desired result
whatever it may be

take the time
upon the prayer mat of the flesh
to ask for guidance
from within

making love is "making love"
from this basic fact
everything else follows

"What I wouldn't give for a piece of ass tonight!"

The words are right; the usual meaning is wrong.

What good will a piece of a woman's body do for that man?

When she wants to give him a "piece of her mind," he doesn't want that.

He wants her mind whole--a piece of someone's mind can be dangerous.

No, he wants peace of ass.

His orgasm will most likely be short-lived.

Intensely pleasurable yet unenduring, such is the orgasm.

How can it be his goal?

The greatest gift of woman to man is her peace.

Peace, contentment, relaxation, release, warmth, serenity.

Ejaculation orgasm he can have more or less at will.

The sweet serenity of her boudoir, the calm contentment of her ecstatic peaks, the indescribable peace of her ultimate Jade Palace, her sacred open O, her transcendental mouth, her incredible resting place, her temple of flesh that overwhelms the mind of man.

Here he can bathe in the waters of wholeness. The waves of her passion are the caress of an ocean's peaceful depths. The whole of lovemaking can be this ecstatic peace that is depth, absorption, surrender, descent into nature's endless valley of gravity, just like what is meant when we say fall in love.

Still, after man's orgasm, always, comes this peace he seeks.

This is the moment to be awake. Stay with her. Be with her now.

Here is what you were seeking.

The sweet, cool peace, the soothing lotion of love.

Look in her eyes. It is there. Even if she has learned to hide it, it is still there. It is there.

Peace of ass.

WHAT IS VOLUNTARY CREATIVE CLIMAX?

The word climax has its origin in the Greek klimax, meaning "ladder." Climax implies that an ascension has taken place, that you have climbed the ladder of sexual energy to a higher level, towards heaven. The climax to a sexual act can be something other than a conventional sexual orgasm. This is discussed at length in the Prologue. Including the kind of sexual orgasm that is familiar to you, your perfect climax may range from experiencing wave after wave of endless ecstastic oneness to falling into a deep and wonderfully restful sleep. Also, there are ways to vary your subjective experience of the orgasm itself.

Climax, whether it is of the kind studied by Masters and Johnson or not, can be a fantastically original and expressive act. Like painting or playing music, creative climaxing is an art. As with any other art form, skill and feeling are both essential. With very little effort, you will have immensely satisfying new experiences. Just a slight change in your concept of sexual climax, based on the approach of this book, may trigger these new experiences.

If you want bigger and better sexual orgasms, the skills in this section will help you do just that as well. Voluntary orgasm skills will make mutual genital orgasm during intercourse more likely.

You have a unique sexual potential which is maximized in a unique way. Become intimate with your erotic organs and with your individualized patterns of sexual response. Pursue peak physical, emotional, mental and spiritual well-being. Strive to fulfill your highest potential as a human being. In this way, you fulfill your highest orgasmic capacity as well.

Be all that you can be and you will understand the place of sexual orgasms in your life. You will be at choice about the sexual orgasm. You will be free to take it or leave it. You will be free to explore and enjoy voluntary creative climaxes, whether it is in the form of sexual orgasm or not. Ultra-intimate ecstasy will be yours.

ANGER AND SEXUAL ORGASM

Is there a relationship between anger and orgasm? It may be that people who find it easy to feel and display anger also tend to be very orgasmic. Difficulty with achieving sexual orgasm may be related to a suppression of the feeling or expression of anger. Perhaps developing a better relationship with anger enhances sexual orgasm for people who already orgasm with ease.

Rage and orgasm are very similar physiologically. When a person goes into an expressive rage, the blood rushes to the organs of expression, such as the face, hands and feet. The voice increases in volume. They may make moaning and groaning sounds. Their face may contort, as the faces of many do when they orgasm. Some people who are skilled at getting angry acknowledge that it can feel as good as a genital orgasm. Getting angry and expressing it may be a socially acceptable way of having an orgasm-type experience in public, a sort of "angergasm."

Maybe hitting a pillow before masturbating or staging a mock argument before making love will enhance your orgasm. Expressing anger in this way will liberate energy without hurting anybody.

When stored anger is released, orgasm may become fuller as well as easier. The release of anger liberates energy from the adrenal glands and the solar plexus. The next stop for this invigorating flood of life force is the Love spot and the thymus gland in the chest. From there, a tingling warmth, energization and a feeling of well-being may flow to the rest of the body, the neck, head, hands and feet especially. When orgasm is allowed to expand out and up and down from the erotic organs, more of its healing power is released.

Anger is a beautiful emotion that can accomplish a great deal under the right circumstances. By making anger more consciously a part of your love life, you will be able to use hidden energy for your chosen purposes, including genital orgasm.

CREATIVE SEXUAL ORGASM

Genital orgasm is an opportunity to be creative and inventive. It is a state of both mind and body. You can extend and enhance the conventional orgasm by changing the quality of your participation in it.

A sexual orgasm can add to your growth as a person. It can be a peak experience that will be remembered as one of the most dramatic, rewarding and beautiful moments of your entire life.

You can use your imagination to enhance orgasm apart from being sexually stimulated. Practice remembering the orgasm sensation while relaxing in a sitting or lying down position. Spread the feeling throughout your body-mind with your imagination. Psychological research has shown that vividly imagining an experience affects the nervous system nearly as much as the actual event.

Here are some powerful techniques that are aimed at changing your state of mind as you enter sexual orgasm. Just as you have eating habits and talking habits, you have genital orgasm habits. With these techniques you will be able to develop new orgasm habits and increase your options for ecstasy.

Affirmation: Mentally repeat "We Are One," "I Am You" or similar thought as you enter and ride the orgasm wave. You can agree on and practice ahead of time a oneness thought and image to share at mutual orgasm.

Afterglow: As the intensity of your peak fades, encourage the waves of life-giving pleasure to spread through your entire body-mind, filling your chest, your belly, your arms, your legs, your head. Feel the tingling or other pleasant feelings spread to the very top of your head and the tips of your ears, fingers, toes and tailbone. These waves of energy can be imagined in the form of rolling waves of white light or a shimmering golden mist that fills and surrounds you.

Afterglow is one of the best parts of making love. Lie still together for up to twenty minutes before you separate.

Some of the most beautiful sensations happen after genital orgasm. Consorts who quickly move into activity tend to miss out on this unexpected bonus.

Crying Release: This is not really a technique, but it is a wonderful thing.   Men as well as women may cry as part of having an orgasm.   Emotions are being released as the pulse waves of the orgasm loosen up internal blocks. Tears may fall afterwards, too, sometimes many hours later.   This is a special sign that the deep feeling core, or heart, is opening, that you have tapped the hidden power.

Dream Come True: Choose a visual image or symbol of something you would like to have in your life, such as a car, a vacation, more love, a higher state of consciousness. Imagine this image rushing out the top of your head on a wave of orgasmic bliss and winging away like a carrier pigeon to do your bidding.   Use this technique to bring into your life whatever you like, but not at someone else's expense.

Expand It: Expand the size of the pleasurable sensations of orgasm with your mind.   Make them much bigger. Use your imagination to puff them up like balloons.   You will feel that these pleasurable sensations fill up much more space than before.   The feelings and spaciousness may seem to extend far beyond your physical body.   A related technique is to imagine that the explosion of your orgasm extends far beyond your body-mind to fill up the whole room, perhaps even the whole house, the whole world, the universe.

Eyegasm: Maintain eye contact during sexual orgasm. Orgasm does not have to be mutual.   This technique may provide some of the most intimate and thrilling moments of your life.

Fly Through The Air: Genital orgasm is often compared to a rocket in flight.   Encourage the feeling of flying or going through space that may occur. See if you can go beyond the usual limits of your body-mind space. You may have the experience, for example, of being an eagle circling through the air high above the earth.

Give Your Orgasm: The pleasure of genital orgasm expands when it is given to the consort.   Rather than focusing on the pleasurable sensations in your genitals, give the bliss and energy you are feeling to your consort. Completely remove your attention from your own pleasure

and concentrate on transferring your enjoyment to them. You can do this for each other, which can create a truly amazing climax of blissful unity.

It may help if, as you approach orgasm, you place one palm over their Love spot and one on their head. Identify with them as completely as possible. Become them. Give everything that you are feeling to them as if they literally are you and their body-mind is your body-mind. In religious language, you are blessing them (see Love Spot.)

Ignorance Is Bliss: The next time you are about to have genital orgasm, blank from your mind all thoughts of expectation. Forget everything you learned about what orgasm is or is supposed to be. Approach the orgasm as if you've never had one, as if it is entirely new to you and you have no idea what to expect.

Jellogasm: If your usual way of enjoying an orgasmic rush is to tense and tighten your body-mind, try the opposite next time. Go completely limp. Become like jello. The orgasm is simply happening. You are not trying to control it in any way. You are just jello.

If your usual habit is to go limp, then try tensing your whole body instead. Yet another variation is to make your body-mind completely stiff. Be as rigid as a metal bar.

Let It Go: You may find that one ticket to memorable orgasm is to avoid concentrating on the sensations localized in your genitals. Keep your attention on another part of your body, such as your Love spot, or above your head. This may take some will power. Concentrating on the genital pleasure too much can prevent the spread of energy to the rest of the body, reducing pleasure and benefits.

Passive: One consort is completely passive and is brought to genital orgasm by the other. The passive consort uses whatever means he or she likes to deepen the experience and eliminate distractions, such as listening to music through headphones, a blindfold, ear plugs or going into a deeply relaxed state beforehand.

Stand On Your Head: Be masturbated to orgasm by your consort as you stand on your head. Use the wall for support unless you are good at headstands. The easy variation is to hang your head over the side of the bed. Sitting up in YabYum or standing up in Statues as you orgasm will also make you experience orgasm in a different way. In general, variations in position create variations in the orgasm experience, although these differences may be subtle.

White Light: Imagine that your orgasm is a blinding white light that is roaring through your body. You may want to direct the light up the spine into and above the brain. Try electric blue, solar gold and ruby red too.

EMOTIONAL CLIMAX

If you yield with sufficient sincerity and emotional intensity to your consort, you may experience what we call an "emotional climax." The intensity of your feeling is so great that it eclipses interest in or need for conventional orgasm on that occasion. Even if genital orgasm occurs, it may only be barely noticed as it melts into the larger drama of emotional surrender with the consort.

GRAND ORGASM

Even if you like to have sexual orgasm every time, build up the juice before you let it loose. Make the universal tension-relief principle work for you. One of the best ways to guarantee a grand sexual orgasm is to build up plenty of tension, or energy charge, before.

The intercourse strategies of the Imsak and Kabbazah styles are great for building up that erotic tension. Even if you plan on having a conventional orgasm, try not to think about it. Fool yourself into feeling you have no back door. Then, when sexual orgasm does arrive, it will be fantastic.

You have a pleasure threshold as well as a pain threshold. The more pleasure you can sustain, the more energy ecstasy you will be able to enjoy. Make a commitment to go past your usual tolerance level.

Sexual orgasm can be planned or be a surprise. Our experience has been that avoiding orgasm on some sessions will make it all the sweeter other times. Reserve the non-orgasm sessions for when you are low energy, working hard or just not in the mood.

Taking a break from having genital orgasms is not self-denying at all. You are just exploring other dimensions of your lovemaking world. When you go back, you can pretty much count on it being a grand orgasm.

One way to get more out of a quicky is to stop and wrench apart from each other as steam is building up for the actual genital union. This can be done before or after he has entered her. Since there is so much drive under these circumstances to get to orgasm, brief dramatic separation has the effect of driving you both absolutely crazy. If you stop too long, you could start analyzing, which may flatten your jungle fever beyond repair.

VOLUNTARY SEXUAL ORGASM

Achieving genital orgasm is a major concern for men and women. Here we will look at holistic strategies that can be used by both men and women. We recommend that you read all three sections on voluntary orgasm, though, because many things that work for men can work for women and vice versa. Other sections, such as Inspire Yourself or Make Love With Your Mind, include more approaches.

Bach Flower Remedies: The flower essence remedies developed by the late English physician Edward Bach are experiencing widespread acceptance. The potential sexual benefit of these remedies is great. Holly is said to eliminate suspicion, negativity and helps to open your heart and keep it open. Aspen may be taken for anxiety. Walnut is said to assist supersensitive individuals. These remedies, especially Holly, may be of value in achieving orgasm for the first time or more consistently or more fully. Bach remedies are thought to act on physical conditions through the emotions. Bach remedies are said to be completely harmless and non-toxic (see Appendix.)

Breathe Deeply and Completely: Breathe deeply and completely with every breath you take. Consistently deep, complete, rhythmic breaths through the mouth and/or nose while making love is probably the most valuable technique of all. A useful variation: think "fill up" when you inhale, "let go" when you exhale (or "charge up" and "radiate.") There is a direct cause and effect relationship between inability to breathe deeply, completely and rhythmically during lovemaking and inability to build up and contain sexual energy charge. Achieving genital orgasm during intercourse and achieving and maintaining erection during intercourse depend upon the breath, though PC muscle development, attitude, consort chemistry, nutrition, personal energy level and concentration are also major factors. See Complete Breath, Co-Inspiration, Inspire Yourself.

Close Your Eyes: Close your eyes and let your senses of touch, hearing, taste, smell and kinesthesia (movement) wake up. Tune in to the hundreds of physical and emotional sensations that are happening inside you, especially at your genitals. Instead of watching outside events feel around and inside of you. Also, tune in to the events in your consort's body-mind world. All of this may be much easier with eyes shut.

Crescent Pillow: In missionary position a crescent-shaped pillow under her buttocks affords maximum penetration and stimulates her clitoris. He can place his hands under her buttocks or sacrum (base of the spine) instead.

Dancing: Take dance classes on your own or just dance to music at home. Dance together as if you are making love, not by grinding pelvises but by enacting the entire erotic ritual non-verbally with body movements. Mirroring each other's movements, dancing in traditional styles such as the tango and simultaneously doing a movement sequence from karate, t'ai chi, yoga and so on together can be very powerful. Consorts who have mastered the art of communicating subtle erotic energy via dancing can experience a totally fulfilling sexual experience together with little or no physical contact. Of course, you can have as much physical contact in your dancing as you like.

Enter Soft: This is possibly an obvious one to most readers and it is one of the best. With a little practice and adequate lubrication, be it nature's own or not, entry while completely or partially soft is perfectly feasible. The advantage is you are starting from scratch. The treat for some women is to feel his manhood grow inside. Vegetable oil on either or both sex organs may ease penetration. Soft entry may be easier if she lies on her side and he enters her vagina from the rear. The ancient Chinese formula for ejaculation control was "Enter soft, leave hard." Typically, men enter hard. By entering soft instead, time spent achieving erection is time spent stimulating her as well.

Go Fast: Ha, ha. Fooled you. Fasting tends to create a state of emotional and physical serenity. When we make love while fasting it usually is an exceptional experience. Make love in the evening or the following morning after one day without food. On a one day fast avoid liquid food like fruit and vegetable juices as well. Just drink water or herbal tea. Longer fasts intensify the effects. We avoid conventional orgasm during a fast.

Herbs: Herbs are a whole study in themselves. There are plenty of good books. Ginseng and damiana are said to aid erotic arousal and orgasmic capacity for both male and female (may stimulate estrogen production). David likes "Four Ginsengs" from East Earth Herb. Ginseng is a stimulant and should not be taken every day. One approach is to take it for several months when its properties are needed most, then stop for several months. Herbal Kingdom puts out a damiana tea concentrate. Just add some drops to your drink shortly before making love.

Histamine Release: Pearson and Shaw report that taking niacin (vitamin B-6) fifteen to thirty minutes before the sex act stimulates histamine release in the body. This can intensify orgasm and may help men and women achieve orgasm who could not do so before. Try 100 milligrams to start. Walker and Walker suggest taking 50 mg three times a day (150 mg of niacin total) plus 50 mg before sexual activity. They also report that high daily doses of vitamin C may increase sexual desire and intensify orgasms. Take plenty of the B complex, too, if you follow this plan.

Negative Ions: An abundance of negative ions in your lovemaking environment may relax, reduce stress and improve reponsiveness (see Boudoir Basics.)

Pelvic Press: He enters but does not thrust. He pushes with his penis and pelvis against her as firmly yet comfortably as he can. He will get added leverage by pressing his feet against a wall or couch. He or she can manually stimulate her clitoris. Combine with pompoir (see Pompoir and Imsak.)

Pure Sensation: Become the sensations of your body completely. This is more than just focusing. We're talking becoming. Your intellect has temporarily ceased to function. Explore the body sensations just for their own sake and you will discover a new universe within you. It will help to move extremely slowly, at least at first, if you want to catch every nuance.

Relax (Meditate): Do you know how to achieve a state of deep relaxation? If you don't, why not learn now. Deep relaxation before sexual activity achieves impressive results because it makes tuning into your body-mind much easier. Achieving orgasm and making it more voluntary are mainly a matter of tuning in to your body-mind.

Relax and Energize During Intercourse: Let go of any tension in your breathing. Feel the breath go from the nose or mouth to the upper chest, middle chest and belly, then back out. Breathing through the nose deepens and helps you contain energy. Breathing through the mouth stimulates and helps you release energy. Let go now of the pelvic area, hips, thighs and buttocks. Now relax the hands, feet, fingers and toes. For the fourth step, as you exhale the breath out, squeeze your sexual muscles. Keep the muscles tight as you take 2-5 full inhalations and exhalations, then release. Repeat step four 10-20 times.

Share An Aphrodisiac: Much of the effect of an aphrodisiac preparation is due to the power of suggestion. The effects are enhanced when the preparation is taken as part of a well-orchestrated ritual. Champagne is reputed to have aphrodisiac properties (see Food.)

Spreading: Purposefully spread the energy away from the genital area towards your torso and extremities with your mind, breath and/or hands. You can gently stroke each other. This will probably be easier when moving slowly or during a full stop (see Full Stop, Spreading.)

Take Stress Levels Into Account: What's happening in your life definitely affects your sexual behavior. If you're really stressed out, don't hold lofty expectations for your performance. Be honest with your consort about any tension that you are under. They will more than likely understand. Your emotional sharing will bring you closer.

The next time you have a chance to vacation a week or two, try a tropical vacation of doing absolutely nothing. Lie in your beach chair day after day. Gaze at the ocean. Drink Mai Tai's. Read novels. After a week of this you will begin to really unwind. Another rejuvenating vacation is a one or two week supervised fast at a holistic health resort.

Woman On Top: You are probably already aware of the benefits of woman on top. This is a tried and true way to delay male ejaculation and increase female satisfaction. He will not be tensing his muscles to support himself and thrust in and out of her. If she is sitting up, either of you can caress her clitoris. For some couples, this will enable mutual orgasm with intercourse. Woman moving on top supplies an array of unique and delicious sensations for both of you. Woman on top may stimulate her G spot more. Also, by mutual agreement, this can put her in control of the pace. Making love lying on your sides offers some of the same advantages.

VOLUNTARY SEXUAL ORGASM FOR MEN

The male genital orgasm usually combines ejaculation, pulsations of the prostate gland and contractions of the PC muscle with intensely pleasurable but short-lived sensations. Pleasurable alternative male orgasm experiences do occur and are discussed elsewhere in this book, but so far scientific investigators have concentrated their research on the conventional male genital orgasm.

The issue of voluntary orgasm cannot be separated from the personal, economic, political and spiritual realities of man's place in the world today. As individuals, it is important for men to be more aware of the feelings of others and to express their emotions more freely, to develop their deeper identities apart from the expectations and demands of women and of each other. As a group, men can support and guide each other, creating an expanding circle of peace-loving masculine force that benefits not only men, but women and society as a whole. As men and women express more ecstasy and intimacy privately and publicly, the world will become happier, freer and more peaceful. See Voluntary Sexual Orgasm (including For Women), OTV, Tao of Sex, Imsak.

Voluntary Ejaculation

Voluntary ejaculation is a term introduced by Michael Castleman, an editor of Medical Self-Care magazine. It replaces the older and less descriptive term ejaculation control. The word control implies a state of tension to many men, when in fact the key to making ejaculation voluntary, to having control, is relaxation. This is true whether you seek to delay or achieve ejaculation.

The purpose of voluntary ejaculation training is to make ejaculation a choice, a voluntary act. This does not mean you no longer can be surprised by the ejaculation orgasm. You can choose that, too. Masculine self-esteem usually gets a boost as ejaculation becomes more voluntary.

An important first step in making ejaculation voluntary is to realize that you do not need to ejaculate every time you have intercourse. If you believe that you must ejaculate every time, then for you ejaculation is involuntary. To paraphrase Shakespeare's Hamlet, you can enjoy freedom of choice "To ejaculate or not to ejaculate?" Among those that criticize the "every time" belief are Michael Castleman, who was the founding Director of the Men's Reproductive Health Clinic in San Francisco, and prominent sex therapist Bernie Zilbergeld.

We met a young man who delays ejaculation by creating a map of the United States in his mind and mentally visiting each state. Men who try to use mental concentration techniques usually become spectators instead of participants and miss out on a lot of fun and satisfaction. Many times the technique fails anyway.

You can let go and still last as long as you want.

Getting to that place where ejaculation is voluntary is not just a mental activity. It is a body-mind process. Below we look at some of the skills that may help you to maximize your penis power, whatever your individual need.

The Training

You must be ready to work out regularly, daily if possible, for at least a month or two. You may choose Kegel exercises, the male Deer exercise, the Root Lock with the Thunderbolt Gesture or some other training. Some kind of regular training program for developing the muscles used during sexual intercourse is a must. These muscles are the pubococcygeus (PC) muscle and the muscles of the anus. If you have a sedentary job or drive a great deal in your work, why not do them on the job?

Make an effort to maximize your skills. You probably place lovemaking near the top of your list of favorite activities. How much time did you spend last year learning how to become a better lover? Compare that with how much time you spend improving your job skills or learning how to fix your car or do some other favorite activity. A little homework and do-it-yourself training can really go a long way. Your sacrifice in terms of time, effort and energy will be peanuts compared to the results.

There is another trap, though, and that is to emphasize

skill too much.   Men already tend to believe that all they need is the right technique at the right time.   Just push the right buttons and sexual fulfillment will follow automatically.   You may be a great performer then, a fact some partners will certainly appreciate, but your experience will probably stay on the surface.   The depths of pleasure will escape you.

Skill is not at all the only thing that matters.   What and how much you are able to feel matters at least as much.   The ability to feel--and to express those feelings with sensitivity--is what being human is all about.   There are, in fact, men who are able to feel so deeply and share so much of those deep feelings that women are drawn to them like thirsty desert travelers to an oasis.

George Leonard illustrates this point beautifully in his book The End of Sex.   Charles, an old black jazz pianist in the North Beach area of San Francisco, was renowned for his success with women.   When asked about his secret, Leonard was astounded to hear Charles reply that he cried. His tears flowed, Charles said, because of their beauty, because it felt so wonderful.   Charles said he couldn't help it.   He covered their bodies with his tears, and they loved it.   No man had ever cried for them before.

If you are already emotionally vulnerable with women, you have probably found that they respect and desire you greatly for it.   Emotional vulnerability increases your personal and sexual magnetism.   The word vulnerability has a scary sound to it, but in practice it simply means to relax and soften the mind, the emotions, the body.   Soft style lovemaking makes vulnerability easier.

On the job, competition is fierce.   Vulnerability like that is undesirable.   When it is time to make love, it is time to make a shift from invulnerability to vulnerability.

In medieval times, a knight had to take his armor off to make love to his lady.   This didn't make him a target.   To take your armor off just means that you are willing to be affected by your consort, ready to make love.

Maximum penis power is based on a lot more than emotional vulnerability, though.   It is a synergy of many seemingly unrelated factors, including your awareness of your body-mind, general health, diet, drugs, allergies, exercise, hormone levels, energy level, self-suggestion, life stress level and consort chemistry.

How Do You Achieve Ejaculation?

Take some time out to experiment with arousal, erection and ejaculation. Probably the most convenient way to become more aware of what is happening within you is solo masturbation. Using a lubricant, masturbate for at least 20 minutes. Approach orgasm at least three times. You may ejaculate at the conclusion or you may allow your erection to subside. Do this on several different days. Do it dry, no lubrication, also.

What do you notice happening in your body as you approach orgasm? What is your breathing like? Are you holding your breath? Are you panting? What muscles are you tensing? Are you contracting your pelvic and genital region? These are ways of speeding up ejaculation orgasm.

Men often learn how to achieve orgasm under stressful circumstances. Did you furtively borrow one of your dad's dirty books and masturbate in the bathroom, making no noise in order to avoid being discovered? This is only one pattern out of thousands, but the result is the same. Adolescents learn to achieve ejaculation orgasm as quickly as possible, to build up tension rapidly, reach the peak and quickly go over the edge into the relief and pleasure of orgasm.

The high school sex scene wasn't much of an improvement. Sex was a thick muggy tension in the air. When you had a chance to have some sex, you grabbed for it. Once again, time felt short. Having sex in the car meant make it fast. You might get discovered. Sex was in short supply and when you got some, you wolfed it down, even if the object of your affections was a new porno magazine you consumed in an afternoon of marathon masturbation.

The most valuable step you can take is to develop a detailed knowledge of how you achieve ejaculation orgasm. This means taking it slow. Be aware of the tendency to rush, the compulsion to get there. Enjoy the preliminaries. Explore the delight of just very mild arousal, the pleasurable feelings that occur long before ejaculation feels inevitable. Do this with yourself and/or with your consort's help. Pay special attention to how your breath, your muscles and your thoughts work together to build up arousal and bring on your climax.

Techniques To Use During Intercourse

These techniques should increase your ability to enjoy intercourse and satisfy your consort. They are not just techniques for achieving and maintaining erection and for making ejaculation more voluntary. They invite your full mental and emotional participation as well. Some of these techniques are dealt with more elaborately elsewhere in this book.

Breathe Through Your Nose: The man's tendency is to rapidly heat up and explode, not unlike a volcano. The single most effective way to stay cool under pressure is to breathe slowly and deeply and rhythmically through the nose. To make this work you must breathe very deeply and completely and be consistent. A few deep breaths here and there while making love may help, too, but don't count on it. Some men find this technique is made even more effective by concentrating on extending the exhalation time.

Clove Oil: Apply a very tiny drop of clove oil to the head of the penis before intercourse and spread it around with your fingers. Avoid the urethral opening. Do not do this just before entering her as you may get clove oil on her genitals. This may not be to her liking, so you should ask first. You may enjoy the tingling sensation. The mild anesthetic effect may help delay ejaculation. Some men apply Nupercainal® Anesthetic Ointment or similar non-prescription products to achieve the effect. This technique is not a substitute for developing ejaculation control, but it can be a fun variation.

Condoms: Aside from their birth control applications, condoms offer the advantage of reducing the stimulation to the penis, delaying ejaculation. Some ultra-thin Japanese imports offer protection with only a slight loss of penile sensitivity. Don't use a petroleum base cream at the same time. H-R or K-Y lubricating jellies are excellent. Avoid condoms in a packet that is not perfectly sealed. Buy condoms that have the nipple-shaped receptacle at the end. Put the condom on before you go in. It is possible for her to pull the condom off the penis when she is on top.

Emotional Detachment: Emotional involvement is certainly stressed in this book, but emotional detachment has its uses, too. The excitement and pleasure that is felt in

189

sexual activity is largely emotional for both sexes. Play with this fact. Be cool, a little detached, a bit flip in your attitude and see what happens. Don't be cold or selfish, just, well, cool. These seem to be attributes that make some men very sexy. Most of the macho superstars of the movie screen display them in their characters.

Here is one piece of advice that works best in small doses. Some of the old Chinese schools recommended that the male Tao Of Sex aspirant think of the woman as ugly and disgusting to avoid getting overheated and ejaculating involuntarily.

Fellatio For Dessert: We would all like to be sexual supermen and first be fellated for half an hour and still be able to give the woman who has just so expertly honored our instrument the best time of her life. Let's be realistic. It all depends on what you want, both together and separately. If what both of you want is for you to last as long as possible inside her, so that you can orgasm together or succeed at Karezza (see Karezza) or whatever, fellatio as dessert or fellatio solo may be necessary. You rarely see fellatio illustrated in the ancient Chinese erotic art for this very reason--it is so arousing for a man.

Fierce Expression: Fierce expression happens to be one of our personal favorites because it is just such a crazy thing to do while making love. It is an inheritance from the old Chinese experts. Make a face that embodies the RAHRRR feeling that you may have bottled up inside you during lovemaking. Go ahead and roar. This roar is not only a tension release but it is also your cry of victory and exultation at taking your woman. You may feel timid the first few times, but most women will love this.

Here is a fierce face. Open your mouth wide, stretch out your tongue like a lion, and bug out and roll up or cross your eyes as you tense your facial muscles. If you've seen the horrific faces of Oriental temple guardian statues then you know what this expression looks like.

The logic behind this action is that the face is one of the areas of the body-mind most under the control of our self-conscious social ego (as in the phrase "to lose face"). It may need loosening up for you to get in touch with the irrational primal powers released in lovemaking. A penetrating facial massage before making love has much the same effect. You can make a game out of doing these grimaces alone or together as a way of working out negative emotions before, rather than during, lovemaking.

Focus Physically: Focus on your physical movements with all of your attention. Focus on your physical sensations fully, especially your sense of touch. Making love is a touching experience. Leave your mind behind and stay at the cutting edge of the sensory present. Nothing else is needed. Just touch.

Frequent Intercourse: Frequent intercourse with or without frequent ejaculation orgasm is helpful. What would be frequent for you is not necessarily frequent for another guy, though. The key is to establish a rhythm in your sexual relations. To a point, having a routine is beneficial, just as going to work at the same time makes life smoother--but only to a point, of course.

Heavy Belly: A heady uprushing sensation often occurs just before ejaculation takes place. This is just one bit of evidence that ejaculation requires a shift in the direction your personal energy is moving. In an ordinary ejaculation, that direction is first up and then out, at least in David's experience.

Imagine that your body-mind is a well and you have thrown a small but very heavy stone or iron ball into it. This ball sinks deeper and deeper and deeper into the well of your body-mind. As this ball sinks lower, your attention goes with it. It continues sinking and sinking and sinking. Finally, it hits bottom with a resounding and very solid thud. It is there to stay.

The location of your physical center of gravity is about two inches below the navel. This is also the location of the pelvic body mass center point. You may have seen the dolls that are heavy in the base and so can not be knocked over that are popular in Japan. As long as you stay collected at your body's center of gravity, your energy will not move from its place. A similarity between ejaculation and fully expressed anger is that both seem to require this upward energy movement followed by an explosive dispersal of the energy. This can be observed if your physical center of gravity is maintained under these circumstances.

A special breath will help you stay in your center of gravity. When you exhale, pull your lower belly in firmly. The muscles of your stomach will force almost all of your air out, and your inhalation will happen automatically.

191

In Deep and Circle: In and out again and again is not necessarily the winning thrusting strategy. Put your hands underneath her buttocks. A pillow there may work as well. It helps if you have something to push against with your feet, such as the wall. You can even grasp her shoulders and pull if this is comfortable for her. Circle and dance with your pelvis. Your penis is less stimulated but your satisfaction, as well as hers, may be more.

Intensive Exercise: One of the best ways to prolong erection and easily control ejaculation during intercourse may be to engage in a vigorous daily exercise program. Athletes are known for their ability to delay ejaculation during intercourse. Though they may be more gifted to begin with, their intensive exercise schedules could have something to do with it. Be sure to obtain your physician's consent before embarking on such a rigorous exercise program.

Cardiovascular exercise is not the only kind of exercise that may have this effect. Intensive daily hatha yoga, T'ai Chi and other soft exercise styles may have a similar effect. Intensive daily exercise may contribute to ejaculatory control by releasing mental and sexual tensions, balancing and harmonizing physical energies and burning off toxic accumulations in the system.

Focused exercise just before making love has also been reported to increase potency and ejaculation control. The key does not seem to be any particular kind of exercise. Concentration of mind in body as you move and choosing movements that bring you real enjoyment seem to be the key factors.

Perineum Point: Here is a concentration technique that successfully delays ejaculation orgasm. It may lead to some unusual and most delightful alternative orgasm experiences. Midway between the anus and scrotum visualize a small red dot. Concentrate on this dot. A major body energy center is located in men just above this point. (The equivalent point in women is located at the cervix.) Concentration on this point may give you a completely new perspective on how to enjoy and use arousal energy. Voluntary ejaculation and achieving and maintaining erection may become much easier.

Pull Out: That's right, just pull out. Pulling out hard is an effective easy way to reduce ejaculatory urgency and prolong intercourse. Not only that, it can add to the erotic tension, a factor the Imsak style translates into a fine art. If just pulling out doesn't reduce your ejaculatory urgency enough, apply the Masters and Johnson squeeze technique. She puts her thumb behind the head of your penis and squeezes firmly. In other words, her thumb is at the top of the penis of the side facing your body and her fingers are on the side facing the other way. This can be done with one or two hands. She needs to do this firmly and your verbal feedback is helpful if for no other reason than she may think she is hurting you. This method of pulling out is used if you want to re-enter her. Pressure on the pubic region immediately above the penis will also delay ejaculation.

Relax Before: It can take hours to prepare a good meal at home so why not take half an hour to prepare for making love? Part of the problem is that taking time to relax just isn't that well understood by our society. Massage, especially acupressure massage, deep muscle relaxation techniques and meditation are just a few of your options. Hot baths and jacuzzis relax, however, they also tend to devitalize, so don't overdo them, and follow with a cold shower. In fact, a cold shower or bath by itself just before making love stimulates erotic drive.

Swallow Saliva: This may seem like nonsense but the principle is sound. A man burning up from being in the sun all day will really be helped by a glass of water. Likewise, saliva will help cool a man down in the heat of lovemaking. Swirl the tongue around the mouth to get more saliva. Pressing the tongue against the soft palate will increase saliva flow. According to tradition, you swallow the saliva in three gulps. It may seem more genteel to reach for your glass of Perrier with a twist of lemon, but this is not good form in the middle of battle. Also, recycling saliva is believed to have healing properties. Sharing saliva is also said to be good for both of you, so exchange saliva as you kiss.

Testicle Tug: For some reason, this feels much more pleasurable when she does the tugging. She will want to get a firm grasp and then tug harder than she thinks she should. This helps delay ejaculation because the testicles must elevate close to the body for most men to ejaculate, though this tends to be less true in older men.

Thrusting Sequences: Thrusting sequences put a method in your madness. This stylistic choice has been receiving rave reviews from women for many centuries now, so on that basis alone it is worth trying. What we call "Chinese Nines" translates in practice to nine shallow-one deep. Three, five and seven shallow is also good. Variations in depth, angle of penetration as well as speed of thrust or withdrawal are also worth consideration.

Mentally divide vaginal depth into three or more levels, such as shallow, middle and deep. The ancient Chinese experts set up eight divisions. The deepest was called, appropriately enough, North Pole. Angle of penetration can be varied on both entry and withdrawal and can be straightforward, diagonal, zigzag and so on. Some women will prefer that you continue thrusting after your ejaculation. See Imsak section and the books of Jolan Chang.

The Turtle: The Turtle is an ancient Chinese health exercise so named because it imitates the craning movement of the turtle as he sticks his head out from his shell. To perform the Turtle, pull out so that you are just barely inside the vagina. Arch your back, stretch your neck, roll your head back and lower the shoulders. Close your eyes and mouth, mentally go within, press the tip of the tongue against the soft palate (the tongue press), flare your nostrils and take several complete breaths. Perform the Turtle when you are highly aroused to delay ejaculation. It is said to send energy up to the thymus, thyroid and brain.

A simpler Taoist technique is to suddenly lift your head, pop your eyes wide open and look to the right, left, up and down. At the same time, contract your lower belly. This should help delay ejaculation.

The Taoist sex experts also advised the man to roll his eyes in circles and to click or grind his teeth 24 or 36 times during intercourse to avoid ejaculation. In The Classic of Immortals grinding teeth, long exhalations and pressing firmly on the prostate point with the index and middle fingers of the left hand are combined for the purpose of returning semen energy to the brain.

These techniques were believed to move the vital force up into the brain and around the body-mind rather than leaving it stuck in the genitals. If nothing else, the novelty of these techniques will distract and entertain you.

Vaginal Veneration: Cunnilingus is an oft-neglected art. Based on current research, women need to be aroused for an average of 20 minutes before they can achieve orgasm, at least during intercourse. Fully arousing her well before you have your ejaculation orgasm may turn out to be more satisfying for you as well. This may take more time than you would like, but your unselfishness will probably be very amply repaid. Skill with the penis during intercourse is important, but you must be sensitive to her unique needs to satisfy her. Ask her what she would like you to do. A simple reliable technique is to **very** gently and lightly move your tongue or moistened middle finger (use oil or saliva) side to side on the clitoris. The Taoist sex experts rated cunnilingus very highly as they believed that lapping up the woman's "tide of yin" (genital orgasm) added masculine force and healthy years to the lucky male.

The Prostate Point

Sexual stimulation causes the prostate to swell up with its own juices. At this point, the prostate must be relieved. It can pump itself, or you or your consort can do the pumping manually. When the prostate has reached this stage and begins pumping or emitting on its own, you are approaching ejaculation. Soon the urgency in the prostate for relief will reach a peak, helping to trigger ejaculation orgasm. Provided you begin doing the pumping for the prostate well before this peak is reached, and pump frequently and firmly, your ejaculation can be delayed indefinitely. If a man's PC/anal muscles are exceptionally strong, he may be able to accomplish the same result by flexing his sexual muscle. In this way, the need for external intervention is eliminated.

The male prostate is a muscular gland the size and shape of a chestnut. It is located at the root of the penis inside the body. It contributes to the pleasure felt during arousal and ejaculation orgasm. The neck of the bladder passes through it. One side of it can be felt manually through the wall of the anus facing the penis. A physician will do this when performing a prostate examination. Pressure can also be exerted on the prostate on the perineum between the anus and the scrotum. This is the location of the prostate point.

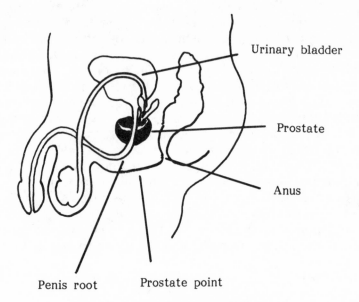

Urinary bladder

Prostate

Anus

Penis root   Prostate point

The Prostate Pressure Point

The prostatic fluid secreted by the prostate is the main ingredient found in semen. The prostate performs a mixing function, combining secretions from the epididymis in the testicles and the seminal vesicles with its own. Secretions from Cowper's glands, which lie just in front of the prostate along the urethra, are added. Together, these four ingredients make up what we call semen.

Ejaculation is a two-stage process. During the first stage, emission, the prostate gland and the seminal vesicles begin contracting and empty their ingredients into the urethra. The second stage is expulsion, the muscular pulsations that move the sperm out of the body, usually accompanied by intensely pleasurable sensations. Emission and expulsion can be experienced separately without difficulty by masturbating close to the point of no return and then relaxing. The contractions of the prostate and seminal vesicles will be clearly felt. A clear fluid may appear at the end of your penis, which is part of the emitted substances.

Although the prostate point pressure technique has been around for a very long time, it has not been medically tested.   It is an experimental technique. You may want to consult your physician before altering your sexual patterns to incorporate this technique.

The technique itself is quite simple.   Push with one or two fingers up and into the perineum.   The correct point is central between the anus and the scrotum just behind the root of the penis.   Acupuncture locates a major point (CV1) there.   According to Chinese sexology, if the man does it for himself he should use the index and middle fingers of his left hand.   Some couples will find this technique easier to apply if the man withdraws briefly.

The push can be a long and firm pressure, accompanied by exhalation.   Encourage yourself to feel a sense of relief as you do this.   Or the push can be a rhythmic pulsing action.   You will probably find it more pleasurable when she applies the pressure and does it for you.   This is the way the Arabs have done it for many centuries.

As an added bonus, the manual pressure causes the penis to swell and emboldens the erection, a fact which she will find delightfully noticeable.   For this reason alone, her application of the technique in the middle of the heat of lovemaking fits right in.   This further reduces the male need for self-conscious controlling in order to delay ejaculation.

What happens to the unejaculated contents of the prostate?   The male body readily recycles the preserved seminal ingredients via lymphatic ducts, which in turn delivers these hormonal treasures to the blood for the service of the whole body.

Rhythmically pushing on the prostate point imitates the rhythmic pulsation of the prostate when it approaches or participates in climax.   The method can also be applied directly to the prostate by inserting a lubricated finger into the anus and pressing towards the penis.   In addition to reducing prostate tension and thereby delaying ejaculation, these techniques are quite pleasurable provided you are sufficently aroused.   The appearance of small amounts of prostatic fluid at the tip of the penis is quite normal and is not a cause for alarm.

Some bestselling sex guides, including ESO and The G Spot, stress the pleasure that stimulating the prostate in this way can give. It is indeed pleasurable for many men to have the prostate stimulated via the prostate point or directly through the rectal wall. In our opinion, though, this stimulation tends to delay orgasm when a man is not yet close to orgasm and can bring on an orgasm if a man is highly aroused. Pressure on the prostate point can help make ejaculation more voluntary by prolonging the stage of excitation and arousal that a man enjoys well before he reaches the point of no return.

If you have not ejaculated in the course of a vigorous lovemaking session or have no intention of doing so, it is common sense that you or your consort employ one of these techniques to reduce the swelling of your prostate gland. Repeated acts of intercourse in which you push yourself to the verge of ejaculation without actually ejaculating, however, may result in a congested prostate, enlarged prostate and/or prostatitis. If, on the other hand, your lovemaking is very leisurely and you are not approaching the point of no return, frequent ejaculation may not be necessary.

The prostate point pressure technique is completely different from coitus saxonus, which is advocated by some Eastern sex experts. Coitus saxonus is accomplished by pressing on this same point just before ejaculation. The ejaculate is blocked and forced into the bladder.

Although we believe that loss of energy is largely prevented by coitus saxonus, we do not agree that the technique is without danger. We recommend it only be used in a clutch by the man who is committed to conserving and recycling his life force (see Tao of Sex), or as a fun experiment to try a few times. It can change the way a man's orgasm feels in some interesting ways.

A "look ma, no hands" version of coitus saxonus is what we call semen stopping. This can be performed during intercourse and is made much easier if the man is on his back. Immediately before ejaculation, clench your PC and rectal muscles and hold your breath. You will experience all of the sensations of orgasm with very little if any ejaculation.

This technique is much more dramatic when performed as a masturbation because nothing comes out even though you felt the orgasmic sensations. Like coitus saxonus, this is an interesting item to play with a little; however, you can overstress the prostate and other parts of your urinary and genital ducts doing this. If nothing else, though, semen stopping is a vivid demonstration of the power of the sexual muscles in the man.

Neither **coitus saxonus** nor semen stopping should be used as a means of birth control. Both can be used in a pinch for the conservation-oriented man, but their place is in the early stages of training.

VOLUNTARY SEXUAL ORGASM FOR WOMEN

Achieving orgasm is a major concern of many women today and rightly so. Some women can achieve orgasm on their own but have difficulty orgasming during intercourse. Below we make some practical suggestions for achieving conventional orgasm more voluntarily which may be new to you. Methods for achieving alternative orgasmic experiences are discussed elsewhere in this book.

The issue of voluntary orgasm cannot be separated from the personal, economic, political and spiritual realities of woman's place in the world today. As individuals, it is important for women to become more assertive and expressive, to develop their identities apart from the expectations and demands of men and of each other. As a group, women can support and guide each other, creating an expanding circle of feminine force that benefits not only women, but men and society as a whole. As men and women express more ecstasy and intimacy privately and publicly, the world will become happier, freer and more peaceful (see Pompoir, Sexercises, Voluntary Sexual Orgasm, Voluntary Sexual Orgasm For Men, Kabbazah.)

Easy Orgasm

Many excellent guides to achieving orgasm, such as **Woman's Orgasm** by Kline-Graber and Graber or **For Yourself** by Lonnie Barbach, are available. Qualified sex therapists are located in your area. The American Association of Sex Educators, Counselors and Therapists publishes the National Register of Certified Sex Therapists if you would like assistance (see Appendix.) You may order the Register from them. It is also available at some libraries. We strongly recommend making use of short-term sex therapy resources. Current studies show that short-term sex therapy offers a success rate of about 80%.

"Know thyself" is the cornerstone of voluntary orgasm. Vaginal self-examination especially can be an important step towards increasing orgasmic capacity. The feminist movement has created an invaluable network of services and resources. A New View of a Woman's Body by the Federation of Feminist Women's Health Centers is an excellent guide.

How Does Your Orgasm Happen?

You are probably familiar with the Masters and Johnson four-stage model of human sexual response (excitement, plateau, orgasm and resolution). Valuable though this model is, it leaves out the fact that orgasm is a two-step dance for the nervous system. The part of your nervous system most involved in building up to and delivering orgasm has two divisions, only one of which is usually dominant at any time.

The parasympathetic half of your (involuntary) nervous system is mainly responsible for the excitement and plateau phases. The crucial transition from plateau to orgasm, however, is handled by the sympathetic half. Look at the light switch on your wall. To turn on the light, you must flip that switch. To turn on orgasm, you must flip the switch that moves you from the parasympathetic to the sympathetic.

The sympathetic nervous system handles your fight or flight responses. Anger, stress, survival, aggression and so on are under its management. Though a form of stress and tension like anxiety may interfere with the achievement of orgasm, stress in the form of force or intensity that is under your control is very desirable. Muscular, emotional and mental force applied at just the right time is the straw that breaks the camel's back, the hand that flips the light switch and turns the light on.

Force at the right moment will trigger the transition from plateau to orgasm. Applied too soon, focusing force will tend to reduce arousal. An example of focusing force is tensing the whole body, especially the muscles around the vagina, and moaning out loud.

Another way to look at the situation is in terms of softness/hardness and coolness/warmth. The body-mind energy of a woman who is experiencing difficulty achieving orgasm may be too soft and too cool. She may need to toughen up physically, emotionally, mentally and display more energy overall. A hardening activity such as martial arts or assertiveness training, preferably taught by a woman, may release her inner hardness and heat. Aerobics classes are also good in this way, and Kegel clenches can be done with the butt tucks. This additional hardness and heat can contribute to sexual arousal and take her over the edge into orgasm. It will make orgasm more voluntary if she already orgasms frequently. Of course, a few women are too hard and too hot and need to soften and cool down. This may be the result of too much smoking and red meat. Yoga is excellent for maintaining hormonal balance, and may be of special value for the hard, hot woman doing intense cardiovascular exercise. Too much of a good thing is still too much. Find the balance between hard and soft, warm and cool that is ideal for you.

Blood plays a major role in making orgasm possible, and your blood flows where your attention goes. Improvement in your ability to focus thought and emotion in your sex organs makes orgasm more voluntary for you. Since the oxygen carried by the blood is also vital for pre-orgasm buildup and orgasmic release, deep breathing in many varieties may be helpful. You can visualize the robust cherry red healing blood full of oxygen and erotic feeling rushing to and engorging your sexual organs in the buildup phase.

The PC muscle is the star of the genital orgasm achievement team. Your voluntary contractions help build up arousal to the necessary peak, and will further strengthen them. They bring blood, feeling and energy to the vagina, clitoris and G spot. During genital orgasm, the PC muscle contracts once every .8 seconds. If you want to make your orgasm more voluntary, PC muscle exercises are a must (see Sexercises.)

Set up the right conditions and you will orgasm. By paying attention to the sequence of events that leads to orgasm in your body-mind, you will know learn to repeat the experience more or less at will.

Orgasm results when excitation builds up sufficiently in the genital and pelvic areas. Orgasm is based on the tension-relief principle: in order to feel relief, you must first experience tension. This is not tension in the sense of stress, of course, but rather the muscular tension of a clenching fist. Allow your clenching genital fist to expand into explosive orgasm.

Some women who are able to achieve orgasm while masturbating have difficulty doing so during intercourse. There are many reasons for this. Sexual scientists are not certain that every woman is able to achieve orgasm during intercourse even under ideal conditions. In several recent surveys, for example, less than half of the women reported having orgasms during intercourse. Some women who frequently masturbate with vibrators are concerned that using the vibrator has raised their tolerance for erotic stimulation too high for orgasm during intercourse to occur.

The notion that orgasm must occur with every act of intercourse may be part of the problem. This expectation sets up an unrealistic goal demands that only succeeds in creating more undesirable stress. The pursuit of such a goal can take on an obsessive quality, which may take you even further from real total sexual fulfillment.

One of the best ways to be assured of having an orgasm during intercourse is to forget about the whole idea and just get into it as sensuously and feelingly as you can. By being here now you may eventually find yourself having an orgasm. You are now feeling so good that you couldn't care less if you had one or not. Though the skillful application of force may help you achieve genital orgasm when and how you like it, body-mind relaxation is the key to voluntary sexual orgasm.

Practice the sexercises described in the beginning of this book. Everything you do to tune and tone your body-mind contributes to your success. Voluntary orgasm is a self-assertive act. Work with your body-mind several times a week, daily if possible. Relax it, strengthen it, develop it, get to know it better.

What at first may seem like burdensome discipline will become your path to freedom. Behind the issue of voluntary orgasm for women is the issue of fulfilling self-expression for women. You can network with other women more freely and more extensively than in any recent time in history.

Voluntary orgasm means the ability to delay orgasm as well as bring it on. This ability to delay orgasm develops automatically as you experience more finely and deeply your arousal states, especially leading into the orgasm. Delaying orgasm may help you time your orgasm so that you and your consort orgasm together.

There really are many beautiful lovemaking climax experiences that are possible which are not genital orgasms. But the first step for you may be to achieve a personal peak of genital orgasm expressiveness that you feel really good about. Then you can ask "What's next? Is there more? Do I have other options for sexual ecstasy that are different from genital orgasm?"

As you continue to experiment with your orgasm options, you may begin to enjoy blissful energies during lovemaking and apart from lovemaking that are not connected to the genital trigger at all. By fully exploring the potentials of your genital generator, though, you can get in touch with these blissful, healing energies of the body-mind. You discover wonderful reasons to love and esteem and trust yourself. You become you.

Holistic Self-Help For Voluntary Orgasm

Here are some holistic suggestions that may help you set up the right conditions more easily. You may find this information helpful regardless of the ease with which you currently reach orgasm. After all, genital orgasm is not just a physical response. Your mind and heart participate too. You may want to look at the other chapters on Voluntary Sexual Orgasm, drugs, diet and exercise as well.

Practicing with these techniques will also show you how to delay genital orgasm. You may want to delay it in order to assure mutual orgasm, to build up more charge to get a bigger bang or to store the accumulated energy if your health, energy level or mental attitude are under par. The ability to orchestrate orgasm includes learning how to start, stop, delay, alter and extend orgasm, all skills which you will acquire as you continue to experiment with the techniques in this book and explore the endless variety of genital orgasms and of climaxes of other kinds.

Arousal Before Penetration: The more aroused you are before coitus, the better chance you will have of orgasming when he is inside you.   Be verbally specific about what you like.   For example, suggest that he massage your vaginal lips and clitoris very gently with cocoa butter.   Let him know exactly what feels good, and thank him for it.   Also, you don't have to be shy even about stimulating yourself. Some men love to watch and can learn a lot this way.

Suggest that he tease you with his penis at your vaginal entrance for awhile before before entering, long enough to get you asking for more.   Be willing to do something to relax him first.

Belly Dancing: Belly dancing training develops awareness and strength in many of the muscles vital to full sexual satisfaction.   It is a beautiful whole-body exercise approach.   If belly dancing is offered in your area, leap at the chance.   Stomach churning, a yoga exercise, offers a similar benefit.

Breathing: Continuous deep energizing breaths during lovemaking can be an enormous help for increasing arousal and bringing on genital orgasm.   Hyperventilation will not occur if breath is rhythmic and easy.   Open the belly and chest and take in plenty of air, but stay comfortable. Straining and over-efforting only delays good results.   See Complete Breath, Inspire Yourself and Co-Inspiration.

Cervix Point: During intercourse imagine a red dot at the entrance of your cervix or just concentrate your attention in your cervix.   A major body energy center is located there which can greatly increase the intensity, duration and pleasure of your orgasms.   You may also have more alternative climax experiences as a result of intense concentration here as well.

Es Sibfahheh: Get on top and face him.   This is the position known as es sibfahheh, "swimming."   The position gets its name from the ease with which the clitoral bud is manually stimulated by you or him and intense arousal is achieved, especially in conjunction with pompoir.   This position enables you to control your arousal level manually and may also stimulate your G spot (see Pompoir, Imsak.)

Energy Level: Genital orgasm is a release of energy. Your body-mind won't want to release energy if it doesn't have enough to go around to begin with.   A surplus of energy ranks with PC muscle training as one of the major secrets of sexual fulfillment.   Women are conditioned from an early age to behave in a subdued fashion.   Claim your energy via exercise, nutrition, relaxation, meditation, women's support groups and so on (see Body-Mind section.)

Iron: The presence of richly oxygenated blood is essential for orgasm to take place.   Adequate iron is needed for blood to carry oxygen.   Yet nine out of ten women were found to have iron deficient diets in the first Health and Nutrition Examination Survey mandated by the United States Congress in the early 1970's.   Take a minimum of 10 or 15 mg supplemental iron a day to replace the iron you lose during menstruation.   Women can exceed 50 mg a day but men should not.

Martial Arts: Aside from increasing power and heat, self-confidence and self-defense skill,   martial arts training teaches you how to focus the body-mind for a brief, intense moment, the same skill that is used to go over the edge from pleasurable arousal to resounding orgasm.

Pompoir: Pompoir power maximizes female orgasmic potential.   Our society undervalues it and suffers the result but you don't have to.   Coordinate PC clenches with inhale or exhale and affirmation, visualization and so on.

Prostate Point: His prostate point is located in the middle of his perineum just in front of his anus.   Although he can press it himself, if you press it for him his enjoyment of the technique will probably increase.   In fact, he may find it is literally ten times more enjoyable when you do it.   Use rhythmic firm pressure or sustained firm pressure.   Although this technique is used to stimulate the prostate and bring on orgasm, it is equally effective as a means of delaying orgasm by compressing the prostate and literally deflating it.   This ancient technique has been practiced in China and the Arab countries for centuries.   You can be physically assertive with this technique without making open demands.   You will be giving him pleasure and delaying his ejaculation, increasing the likelihood of full satisfaction for you as well.   Also, your knowledge of this technique may impress him favorably.   You can also insert your finger in his anus and press directly on his prostate gland on the side facing his penis. Either position may be used to create an exotic and more intense orgasm for him. You may also enjoy rectal stimulation during orgasm. The prostate point pressure technique has been used with great success by prostitutes in some countries to guarantee repeat customers (see Voluntary Orgasm For Men, OTV.)

Soft Styles: The soft styles and pair bonding and tuning skills described in this book may attune the two of you more deeply and sensitively than the more familiar hard style of lovemaking. Many women find that this attunement with their consort is a prerequisite to having an orgasm with him, especially through genital intercourse because women especially must feel comfortable with and trust their consort to be able to open up and/or orgasm.

It is easy to get trapped into excessive efforting and block the natural high that is intrinsic to sexual communion. Just settle back in body and mind and the richness that you seek will be yours. You can have the best of both worlds and enjoy ecstasy with intimacy.

Wild Woman: A popular theme in today's books, songs and movies is the wild woman. There is an old saying: the ideal woman is an angel in the kitchen and a devil in bed. Though the kitchen reference certainly dates this aphorism, it makes an invaluable point. Be a wonderful, caring, nurturing woman outside of the bedroom, of course. But in the bedroom? In the bedroom, go crazy, go bananas, go nuts, go mad, go for the whole thing, go for ultimate, supreme, no mind ecstasy. Lovemaking taps the most primeval--and powerful--forces available to the human race. Lovemaking is an atomic explosion. Allow your wild woman to emerge. Synchronize your erotic awakening via sexercises, meditation on sex energy, masturbation (if you like), and plenty of lovemaking.

Be willing to take the lead in a sensuous, non-verbal way and be assertive. Aggressiveness, by the way, is different. Aggression involves interfering with the other person's space, integrity and freedom of choice and expression. Assertion simply means that you have expressed exactly what it is that you want from that person and that situation. Perhaps participating in consciousness-raising activities with other women will be of value to you also.

PART 5
STYLE

Making love involves both pleasure and pain.

A certain amount of pain often accompanies making love, such as bites and nail scratches.

Somehow, these usually painful events are experienced as enjoyable.

During sexual intercourse, what was pleasure a moment ago can suddenly become pain, as well as what is ordinarily painful become pleasurable.

The meaning of pain can be transformed. This is shown during sex.

The futility of pleasure is that it will end, just as orgasms do. The reality of pleasure is that it will be transformed.

Pleasure becomes Pain. Pain becomes Pleasure. And then there are neutral states, also.

What has made the pain experienced while making love pleasurable? It is the intensity of the involvement. We are most fully involved at the time, more than almost any other time in our daily lives.

Can it be that a truly maximum participation in this sensory moment has the power to transform pain and extend enjoyment? Can it be that there is a condition of being that is beyond the cycle of pleasure and pain, yet not above or below them, but right there in them?

Making love is a model for living. Live as if you were making love every minute. Make love to this moment, to the car as you drive it, to the book as you read it, to the food as you eat it, to the bed as you sleep in it, to the clothes as you wear them.

Make love with the world and it makes love with you.

WHY STYLES?

If the soft styles of lovemaking are new to you, be prepared for one of the most exciting and satisfying adventures of your life. Even so, you may find this to be true only after you have broken through the inertia of old habits. There may be a period in the beginning when it all seems like complete nonsense and an utter waste of time.

The process is not unlike what author Mary Shivanandan reported happens to couples when they go on a "natural sex" birth control program. This program requires up to two weeks of abstinence from sexual intercourse every month. Though agreeing to the concept in theory, in practice couples often go through stages of confused separation, then anger and finally self-deception before reaching the fulfillment stage.

Don Kramer, who is a full-time Natural Family Planning Center director, outlined these stages after observing hundreds of couples. He found that men especially have difficulty making the adjustment. Still, the rewards are great for the couple who goes all the way.

The fulfillment stage is frequently experienced by the couple as a profound deepening of their erotic life. A startling refinement of their emotional attunement can also occur. The voluntary abstinence period becomes a blessing as the couple realizes that they have passed beyond the usual dependence on simple physical release into a realm of loving communion.

A simple touch, which before may have only meant an invitation to intercourse, now expresses a universe of tender feelings. A kiss becomes a magical life-giving act. The consort's entire body-mind, and not just the genital organs, is the love object.

Mutual respect and commitment grow in the light of this elevated enjoyment. What before seemed like much to give up is now eclipsed by an intimacy so rich the couple may feel embarrassed when they recall their earlier attachment to old habits.

As far as we know, these couples did not abstain in order to experience these benefits. They wanted a way to make love safely without resorting to methods that they believe are artificial.

They discovered that their relationship was enhanced and that their erotic interest in each other expanded and became more steady. They found that their need to endow the sexual act with a sacred quality was met. By following a natural cycle of indulgence and abstinence, they tapped a mysterious power which enabled them to feel--and this is almost a miracle--those feelings of wonder, glory, excitement and awe that they shared in the very beginning of their relationship. By accident or design, they discovered a universal secret for restoring the virginity of their union. Sexual relations became fresh, exciting, magnetic again.

Sexual Energy Ecstasy makes use of voluntary abstinence and it also makes use of voluntary indulgence. Sexual Energy Ecstasy is a way to refine and redefine the way we make love so that the reality of sex in our lives becomes a growing source of joy and clarity.

The principles that bring success to the refinement of the sexual drive are universal, as the experience of the "natural sex" practicioners illustrates. Dozens of examples could be given, but what good would that do? What is left is for you to do it.

Based on our own experiences in making the transition, we decided to take this approach of giving instructions for a wide variety of styles. The reasoning is simple. Hard style habits are often so strong that only direct intervention will bring about changes.

It will not be enough to suggest some exercises. Would you do these exercises at home? Possibly not. Or if we say "Breathe deeply, go slow, feel, really feel your consort," you may think to yourself "So what? Big deal."

We want a positive reaction. We really want you to do it.

Why do we want so much for you to do it? Because it's wonderful, simply wonderful. But you've got to get past the rough terrain at the beginning somehow.

Of course, you can use the techniques and principles of the different styles immediately. For example, you can apply the key to the Imsak style--the man pulls out and re-enters several times to build up erotic fervor--right away.

Conservation of the genital orgasm is more likely with soft styles. You may find that soft style sexual union without orgasm energizes, uplifts and inspires you. It may bring you and your consort closer together. However, it is very important that you take certain actions if you are having arousal without orgasm. Do spreading, practice deep relaxation, direct the life energy with your attention, share energy with each other. The practice of meditation, prayer or some other method that brings you peace and insight is also good.

If you are without a consort and want to practice these styles, you may want to try masturbation without genital orgasm. We have found that doing this frequently can greatly increase personal and sexual magnetism, quickly drawing a suitable consort to you. When you masturbate place attention on the Love spot and draw energy to that area. Be sure to conclude by spreading the energy with your hands and attention and by relaxing and breathing deeply.

The other side of sexual freedom, of the sexual adventure, is exploring the subjective dimension of love-making with each other. You may find that one touch is literally an explosion of mind-bending textures, a ripeness of sensation more overwhelming than full penetration in intercourse.

There really are no limits other than the ones we have in our minds.

RECIPES FOR ECSTASY

Reading the styles is a little like reading a cookbook. Each style is a recipe for ecstasy. You don't have to read one recipe after another. Feel free to skip around, as you would in a cookbook. When you find a recipe that you like, then it is time to cook.

We recommend that you follow a recipe for ecstasy to the letter the first few times you try it, since there may be much in it that is new to you. Then play with it, create variations, improvise as you make love. Design new recipes, new styles, that are tailored to your appetite.

A Quick Overview Of The Recipes For Ecstasy (Styles)

Sleeping Together: You can make love without genital contact.

Extrasensory Sex: If you unite genitally and then do absolutely nothing for half an hour the result can be a memorable lovemaking experience of a different kind or at least deep relaxation and energization.

Bio-Electric Sex: You can combine Extrasensory Sex and moderately active intercourse in equal amounts and enhance both, especially if you stay in a position that accents consort equality.

War And Peace: One of the secrets for delighting the senses is to alternate between extremes, such as very active and very passive lovemaking, concluding with relaxation and release (unless genital orgasm is preferred.)

Magnetic Sex: By massaging each other in specific ways you can reach into each other's biomagnetic energy and relax and energize so much that making love becomes a new experience.

Karezza: The man moves only enough to keep his erection. As heart-felt and energy-giving caresses are shared, a quality of intimacy and aliveness is enjoyed so delightful that many advocates of this style make a point to describe the effects as a spiritual experience.

On The Verge: The moment of being on the verge of orgasm can be made to last much longer with practice, resulting in intense pleasure.

Tao Of Sex: Assuming the role of pilot, the man guides the woman through nine stages of arousal until she reaches the fulfillment of total letting go. He delays his climax in favor of multiple almost-ejaculation orgasms.

Imsak: With or without the erotic incentive of vaginal muscle contractions, a strategy for erotic intensification is put into action in which the man withdraws, an affectionate break is enjoyed, he re-enters, another break follows and so on in a rising spiral of erotic fire that ends only by your choice.

Kabbazah Sex: Development of the circumvaginal muscles enables an extraordinary lovemaking experience in which the arousal is created and controlled by the woman alone. Maximum relaxation and maximum arousal are artfully combined, making TRO more likely.

212

SLEEPING TOGETHER (The First Style)

Is it unmanly or unwomanly to hold each other and just fall asleep together? Do you have to "have sex"?

What is really happening when you "just" sleep with someone?

Although, obviously, not as overwhelming as genital union, a form of "sexual intercourse" is taking place. Mahatma Gandhi, for example, is reported to have slept with young women--while remaining celibate--to boost his energy level during long protest fasts.

According to the story, Gandhi slept with a young virgin in front of him and one behind him. Whether this story is true or not, the message is clear: bodies asleep in a bed together are sharing, or "intercoursing" life energy.

It is recorded that in eighteenth century Paris, elderly men paid good money to a Madame Janus in the hopes of experiencing rejuvenation by sleeping in exactly this manner with two young women. Is "sleeping together," in other words, a form of very subtle sexual union?

There is a long-standing and suppressed tradition in the West of "just sleeping together." More than 1500 years ago in Europe, some Christian monks were in the habit of sleeping with young Christian women. Although nude caressing, embracing and sleeping together was often all that took place, some of the monks probably also practiced a form of **coitus reservatus** (sexual intercourse without ejaculation). Evidently, this kind of relationship satisfied their need to elevate sex to the level of a sacred act.

This practice of monks enjoying **agapetae** or **virgines subintroductae**, as the young women were called, was eventually stamped out as the organized Church grew in power. Around the twelfth century, a similar practice popped up in Europe.

Young knights offered "courtly love" to women who were not only married but wedded to a nobleman or other male power figure. This was known as a donnoi relationship.

Again history is vague as to the details, but in addition to sleeping together in the nude, nude caresses, nude embraces and ravishing the naked noblewoman's body for hours with their eyes, the young knights may have also practiced coitus reservatus on occasion or even frequently.

Were these monks and knights torturing themselves and their lovers?

According to their own reports, these relationships fired their imaginations and lifted their psyches to planes of feeling much higher than ordinary sexual relations usually did. In fact, the knight's "courtly love" relationship is probably the predecessor of our contemporary romantic love ideal.

The lyrics of many pop music songs are about some of these very same emotions. What is lacking is the practical knowledge of how to go about maintaining such a high pitch of emotional intensity. A thousand years ago, this may have been common knowledge, transmitted by troubadors (who also practiced a form of donnoi) across the Continent.

It would appear that by not getting what you want you can get something even better.

Experiment with features of the donnoi arrangement that appeal to you. You may discover it is more fun--and more natural--than you thought. Romantic passion is, after all, a form of creative tension.

As for "sleeping around," the next time you want just to sleep with somebody, why not?

You may discover that the urge we tend to automatically label as the need to "have sex" is in fact a bundle of needs. Included in this bundle are needs to be touched, held, caressed, cared for, breathed upon, smiled at, and perhaps even to smell each other.

If it would endanger your primary relationship to have sex with someone else, definitely give this idea your consideration. You may discover that a lot of what you are looking for in your encounter is not intercourse but intimacy.

Holding each other, cuddling, can be a profound sharing. Some happy harmonious couples share a feeling of oneness or confluence (flowing together) by simply holding and feeling each other for ten minutes or so. In fact, they may find this is more fulfilling than genital intercourse usually is.

Some people find that breathing in unison while holding each other brings them closer. Others find this too artificial. You will notice, though, that when the two of you are already in tune you tend to breathe together without trying.

One ancient sexual practice takes this a step further and recommends an hour-long embrace during which man and woman tune into the river of energy moving back and forth between them. This natural flow is already happening. The challenge is mainly in becoming aware of it. Back to back or belly to back contact, instead of the usual embrace, will also do the trick.

By allowing the breath to slow down, by actively imaging this force between and around you, by feeling or sensing internally for this flow, tuning in is achieved. Physical stillness is needed.

Usually, mind and body is prepared for several days in advance by contemplating the beauty and mystery of life. The special event is looked forward to with delight and respect, even awe.

The end result can be a peaceful, luminous ecstasy that even poetry does not describe. The experience may linger for days, weeks or even months, permanently enhancing the quality of life for both consorts.

This really is an experience that ordinary people have had. The crucial ingredients are patience and a desire to really be with the person.

Whatever you experience, you will find that there's much more to sleeping together and cuddling than keeping each other warm.

EXTRASENSORY SEX (The Second Style)

Sexual intercourse is complete when you join genitals.

The word coitus is simply the Latin for "meeting." To copulate, according to its roots, means to create a bond or link.

The word intercourse has come to us from the Latin intercurrere, "to run between." What is it that could be running between lovers? Life energy, love feelings, bio-electric impulses, hormones and glandular secretions, to name a few good things.

Another word for running back and forth is exchange. Some kind of valuable exchange between lovers is an automatic outcome of genital sexual union. No movement is necessary for "sexual intercourse-coitus-copulation" to be complete.

However, if you treat the act of genital union without movement AS IF it were incomplete by itself, naturally it will be.

We first heard about "stuffing," a therapeutic technique taught in Sexual Surrogate Training, from a doctor who took one of our workshops. The sexual surrogate and the person he or she is working with stuff the man in the woman. Then they watch TV or share some other low stress situation together.

The resemblance between this technique and Extrasensory Sex is on the surface only. Even so, some of the benefits of Extrasensory Sex may take place anyway. This probably accounts for some of stuffing's effectiveness. Though the form hasn't been followed to the letter, stuffing does encourage the most important ingredient of all, relaxation.

The bare bones of the Extrasensory Sex method is that a man and a woman unite genitally in a position that is extremely comfortably for both of them and lie completely still for about 40 minutes (see Peaceful Positions, illustration of YabYum On Chair on page 218.)

Curiously enough, once the couple are securely united genitally, the penis doesn't slip out. The vagina contracts around the penis, assuring continuous genital union. Also, it isn't necessary for the penis to be buried deep within the vagina. If just the tip of the penis is within the vagina, even if only mere contact between the organs is maintained for 30-40 minutes, that will be enough to produce results.

What are we looking for in an experience like this?

You can forget about conventional genital orgasm.

How many times have you come home from work too tired to make love yet wishing you had a way to unite and harmonize with your consort? Extrasensory Sex says unite genitally and fall asleep. The magic of sex is still at work even when you're not.

Extrasensory Sex can be wonderful. Some couples report that they share a beautiful natural high in this way. Lovers may discover that it deepens their feelings of intimacy in a way that hard style lovemaking does not.

Extrasensory Sex is thought to offer many practical benefits as well. For example, some people have reported that sexual dysfunctions disappeared, that stormy relationships found peace, and even that health problems vanished after taking up Extrasensory Sex on a regular basis (once a week). The charge up technique was developed by Betty Bethards of the Inner Light Foundation in Novato, California (see Charge Up.)

Extrasensory Sex Step-By-Step

(1)   Unite genitals. Charge up (optional).
(2)   Find comfortable positions, lie back, relax and enjoy.
(3)   Remain motionless for 30-40 minutes (or longer).

Practical Pointers

You may want to prepare by taking a cold shower together (yes, cold). Semi-soft and even soft entry are feasible provided lubrication is adequate. To ease insertion, use saliva or vegetable oil. Other kinds of lubrication may be too greasy or slippery and the penis may slip out.

If full insertion is not feasible or desired, simply place the penis just inside the lips of the vagina. The moist membranes of the two organs will then be in contact. This is all the genital union that is needed.

Do Extrasensory Sex after active lovemaking if you like. If male ejaculation has just occurred, though, the penis may slip out.

It is essential that neither one of you fidget or move. As the senses fatigue and the body image defocuses, you may, for example, experience the sensation that the two of you are one body. But this probably won't happen unless you stay motionless as well as relaxed.

Unconscious movements, such as hand twitches, can distract your consort much more than you. Simply rest your hands on your stomach or on the bed next to you.

Following a suggestion of a Bengali teacher, recorded in

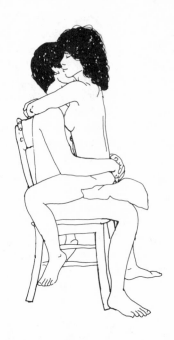

Omar Garrison's **Tantra: The Yoga of Sex,** you may want to imagine currents of life energy flowing between you during the long stillness phase. See this flow mostly but not only at the genitals. Also, the teacher recommends an effortless, almost indifferent, reverie state.

However, you may find that any kind of mental activity, visualization included, makes you less able to let go and enjoy the experience. Feelings very new to you may appear. Tuning into and encouraging these new feelings will be more than enough activity. The key is, after all, to relax, let go and allow your natural state of fulfillment to reveal itself.

Extrasensory Sex is a deceptively simple technique. It can be a very powerful experience even though it does not depend on the more familiar genital arousal and orgasm for its results. You may discover that you become very "high" or "spaced out" using this method. If this state is uncomfortable for you, try some of the grounding skills offered in this book (see Ground.)

Feel free to use Extrasensory Sex, with or without the charge up, as a prelude to or aftermath of more active lovemaking.

BIO-ELECTRIC SEX (The Third Style)

Rudolf von Urban, M.D., whose book **Sex Perfection and Marital Happiness** was published in 1949, devised his own approach to making maximum use of the subtle sexual energies. He made a number of claims for his technique based upon the numerous physical, emotional and mental benefits he observed in his patients who used his "bio-electric" method of intercourse. We will call his method Bio-Electric Sex.

For example, von Urban reported that health problems as diverse as high blood pressure, skin disease and sleeplessness were totally cured in some patients after just a couple of weeks of Bio-Electric Sex. He also reported that the technique was found to be extraordinarily relaxing.

Von Urban writes that some experienced renewal of their marriages. Those who were in love became even more so. Some long-term relationships that had been full of discontent suddenly enjoyed peace.

Some lovers shared a special ecstasy during the Bio-Electric Sex sessions. Von Urban realized that something very valuable and wonderful was taking place. Beyond any immediate personal pleasures a man and woman might experience with this technique, benefits were being experienced by some participants that they had not enjoyed with conventional hot, hard style intercourse-to-orgasm.

At some point, von Urban developed a theory to explain these effects. Von Urban had worked out his theory and was prescribing this technique to patients as early as the 1920's here in the United States.

In brief, von Urban's theory was that the cells of the male body-mind and the female body-mind are of opposite electrical polarity. Via prolonged contact of the skin, particularly between the moist areas of the body, i.e., the genitals, the bioelectric quality of the skin changed.

This change in the skin attracted the unique bio-energy in the cells of the male and female forms to the surface, where they could be exchanged, resulting in benefits and perhaps ecstatic experiences.

Today science has confirmed the electromagnetic character of the human body-mind as a whole and of the human skin in particular. Von Urban's notion of male and female electrical cell polarities will remain a mystical non-explanation until it is studied scientifically. However, his intuition that the best scientific explanation of the process he had discovered would be in terms of human bioelectromagnetic phenomena is remarkably contemporary.

Von Urban also explored the issue of contraception from his bioelectric point of view. He believed that barrier contraceptives made of rubber (an electrical insulator) such as diaphragms, cervical caps and condoms, block the energy exchange at the genital juncture. Technically, Von Urban was probably right. But the barriers within the body-mind are much more important.

Von Urban gave precise, easy to follow instructions.

Take a shower or bath.

Completely naked, cuddle, kiss and otherwise turn each other on.

Adopt the Scissors position (see Peaceful Positions) with the man on his right side.

With or without an erection, his penis is placed just inside the outer lips of her vagina.

Lie in this way for at least 30 minutes. Focus intensely on any genital feelings. Keep attention on the exchange of male and female polarized energies taking place at the genitals.

After the 30 minutes is up, have regular intercourse with genital thrusting but stay in the Scissors position. This should also last for 30 minutes. Male ejaculation is to be avoided. (Note: von Urban said nothing about ejaculation after the second half hour was over).

Should male ejaculation occur, the couple stays genitally fused for 30 more minutes from that point. This is to insure that the bio-electric interchange between the lovers is complete.

A writer acquaintance of ours and his wife have followed von Urban's instructions to the letter for many years. Over breakfast one morning, he described their experience with the method as "the Orgasm beyond the orgasm, the High beyond the high."

WAR AND PEACE (The Fourth Style)

The gist of this approach is to alternate stimulation and relaxation in repeated cycles that last a total of about an hour (or two or three) and conclude in a final relaxation which ends in blissful consciousness and/or sleep.

You will be asked to relinquish the familiar and reliable certainty of sexual excitement leading to orgasm for the unfamiliar and unpredictable joys of ultra-intimate polarized communion and other possible benefits.

Remember, though, you always have the option of orgasm. The enormous energy you build up by shifting back and forth between arousal and relaxation virtually guarantees a great orgasm as the grand finale.

This approach may also provide the necessary ingredients for a woman who has been unable to orgasm during intercourse to do so. A woman can hold on to her level of arousal during the tranquilizing stages, building up momentum with each stimulating stage.

War And Peace gets its name from the repeated cycles of conflict (arousal) and resolution (relaxation). The final and deepest relaxation may take you beyond all dramas of conflict and resolution within and between each other into a wonderful oneness. At any rate, it is believed by some people that a power is built up by making love in this way, a power that this final relaxation releases to heal body and mind.

Each sub-cycle of War And Peace is like one complete cycle of Extrasensory Sex. The arousing phase in War And Peace corresponds to the charge up phase in Extrasensory Sex.

How Much War And How Much Peace?

The purpose of the first arousal phase is to achieve genital union fairly rapidly so that the second phase, relaxation (meditation), can begin.

Just as the first arousal phase of the first cycle is brief

(5-15 minutes), so is the first relaxation (5-15 minutes). It is preferable to keep these two phases on the short side in order to get things rolling. In particular, don't extend the arousal phase or you may never complete your first cycle. It's often a fast track that takes you to orgasm.

After you've completed the first cycle, the time you spend topping (arousing) and bottoming (relaxing) depends to a large extent on whether you have 45 minutes or two or three hours. Arousal and relaxation phases of not less than 5 minutes and not more than 20 minutes should be ideal for most couples. However, the final relaxation phase should last at least 30 minutes (as in Extrasensory Sex) to allow time for the deepest feeling of communion to take place.

You can discuss these details before you actually make love, since this kind of lovemaking requires real teamwork. We find a meditation technique quite useful during the relaxation phases (see Deep Relaxation.)

War

You may want to decide in advance if you want to conclude with orgasm or final relaxation.

If you want to conclude with orgasm, you can do so at the peak of your second arousal phase and never complete a second cycle.

You can complete two cycles and follow the third arousal phase with orgasm and not finish a third cycle.

Even though lovemaking during this phase can be quite vigorous, take your time. Go much slower than you do when you have orgasm in mind. Give much attention to the whole of your consort's body-mind.

Be like a king and queen vacationing on a luscious isolated island making love in an elegant open-air boudoir surrounded by swaying palms and painted skies. Your every need is taken care of. All you have is time, time and more time to enjoy each other. Life is a dream of sensuous peace.

Absorb all the sights and smells and sounds, the tastes and caresses and bites and moans. Especially explore the world of touch together. Tantalize each other. Celebrate your senses. Make love in a truly leisurely way, as if there were nothing else in your life but this moment.

You will find that when you are fully in the present with your lover, you have all the time in the world.

Unless you intend to take an arousal phase to sexual orgasm, avoid pushing yourself to your limit. In particular, it's not a good idea for a man to push to almost again and again without concluding in ejaculation. His prostate is a delicate organ which may become inflamed or enlarged as a result of such practices.

After going through several cycles together a couple usually generates a substantial surplus of energy. Orgasm at this point, particularly if it is consciously directed, will probably not be experienced as an energy drain even by the more sensitive. However, if one or both of you are making love in order to summon and store up vitality, you must avoid sexual orgasm in order to fulfill such a purpose (see Ground and Store Energy.)

Peace

The duration of the peace-filled phase(s) is completely up to you. In our experience, though, a minimum of 5 minutes and a maximum of 20 minutes works best in practice. This will allow for several complete cycles even if you have only an hour or less. As beautiful as the journey along the way will be, all is still a preparation for the final relaxation, which will be 30 minutes long or longer.

Follow the guidelines given in the discussion of Extra-sensory Sex. Penile insertion will offer no difficulty as arousal will be complete.

Bliss

By using the War And Peace format you build up your mutual energy to an invisible and pregnant maximum, which you then fully and sensitively relish during the final relaxation.

The final relaxation, then, is a climax of a different order.

It's best to keep your expectations and ideas about what you may or may not experience to a minimum. Avoid using the experiences of others as your model. The way for you is unique. To follow it, listen to yourself.

Preparation And Position Variation

People think nothing of spending months and thousands of dollars in preparation for a legal wedding.

Making love in this fashion is a wedding of a different kind. It is a wedding of energies and dreams, of aspirations and evolutions.

A little preparation, at least, is recommended.

Improvise your preparation as the chemistry and the occasion dictate (see Do It Rite, Boudoir Basics, Aculoving Massage.)

If you opt for a long encounter of 2 or 3 hours, you will discover that position variety becomes important. In fact, we would go so far as to say that position variety is the spice of prolonged intercourse.

A variety of peaceful positions are described in this book (see Peaceful Positions.) These are some of the positions that are ideal for a relaxation phase.

See Tension Positions for some great arousing positions that need not involve movement. An investment in one of the illustrated manuals showing positions designed for movement is worthwhile if you find that you are running out of ideas.

There is a delight to exploring position variations as a form of non-verbal communication in stillness and tension as well as through movement. We experience a precious satisfaction in exploring and contemplating various two-body postures that don't encourage, much less require, vigorous thrusting. The challenge in many of these positions is maintaining them conscientiously. Arousal is created through a whole-body effort that includes the genital avenue but does not emphasize it.

You have the option of assigning one person the role of leader for the duration of that lovemaking session. This simplifies the transitions which can be choppy and break the mood.

Another option is practicing your positions and transitions ahead of time. Some people make a dance-like sequence out of several positions that flow easily from one to the next. If this sounds like a lot of work, remember that once you've stored these sequences and transitions they will add to all of your lovemaking. This kind of practice is also a good warm-up for what's ahead.

MAGNETIC SEX (The Fifth Style)

In a new unpublished manuscript, described by writer Dio Urmilla Neff, psychologist John Heider, Ph.D., outlines his innovative approach, which we will call Magnetic Sex.

Heider distinguishes between, in his words, "electric" and "magnetic" sexual intercourse.

In electric intercourse, lovers concentrate on two sexual push buttons: the most sensitive part of the penis (the head) and the clitoris. Arousal caused by stimulating these two push buttons increases until the orgasm, in the form of a rapid and pleasurable electrical discharge, brings relief.

The exciting electrical style of lovemaking is the most common approach to sexual intercourse in the West. The journey from genital arousal to genital climax can be a short ride and, judging from modern surveys, usually is. Electric push-button sex definitely brings quick impressive results, i.e., the "big bang" of conventional orgasm.

Magnetic intercourse, in contrast, is energy-oriented. There is no question that it takes more time. Sexual feeling and excitement must permeate the whole body-mind, though the sexual organs still play a major role.

Heider claims that the most magnetic regions of the body-mind are the base of the penis, the perineum (the area stretching between the anus and the genitals) and the vagina. He believes that when these areas are massaged in a sensitive way, the resulting aliveness can spread throughout the entire body-mind. The lovers will then be truly and deeply touched by each other.

Heider recommends the practice of meditation and movement disciplines and/or body work over a period of time to enhance your enjoyment of Magnetic Sex.

Provided the couple is sufficiently in the flow, what can they expect? Heider asserts that the lovers will have the sensation sooner or later of falling backwards or dropping through the air. The feeling of having separate identities then begins to dissolve.

This process of falling or dropping continues until the couple really feel as if they are completely one. Instead of the familiar electric orgasm, they experience sensations that resemble orgasm but roll through them again and again like waves on the ocean.

Heider claims the experience is not only wonderful in itself but also healing and nurturing. He stresses that when the couple finally chooses to end their union, they should do so with extreme slowness. They have built up a powerful energy field together. If suddenly torn, this field could create an unpleasant backlash effect.

Directions For Magnetic Sex

These directions incorporate a few ideas of our own, but the basic procedure has not been changed.

Sit and just be with each other. You may meditate together if you wish. As you sit make an effort to become aware of and to feel the life energy that fills the space where the two of you are sitting. Try to get a clear sense of what your personal presence or personal space is like. How far from your body-mind does it extend? What color is it or is it transparent? Once you have this sense of your personal space, be it real or imagined, choose to extend it to include your consort and the space surrounding the two of you.

This is only one way to go about it. Another tactic is to simply stretch the tactile sensitivity of your skin slowly out away from your body-mind, as if it were expanding like a big balloon. There are many techniques. What is most important is that the technique you use suits you personally and makes use of your unique talents and inclinations.

Using stroking movements, softly and tenderly caress and massage each other's bodies. We recommend using the flat of the hand, with both the palms and fingers. Feel or imagine life energy in your hands and perhaps flowing through your hands as you do this.

How do you know how much to do? One good way is to stroke and caress until you feel that more would simply be too much.

Using your hands in the same way execute the same stroking movements only now gently caress and massage the space near your bodies at a distance of two inches. In other words, four open hands slowly sweep over two bodies at a height of two inches above the skin.

You will feel the life energy around you build up and become thick and compacted as a result. The space between and all around your body-minds will be experienced as being filled with this life energy. The high density of life energy in the air will feel tangible and solid. You will feel with certainty that it is as real as your own flesh.

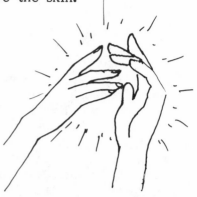

Now you genitally unite. You move only a little or none at all. Movements should be only enough to sustain his erection and her natural vaginal lubrication. By staying still in mind and body, breathing and relaxing fully again and again, the genital energy will not build up as tension but instead spread through your whole bodies.

At some point the feeling of falling backwards or dropping through the air occurs. The usual sense of having separate identities begins to dissolve. Eventually your sense of oneness becomes total. The two of you (at the life energy level) have literally become one. Thrilling oceanic wave-like feelings that are like orgasm yet different course through your bodies over and over and over again. This is a classic TRO.

Eventually, you disunite. You do this very tenderly and sensitively and cautiously in order to avoid suddenly disrupting the powerful energy field you just created.

It can be quite a shock if one of you decides to get up abruptly and leave the scene, even psychologically. Even physically moving apart a little too quickly at this point can feel distressing. Your energy fields are still literally one at this stage. Oneness is oneness, and it makes sense that your separation following such intimacy should not be a casual affair.

KAREZZA (The Sixth Style)

Karezza or Carezza, pronounced "kuh-retz-zuh", is an Italian word which means "caress." It first appeared in English usage in 1883 in a privately printed book, Tokology, written by a pioneering female physician named Alice Bunker Stockham. Her views later appeared in slightly revised form in **Karezza: Ethics of Marriage**, available by mail from Health Research (see Appendix.) According to author Robert Moffett, Stockham was one of the first five woman M.D.'s in the United States.

So widespread was the excitement this little self-published book generated that it was translated into Russian by the great novelist Leo Tolstoi, and also into German and Swedish. Letters of gratitude poured into her office in Chicago. Many of the letters were variations on a single, exciting theme: now, at long last, husband and wife can celebrate the sexual act as a form of sacred communion.

This lovemaking technique was by no means Stockham's original discovery. But the name she gave it has stuck ever since and appropriately so. The concept and practice of the sexual caress is nowhere more highly developed than in Karezza.

Stockham was not the first American to stumble across this approach. In fact, she almost certainly owed the essentials of the method to a social religious revolutionary by the name of John Humphrey Noyes. Himself the author of a popular pamphlet entitled Male **Continence**, Noyes claimed the technique came right out of the Holy Bible itself.

The Putney, Vermont minister was not the sort of man to just publish a pamphlet or two. In 1846 Noyes founded the famed utopian social experiment that found a place in history, the Oneida Community. They made the well-known silverware of the same name. The 250 members of the Community practiced a form of open group marriage Noyes christened "Complex Marriage."

The practice of male continence as described and championed by Noyes supplied the glue which held the radical sexual experiment together. Though Noyes may have first developed the practice as a new birth control measure, he quickly discovered that something new and wonderful was happening for him and his wife. Though the method did offer some birth control advantages for these pre-contraception pioneers, Karezza proved to be a technique that promoted exceptional harmony and fulfillment between man and woman.

The Basics Of Karezza

The prerequisite for Karezza, discovered by Noyes and promoted by Stockham, is the ancient Roman practice of coitus reservatus. The value of male continence or retention in lovemaking had been rediscovered.

As none other than Xaviera Hollander points out in her book **Xaviera's Supersex**, continence doesn't mean denial but refers to the ability to contain something. For thousands of years, men and women, but especially men, have believed that containing the forces of Eros within the body-mind container is a wise and healthy thing to do.

Karezza advocates have developed the art of the loving sexual caress to an impressive degree. Male non-ejaculation simply sets the stage for up to an hour or more of exalted and highly refined interplay between man and woman.

In Karezza, there is no dancing on the brink as in OTV (see On The Verge.) In contrast to OTV's pyrotechnics, a gentle celebration of the very act of sexual communion itself prior to and distinct from the sexual orgasm is enjoyed.

Physiology Of Karezza Lovemaking

Though the psychophysiology of human arousal and orgasm has been studied, this remains an area of major mystery to modern science. Briefly, the current understanding is that in the beginning stages of sexual arousal the parasympathetic nervous system is dominant, while in the culminating stages of sexual arousal, i.e. pre-orgasm and orgasm, the sympathetic nervous system is dominant.

The parasympathetic nervous system is more associated with relaxed and "I feel good" states of body-mind. The sympathetic nervous system is more associated with survival and the "fight-or-flight" reaction.

These descriptions are obviously oversimplifications. The interactions between these two halves of the autonomic (involuntary) nervous system during sexual arousal are much more complex than this. However, these convenient descriptions are accurate enough to make our point: the Karezza practice has a sound biological basis.

As odd as it seems, in order to complete the sexual act through ejaculation, consorts must switch over from the pleasant parasympathetic sensations to the stressful sympathetic sensations.

As we interpret the scientific basis for the claims of Noyes and Stockham, what they are saying can be rephrased in this way: "Stay with the parasympathetic arousal in the beginning. Explore and enjoy and celebrate that." Noyes called it the "social" stage of intercourse.

If you don't shift over to sympathetic nervous system dominance, if you don't shift over to the "fight-or-flight" response in which your hearts race and your lungs heave, then it isn't particularly stressful to either of you to delay or avoid sexual orgasm.

To Caress You Is To Bless You

The word caress comes to us from the Latin carus, meaning "dear, precious."

Magnetic Sex uses the sexual caress as a way to condense and dynamize the life energy in the immediate vicinity of the two lovers during the arousal before genital union.

In contrast, Karezza uses the energized hand to send energy, feeling and arousal to the consort during sexual union.

Man and woman are conceived of as two halves of a profound battery of life.

The hands, which are in some fundamental way extensions of the heart, of the deep feeling capacity in the core of our bodies, act as mobile contacts for the mutual electricity. The arms extend like wires, the hands offer living moving flexible connections.

Many advocates of Karezza conceive of it as a spiritual act and seem to enjoy couching their descriptions of the method in religious language.

In their way of Karezza, to caress you is to bless you.

Being a physician, Stockham was of the opinion that to practice Karezza promoted health and wholeness. In particular, she recommended it in cases of sterility. She also believed that various beneficial biochemicals, secretions and vital forces were exchanged during a Karezza session.

Stockham was quite specific about how to prepare for a Karezza lovemaking session. A few days or even a week before the Karezza union the lovers are especially kind in their daily dealings with each other.

During this preparation period, they read uplifting writings and contemplate their meaning. Ralph Waldo Emerson, the philosopher, and Elizabeth Barrett Browning, the poet, were two authors she recommended.

They meditate on surrendering their individual will to the cosmic will. They seek to lose their individual consciousness in the cosmic consciousness.

She was also quite specific on how to do Karezza.

She recommends an hour of quiet sexual union. Movement is slight. Arousal stays pleasurable. The mood is serene and contemplative. Genital tension beyond pure and simple arousal is given little opportunity to develop. As a result, the need for orgasm is not experienced and the relief that it offers is not felt to be necessary. When genital friction is light, the need for orgasm is diminished.

She also recommends religious affirmations. A contemporary example is "God Is Love." Or "We are spiritual beings and this intimacy of our bodies symbolizes the union of our souls." She recommends doing this before and during the Karezza lovemaking session. This is also the time to practice a religious devotion, to pray, if this is your way. She makes it quite clear that both affirmations and devotions are completely optional.

According to Stockham, the hour allotted is more than enough time for the physical tensions to subside. Although she doesn't mention it specifically as far as I know, it is also enough time for mental and emotional tensions to subside. Once again, that key ingredient of total relaxation makes its debut.

Of course your state of mind at the time--how bright, how clear, how concentrated, how calm, how contented, how centered you are--is very important. In fact, your state of mind in your life as a whole, past and present, has an effect.

Sexual Orgasm In Karezza

In Noyes' Karezza, the man does not have genital orgasm but the woman may or may not.

In Stockham's Karezza, neither the man nor the woman have genital orgasm.

The chief benefits obtained through intercourse without sexual orgasm are an increase in personal energy and well-being, an intensification of the interpersonal bond and an alignment with the higher forces of personal evolution. Both agreed the male ejaculation orgasm was an undesirable dispersal of this accumulated benign energy. In Stockham's view, the female sexual orgasm was also undesirable for the same reason.

J. William Lloyd, also a Karezza master, wrote that if you opt for the conventional sexual orgasm you end up dumping most of the "wine" you have contained in your body-mind bottle. It rushes through you so fast you can't take advantage of it.

Noyes points out in his writings that though men tend to think of ejaculation as being what having sex is really all about, the event of seminal release is the aftermath of the sexual act, actually following after it. When a guy begins his ejaculation, he has already reached and gone past his point of no return.

What is it that he is unable to return to?

He cannot, after passing that point, return immediately to the act of making love. He is now committed to a roller coaster ride as quick as it is intense, self-involving and mind-boggling. Making love has become making orgasm, yet the two can be as different as day and night.

If you stay at the beginning, it doesn't have to end.

Our Karezza

In the style of Karezza that we do, the man moves just enough to maintain his erection, just every now and then. The rest of the technique is to relax and let go of everyday thinking mind (see It's The Thought That Counters.) From deep within ourselves we reach out for and into each other, melting in the ever increasing feeling and sensitivity. The woman uses pompoir, too, as needed.

Lovemaking As Peacemaking

Too often, the instruments of sex are used as instruments of war, however subtly. The goal of Karezza is to transform the penile sword and vaginal sheath into instruments for the cultivation of food and nourishment.

The sword becomes the plowshare. The vagina becomes the field of plenty.

The Karezza relationship, in which the energy of life is accumulated, escalated and recycled, offers the possibility of an insoluble mutual magnetic bond, lasting beyond even the body, or so it is believed.

Ultimately, the issue is not whether to avoid the conventional orgasm or not.

Hopefully, ultra-intimacy and TRO will not become the kind of elusive frustrating goals that bring more sadness than success. Since they are the experiences of real people, these ideas may be useful as gentle guidelines. If these concepts get in your way or cause you distress, just drop them.

The mutual and unquestioned commitment of heart-felt vital energy between man and woman is the condition unconsciously sought by most consorts. It offers sufficient fire with or without the intentional avoidance of the orgasmic act. You want to love and be loved, to feel ecstasy, to be free. Acknowledge this and you will find it.

What A Couple Can Expect

What you will experience is impossible to predict. Experienced practicioners of Karezza describe it as thrilling, inspiring, blissful, ecstatic, regenerating, exalted, spiritual, transcendental, and . . . indescribable.

To find out for yourself you must do it.

If you don't get results the first time, then do it again.

Every time you make love in this way, or simply try to make love in this way, you will grow a little bit as a human being.

You are integrating sex and love, man and woman, hard

and soft, wisdom and power in yourself a little bit each time. Karezza lovemaking is an intentional act of conscious self-evolution.

In fact, any kind of lovemaking, even the hardest, fiercest kind of lovemaking, can have this effect. The key is in the attitude.

Yet, at least at the beginning, it seems easier to reap these benefits from soft-style lovemaking. It's like learning to meditate, which is much easier when you begin by sitting quietly.

Viva Karezza

Without a doubt, Karezza is one of the most enduring and most popular soft or complementary sexualove styles of all time. The great Chinese physician Master Sun described Karezza-type lovemaking back in the seventh century. In his version the lovers adorned their navels with a big imaginary red egg but the basic style was pure Karezza.

Those who find the arousal with a Karezza method inadequate may have neglected one of the essential skills of Sexual Energy Ecstasy: pompoir. Pompoir heats the oven and firms the ol' jelly roll very well indeed.

Karezza offers a practical do-it-yourself way to reconcile the age-old conflict between love and lust: stay in the first (parasympathetic) stage of arousal and emphasize deep heart-felt feelings. The quality of the sexual union may change vastly. Regardless of background, people are moved to describe the experience as sacred, holy, spiritual, uplifting, transcendent and so on.

Always feel free to improvise and change. The methods of Stockham and Noyes may strike you as a bit formal. Personalize them and they will feel natural to you.

Put simply, the Karezza advocates believe that love is the principal food of life, and that one of the principal ways of feeding love to each other is unselfish lovemaking. Here is the Karezza secret: in order to be deeply touched by Karezza, be the person who gives that touch to another.

OTV: ON THE VERGE (The Seventh Style)

Making love on the verge (OTV) can be your ticket into a twilight world of mind-boggling erotic magic.

Let us share with you just one experience of erotic madness provoked in this way. Imagine, if you will, literally riding on top of a volcano as it explodes and explodes and explodes. Imagine skiing or surfing on the rolling fury of a mountainous molten red lava flow. Imagine that all around you, even with your eyes wide open, all you can see is red, red, red. Imagine your body-mind is consumed with a head-spinning erotic fire that burns all of your flesh at once. Imagine pleasure so intense that you actually beg for it to end.

For us that day in 1982 in Topanga, California, it was not imagination. It was real. (And, yes, it was a high from sex--not drugs.)

Riding a volcano is, of course, just one experience of the erotic ecstasy which can be enjoyed when the timeless world that lies between arousal and orgasm is entered. Those who dare to try this technique may discover that the word "erotic" takes on an entirely new meaning for them.

Whenever transiting from one kind of reality to another, as from night to day or from day to night, there is a period of time when it is not the old reality and not yet the new reality. You are in between.

Take a moment now to recall the indescribable appeal of dawn to sunrise and of sunset to dusk in a natural setting. These twilight times of earth have long been felt to offer special value. It is as if what lies normally hidden becomes more visible.

The transitional time from peak arousal to orgasmic release is such another special time. Experimenting with this interval shows that it can be extended indefinitely.

How To Reach OTV

Begin an OTV session from a place of real relaxation. A depth of relaxation will make it much easier to notice the finer gradations of arousal as they show up. This noticing may feel quite rewarding in itself.

Remain relaxed, particularly in the pelvic region, the

genitals and the buttocks. Also relax your hands and feet. When you approach peak arousal, don't squeeze your PC or anal muscles.

Spread the sensation of arousal throughout your entire body-mind as much as possible. A casual, almost indifferent, dream-like attitude works for many people.

You may want to breathe deeply and concentrate on your feeling center at your heart (the Love spot). You may feel waves of energy surge up or you can visualize this happening if you wish. Again, relax.

Another technique is to visualize the energy from the genitals spreading thoughout your whole body-mind. Use your breath to send the energy flow to other parts of your body-mind. Of course, you can always orgasm.

After a few weeks or months of this you learn to love feeling close to orgasm without orgasming a lot. Just listen to your own energy needs. Don't be surprised if your attitude about having orgasms changes a little.

Stroking movements of your hands on each other's body-minds will help a great deal to spread the erotic fire down the legs, up the trunk and to the extremities. The extremities include the tips of the ears, the top of the head, the soles of the feet, the palms of the hands and the tips of the toes and fingers.

Your breath and the emotions of your heart can be directed with the intention of enabling a whole-body response in both you and your consort. To use your breath and feelings in this way, invest them with a quality of expansion, a feeling of spaciousness and brightness, as you give them to your consort.

Also remember to fully take in what your consort is offering you.

The Colors Of Arousal

In a sexuality seminar given in Los Angeles, psychologist Paul Bindrim, Ph.D., made an analogy between the green, yellow and red traffic lights and the situation of someone gradually approaching the point of orgasmic no return. We liked the analogy but found it useful to fine tune our awareness of genital excitedness into five subdivisions, each with its own color and significance.

Green is the first level. Green means all systems are

"Go." Yellow would ordinarily be next, signifying "caution," but it is helpful to identify a new level in between green and yellow, the "lime" level.

In the lime level, it is already time to put your sexual energy management strategies into action. In practice, this means you will successfully undermine the compulsion to rush and bring your lovemaking to an end. You will nip it in the bud, so to speak.

Beneath this compulsiveness lies a vast oceanic space of peace and energy. If you make the transition now, early enough, you may move into a new level of mastery you never dreamed possible. Men, especially, who often are concerned with "lasting longer," will be pleased with this new ability level.

You celebrate the thrill of skill in a moment of great challenge. Like a master surfer or race car driver, your thrill comes from playing the edge. Part of that thrill is a product of the real possibility of a wipe out or a crash. However, with OTV the consequence of going over the edge is having an orgasm!

The yellow level of arousal is the true caution level. At this arousal checkpoint, you decide the outcome of that particular union. If you're doing OTV, now is the time to ever so gently ease into the orange level.

The orange level is the realm of OTV. Since red is the level of orgasmic certainty, to be in the orange level is to be on the verge or at the threshold. When a man enters the red level, he is at the point of no return, or ejaculatory inevitability.

Erotic Magicians At Orange Level

When you are in orange level, the slightest sudden movement can set either or both of you off. You do move, but you move with tremendous tenderness, with super-sensitivity, so that you remain pre-orgasmic. You will find that every sensation is magnified. Because of the enormous expansion of your passion, even a tiny movement, though it doesn't set off an orgasm, results in earthquakes of sensation, in floods of feeling.

Success at OTV requires top-notch teamwork. All the sensational fanfare aside, the joy of cooperating so intimately with another is substantial reward in itself.

When your lovemaking is flowing in this way, you won't feel any sense of strain. You will be like entranced firewalkers, dancing in the flames and feeling only warmth and love.

Of course, you can always exercise your orgasm option. It is fun, though, to choose when and how you will have your orgasm(s), to make it an act in which you exercise complete freedom of choice.

If you are constantly having to use force to hold your body-mind back from orgasmic release, then you have already passed through the orange level and are just fighting off the inevitable red tidal wave. You need to back off, relax for several minutes and try again for the orange level, or let go and enjoy your genital explosion.

Let the erotic madness overwhelm you. Surrender to the excruciating ecstasy of being almost, almost, almost "there." It is an exquisite torture that is bound to bend your mind.

Taking breaks at least a few minutes in length is recommended. Just hold and feel each other, feel your breathing and blending together.

Use this time to taste and savor your union for what it is. Very often, lovemaking is used only as a means to an end like having orgasm, proving yourself or pleasing your partner. The hidden riches of the lovemaking opportunity remain hidden if you stay on the surface. Don't skim over it like a pelican gliding over the waves in search of fish, become the deep-sea diver.

Benefits of OTV

Women may find that with OTV practice they can bring on the orgasm or delay it to a much greater degree than they had believed. Judging from the large numbers of women who are concerned with not being orgasmic, who have difficulty having orgasm during intercourse or who are unable to initiate orgasm without primary clitoral stimulation, OTV may offer a unique skill-building opportunity.

Too often women are trained to be so passive that they forget how to tap their own energy. Fully satisfying sexual activity requires an abundance or surplus of energy. OTV emphasizes the accumulation of energy, not its dispersion. You can't get off on what you don't have.

A man who is OTV may find that he actually can begin the ejaculation process and then stop it midstream. This may happen automatically. In this and other ways, a man can actually experiment with the sensation of "ejaculatory inevitability" and find out firsthand what brings it on. He may discover that this famous point of no return is not so inevitable after all. He may also discover that he can have rushing sensations strongly resembling sexual orgasm without ejaculation, loss of erection or the usual PC muscle spasms. This we call the Non-Ejaculatory Male Orgasm (NEMO). The OTV style grew out of our experiments with Non-Ejaculatory Male Orgasm (NEMO) and voluntary female orgasm during intercourse.

The good news is, yes, NEMO can happen. The bad news is we know of no way to reliably duplicate the experience at will.

Briefly, NEMO may be achieved by relaxing as the ejaculation crisis is approached. Pleasurable orgasmic sensations are experienced without the ejaculation of semen taking place. Maximum PC muscle development seems to be a prerequisite. Male Multiple Orgasm (MMO) on one ejaculation or with no ejaculation seems to be developed the same way.

OTV places stress on a man's prostate gland. Male ejaculation orgasm is recommended at the conclusion of the session.

Both consorts may have extremely pleasurable experiences that are not the conventional sexual orgasm, simply cannot be described by words and must be experienced to be understood (see Sexual Energy Ecstasy in Prologue.)

THE TAO OF SEX (The Eighth Style)

According to traditional beliefs, the Yellow Emperor Huang Ti ruled China from 2697 B.C. to 2597 B.C. Many deeply respected ancient Chinese writings are attributed to him, including the single most important Chinese medical work, The Yellow Emperor's Classic of Internal Medicine (Huang Ti Nei Ching Su Wen, or simply Nei Ching).

Among the ancient Chinese writings which bear the Yellow Emperor's name are several works on ancient Taoist (pronounced "DOW-ist") sexology. One of these, the Su Nui Ching (The White Madame's Classic), disappeared in China about 1,000 years ago. It reappeared 150 years ago in the possession of the Japanese royal family (in Japanese, of course). A Chinese version was finally found in China and the two were compared.

In October, 1983 David attended a seminar based on the Su Nui Ching in San Francisco given by Dr. Stephen T. Chang, one of the foremost authorities on ancient Taoist medical practices and contemporary Chinese acupuncture (see Appendix.) Dr. Chang wishes to make this information widely available and generously gave us permission to quote him at length here.

There are, however, other interpretations of the Taoist sexual wisdom which emphasize different aspects. We recommend the books by Jolan Chang and by Ishihara and Levy in particular (see Bibliography.)

At The Table Of Love, The Woman Dines, The Man Waits

According to the Su Nui Ching, the woman should be, figuratively, served a nine course meal by her man. Idealistically, the man plays the role of waiter and serves her course after delicious course until she enjoys the ninth and final delight, the Taoist total climax or blissful collapse.

But women nowadays are rarely taken all the way. The man usually ejaculates long before she has completed her meal. The result is, not surprisingly, indigestion. In other words, the ideal male Tao Of Sex consort is a servant, a butler, a waiter.

Consistently harmonious sexual relations are possible only when the man makes love with the attitude that serving female satisfaction is his first and foremost goal. The battle of the sexes would suddenly stop if men surrendered in this way. Male satisfaction is also greatly heightened.

Tao Of Sex is a completely cohesive, utterly logical systematic solution to the very real problem which is at the root of the sexual conflict. And what is that problem? Men and women have fundamentally different sexual goals.

Men And Women Are Different

In the Taoist formulation, a man's inborn tendency is to rapidly heat up and explode. For this reason, he is symbolized as fire.

A woman's inborn tendency is to heat up slowly and cool down slowly. For this reason, she is symbolized by water.

But the differences are even more fundamental than this. During sexual intercourse not only does a man not know what a woman feels and a woman not know what a man feels during sexual intercourse, their destinations are completely different.

If a woman is taken to her ultimate destination, the ninth and final course of her erotic supper, she will experience a complete loss of sense of self. She will vanish, disappear, melt into nothingness. She will not know where she is or who she is or what she is during this Tao Of Sex total climax.

This is the woman's Tao Of Sex climax of emptiness.

Paradoxically, this Tao Of Sex total climax of emptiness creates the feeling that she has returned to her deeper and truer self. She is stronger, more independent, more self-directed.

Her contribution to the celebration of sexual union is to lose herself. By acting in accord with the Tao, she also helps bring her man to a deeper sense of manhood, to a more confident and caring and easeful masculinity.

Now her job is to let go completely, what is his job?

To use Dr. Chang's word, he is the "pilot."

She surrenders the she-boat of her body to the he-pilot who will, ideally, sail her beyond herself to bliss. Only a skilled navigator can fulfill his role as pilot. Most men must train their bodies, emotions and minds in order to fulfill this role.

Tao Of Sex couples enjoy intercourse (apart from "foreplay") for half an hour, an hour or even longer. For ancient Tao Of Sex consorts, such prolonged lovemaking was standard fare.

In Tao Of Sex lovemaking, a woman may take 20 minutes or more to reach her ninth course, her total climax of emptiness. On the other hand, it is recorded in Taoist texts that some women have reached that stage in a few minutes.

There are many, many variables. For this reason, the Tao Of Sex draws upon ancient Chinese medical principles to describe in detail the 9 stages (9 courses) of increasing female surrender and arousal ending in ecstatic emptiness.

THE NINE STAGES AND THEIR SIGNS

(1)	Lung	Sighs (Short Breathing)
(2)	Heart	Heart Speeds Up
(3)	Spleen/Pancreas	So Much Saliva
		Even Has A Cold Tongue
		(A Sure Sign)
(4)	Kidney	Much Vaginal Secretions
		Very Juicy
(5)	Bones	Tries To Curl Up And
		Hold Man Tight
(6)	Liver And Nerves	Begins To Bite
(7)	Blood	Heavy Perspiration
(8)	Muscles	No Muscle Tone
		Completely Relaxed
		She Is Soft Like Silk
(9)	Collapse	Total Climax

According to Dr. Chang, conventional orgasm is not the same thing as the Tao Of Sex complete climax of collapse and rejuvenating emptiness. The woman may or may not have regular orgasm with pubococcygeus (PC) muscle contractions. The two kinds of climax can occur at the same time, though.

Dr. Chang told the story of a wealthy woman who came to see him privately about her kidney problems and lack of energy. The solution was simple. When her husband began taking her to the ninth stage instead of the fourth (kidney) stage, her kidney condition cleared up and her energy returned.

Man's Tao Of Sex Pleasure Peaks

For the man, the routine of ejaculation orgasm with virtually every act of intercourse was viewed with horror by the Tao Of Sex experts. Though emptiness is definitely appropriate for and is to be sought by the female, the sensation of emptiness that often befalls the ordinary man after he ejaculates is, according to the Tao Of Sex, a sure sign of significant loss.

However, the Taoists were not against ejaculation per se. The ordinary man was not advised to avoid ejaculation entirely but rather to regulate it according to his age and self-evident health and vitality. A man's semen was regarded as life-giving and life-sustaining personally and merited a thoughtful and individualized conservation program.

The main obstacle to male/female harmony according to the Tao may well be the male addiction to ejaculation orgasm. As long as a man believes that his supreme pleasure can be found only in the ejaculation orgasm, the principle of the man as "pilot" will remain just another good theory.

Fortunately, however, no ascetic sacrifice of man's prime pleasure is implied or required by his taking on the Taoist pilot role. In fact, a significant gain in immediate pleasure and long-term sexual fulfillment (and long-term relationship fulfillment, perhaps) is waiting for him.

Some men do take their women to the ninth and final stage of Tao Of Sex and still ejaculate at the end. These men have discovered that as good as ejaculation orgasm feels, especially when delayed, there is something that feels even better.

What could possibly be even better than the ejaculation orgasm for a man? The answer is repeated almost-ejaculation pleasure peaks. Just as a woman is capable of multiple orgasms, a man is capable of multiple almost-ejaculation pleasure peaks.

The male pleasure peak in Tao Of Sex may be defined as approaching ejaculation orgasm inevitability, following with retreat, relaxation, the male Deer exercise (see below) and, eventually, renewed thrusting.

The cycle is repeated to mutual satisfaction or as long as time or desire permit. Male satisfaction, by the way, is complete with this method without ejaculation. According to the Tao this is the way of lovemaking for the man.

None other than the famed sex researcher Alfred C. Kinsey reported interviewing a number of men who practiced this kind of male climax. Kinsey made the point to his fellow sex researchers that they should not give the experience the coveted "orgasm" label. Still, he reported that these male sex adepts were themselves convinced that their dozen or so almost-ejaculation pleasure peaks during one lovemaking session were, in fact, actual orgasms, though admittedly of somewhat lesser intensity.

In a recent bestseller, writer Alexandra Penney praises this style of lovemaking for the pleasure and satisfaction it brings to both lovers.

These "hold backs" (another of Dr. Chang's terms) are the main course for the man in Tao Of Sex. Male ejaculation orgasm becomes dessert and is enjoyed as an occasional delicacy of great sweetness.

For a man to commit to his pilot role it helps to keep in mind a supreme pleasure other than ejaculation orgasm. This new supreme pleasure is male multiple pleasure peaks.

Whether or not a man chooses ejaculation as a grand finale (having his cake and eating it too) is a personal matter. Here is clear and sufficient motivation for him to last until his woman reaches the ninth stage of ecstatic total climax collapse.

One of the chief objections to this practice of parlaying for multiple pleasure peaks is the stress it can place upon the male prostate gland, particularly if relief is not provided at the end via ejaculation. Amazingly enough, the ancient Taoists had an answer for this one.

Male Deer Exercise In Intercourse

A woman's health is clearly benefited by being brought to the ninth stage. But where is the health benefit for the man in the Tao Of Sex male climax?

According to Tao Of Sex, his benefit is derived mainly from withholding the ejaculate and recycling the vital ingredients to the rest of his body. He may also receive benefit from her secretions and from excess vital energy released by her during orgasm.

However, some beneficial biochemistries are undoubtedly absorbed during extended lovemaking even if ejaculation does conclude the act.

There are men who for organic reasons, often as a result of surgery such as a prostatectomy, do not ejaculate when they orgasm (the ejaculate goes into the bladder). But there is no evidence that these men are any better off than men who emit semen from their bodies regularly.

Western men who avoid sexual activity altogether, such as Catholic monks, generally don't live as long as the average married man. If there is a health benefit gained from avoiding ejaculation, it certainly isn't just a matter of men avoiding seminal emission.

Here the ever-practical Tao Of Sex experts step in with a plausible modus operandi that makes perfect, though mind-stretching, sense. During intercourse the man voluntarily contracts his anal and PC muscles firmly and frequently. This massages his prostate gland, encouraging it to release its hormonal treasures back into the bloodstream (see Sexercises.)

Due to the prostate gland's mixing function, these secretions are a real pot pourri of male hormonal delicacies (see Voluntary Orgasm For Men.) This semen "fertilizer" (to use Dr. Chang's term) is carried via blood to parts of the man's body needing the vital nutrients. Glands, nerves, bones and bone marrow, joints and the immune system are fertilized first by the rejuvenating hormones. This semen fertilizer also favors the hair and skin.

But there is another very practical reason for these voluntary PC/anal muscle contractions. As Dr. Chang put it, "the prostate must pump." Either you pump it or it pumps itself in ejaculation. If it doesn't pump, congestion of the prostate may result.

Dr. Chang suggested a variety of ways to pump. The man can stop completely, relax and pump for up to five (5) minutes. The couple will need to lie still for this. He can also pump as he makes love, contracting the muscles as he pulls out. And he can pump as frequently during love-making as he likes and at any time he likes.

There are two main styles of pumping the prostate, with either establish a pulsating rhythm. The first way is to hold the contraction as long as possible, then totally let go and feel the relaxation. The second way is to do a set of them rapidly with complete relaxation of those muscles following, a set may be 50 repetitions.

Be aware of a tendency to slight the relaxation phase. Maximum contraction will result from maximum relaxation. Performance of this exercise during intercourse eventually enables the man to delay ejaculation indefinitely while intensifying his pleasure. This may or may not be followed by ejaculation.

The basic male Deer exercise is described elsewhere in this book (see Sexercises.) A dedicated Tao Of Sex pilot practices on a daily basis separately from intercourse. However, even occasional practice should provide valuable benefits. This exercise strengthens the muscles as well as intensifies the hormonal reabsorption process.

To summarize, the act of delaying final ejaculation and enjoying multiple pleasure peaks is, in fact, only half of the reality of the male Taoist climax. The other half is the conscious and voluntary act of pumping the prostate and recycling its hormonal cocktail throughout the male system.

Remember, Dr. Chang's pumping technique is an experimental method. It is not intended to replace the counsel of your physician. However, combined with very firm pressure on the prostate point (see Voluntary Orgasm For Men), pumping should aid in relieving prostate congestion and hormonal recycling. Please check with your physician now about the condition of your prostate and get regular prostate checkups. This examination should include a manual examination of your prostate via the anus.

When making love, the sequence of events is to pump during intercourse and follow with manual pressure on the prostate point, which your consort may be willing to perform for you. Or pumping and manual prostate relief can be mixed during intercourse, which is the way we generally like to do it.

Acupressure And The Sex Organs

The Taoist sexology of the Su Nui Ching teaches that sexual intercourse is actually a form of mutual acupressure. The end regions of the body, such as the hands and feet, and the open areas of the body, such as the ears and mouth, are rich with nerve endings and acupuncture energy points. The sexual organs are the richest of all such regions.

When male and female sex organs unite, a wonderful pressing together of acupuncture points takes place. In an acupuncture energy sense, the two bodies have literally become one. Among other things, this arrangement suggests a good match between male and female sex organs may be important for whole body stimulation and release.

In the diagrams below, Lung includes large intestine and skin, Heart includes small intestine and blood vessels, Spleen/Pancreas includes stomach and muscles, Liver includes nerves and gall bladder and Kidney includes urinary bladder and bones.

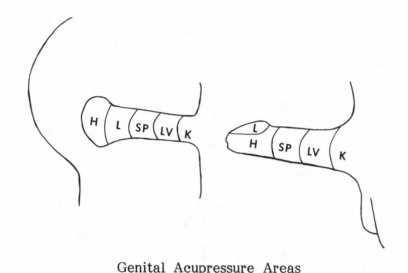

Genital Acupressure Areas

When a physically and emotionally compatible man and woman unite sexual organs, Kidney communes with Kidney, Liver communes with Liver and so on. According to this theory, there is simply no substitute for this all-points alignment. Even if the couple just lie still, abundant bio-energy is exchanged. They are both getting a free acupressure treatment.

Healthy Sex, Whole Sex

Tao Of Sex evolved in a more leisurely, more down-to-earth world that was very different from our own. In fact, we will probably never be able to fully understand how much and in what ways ancient Tao Of Sex couples appreciated lovemaking.

For one thing, they literally made it a part of their daily lives. Free of distractions like newspapers and television, they made love for hours on end daily.

When we get sick today, we receive a medical prescription, usually a drug. Although ancient Taoist physicians certainly did prescribe herbs, they often advised frequent sexual intercourse utilizing very specific positions and thrusting protocols or pelvic movements.

So instead of taking pills one, two, three or four times a day, men and women were instructed to make love one, two, three or four times a day.

It was a very different world, indeed.

On Not Getting Enough

A benefit of making love without male ejaculation that we have found is that romance is enhanced.

It is a common observation that the lightning of love strikes and then is gone. The mysterious magic quickly fades, leaving familiar struggles.

Being in love is a kind of creative tension. To get one's fill, to be sated, this is not the mood of a person in love. To be in love is to be ravenously hungry, to be ever unsatisfied, to be longing, to never get enough. Happy lovers enjoy a paradox of fulfilling non-fulfillment.

According to Tao Of Sex, some of this loss of magic is the result of one or both lovers losing rather than gaining via their lovemaking. Not only the man but the woman also can lose. The two who once felt so full with each other quickly exhaust the gift.

Wise lovers will never get enough of each other. Wise lovers will stay with the tension, the unknowing, the insecurity, the hunger of the beginning, of the fall into love. One way to sustain the magic is Tao Of Sex.

Contemporary Tao Of Sex master Jolan Chang emphasizes in his writings that this is one of the key secrets of bringing peace to the war of the sexes. He is convinced, based on decades of research, that following the Way of the Tao is the natural way. Disharmony between man and woman is largely the result of men and women forcing orgasm and losing the cutting edge of need and desire. When intimacy is the main focus, the ultimate in pleasure is enjoyed as well.

IMSAK (The Ninth Style)

Imsak (also pronounced "im-shak") is an Arabic word that means, literally, "retention." In this respect Imsak resembles Karezza. The man retains his semen by not ejaculating. However, it's difficult to tell from the sketchy records whether this meant ejaculation was delayed only until the woman was satisfied or that it was foregone entirely (or both, depending on the occasion).

According to one tradition, Imsak was developed out of necessity: no ordinary man could satisfy an entire harem of passionate (and bored?) young women. A man who had mastered Imsak could satisfy 10 women or more a night. Such a man might still have had a favorite(s) and, when appropriate, shared the joys of mutual orgasm with her.

All of this sounds irredeemably sexist, and, no doubt, it is. Today, though, a woman stands to gain a great deal by enjoying with her man the prolonged ecstasy that was once shared by an entire harem.

Very little is know with certainty about the details of the Imsak method. The generic label of "retention" can be applied to several of the Sexual Energy Ecstasy styles. Fortunately, freelance writer Robert Meister researched this method and has unearthed what are probably the essentials. The key to Imsak is found in its uniquely systematic way of combining coitus interruptus and pompoir so that higher and higher levels of ecstasy and energy are attained and absorbed.

Since at least Roman times, man has pulled out before ejaculating to avoid (they hoped) impregnating the woman. In Imsak, the man pulls out well before he reaches his point of ejaculatory inevitability in order to achieve cumulative erotic and consciousness-altering effects for the couple together.

Teasing is universally recognized as a way to build passion and desire to such a pitch that the final release is unforgettable. To a point, the greater the erotic tension and frustration, the better the release. Teasing, however, is too weak a word to convey the mind-boggling power of Imsak.

In Imsak, the man enters and pulls out up to ten (10) times, allowing their mutual arousal to build with each successive penetration. Ejaculation is delayed until the final union or, perhaps, altogether.

Some lovers content themselves with two or three re-entries. The sensations that accompany even just this much erotic self-discipline can be far superior to the usual fare. These lovers may believe they have scaled the heights of erotic ecstasy when, in fact, they have only reached the foot of the mountain.

The acme of Imsak is reached after about 10 unions. The exaltation that permeates the lovers who go that far is, according to Meister, the pinnacle of erotic possibility.

All of this depends, of course, on male ejaculatory control as well as female cooperation. Fortunately, the essence of Imsak is also what makes it feasible for just about any man unless he is physically impaired.

Pulling out is a great way to delay ejaculation orgasm. Pulling out is now a popular way to train a man to last longer. Ordinarily, a man feels awkward pulling out. Imsak enables him to pull out as needed, rest and then re-enter and be confident that he is adding to mutual bliss.

What do you do during these rest periods?

First, allow the man a few minutes of non-stimulation so that his erection and his need to ejaculate subside.

Avoiding the genitals, stroke, caress, touch. Show affection while at the same time creating arousal as needed. All is done very gently and with great sensitivity. The skin becomes sensitive due to the accumulated whole-body arousal therefore tender gestures are strongly preferred.

One thing leads to another. Soon you will be kissing and El besiss, "the impudent one," as Sheikh Nefzawi called him, will rise once again. With great care and cooperation, re-entry is achieved yet one more time.

Take enough time in the rest periods, though, that you actually do experience some rest and relaxation and cool down a bit. Also, these rest periods are your opportunity to recollect and focus your heart-felt feelings for each other and spread energy for health and rejuvenation. You may want to use some of this time to go within (meditate).

For Meister's Imsak some pompoir (kabbazah) ability is essential (see Pompoir Power.) Unlike Kabbazah Sex, though, the skill level required is not that great, and many women will have sufficient strength and control without having done regular exercises. If Meister's formula is followed precisely, the first five unions (the man has pulled out and repenetrated four times) are mergers without male thrusting motion.

The woman is in control of their arousal through her kabbazah skill. This way the erotic fire builds and builds as an experience of the whole body and is not localized in the genitals.

Naturally, you are free to deviate from his formula according to your own needs and capacities. But you will know the precise and, perhaps, ideal Imsak formula.

On the first entry, Meister suggests that the man enter but not thrust, though he should push with his pelvis and penis against the woman as firmly yet comfortably as he can. The pressure he can exert in this way is a major stimulating factor and can be used during any unions without motion. To get things going for the female, she or he can manually stimulate her clitoris.

If she is on top and facing him, this is the position known as es sibfahheh, "swimming." The position gets its name from the ease with which the clitoral bud is manually stimulated and intense arousal is achieved, especially when combined with voluntary contractions of the sexual muscles.

She also begins clenching and letting go, starting with delicate little flicks and building up to real manhandler grips and, if advanced in the art, rolling and milking motions.

He is encouraged to work his PC and anal muscles, too.

She will probably need to stimulate her clitoris manually only during the first union. Even though he is not moving his penis, it won't be long before he has to pull out.

At this time begin the affectionate yet arousing rest period. Avoid direct genital stimulation unless it is needed to achieve re-entry. Relax and cool down as needed.

After about the fifth such cycle the couple is now ready for the second half of the technique. During the next cycle the thrusting strategy outlined below is followed.

This cycle is followed by a motionless cycle as above. This cycle is followed by another thrusting cycle and so on up to about ten completed cycles. The man pulls out between each cycle.

Advanced Imsak practicioners capable of completing ten cycles will follow a protocol consisting of five pompoir cycles followed by thrusting, pompoir, thrusting, pompoir and thrusting cycles, in that order. The man voluntarily climaxes on the final thrusting cycle.

In practice, the woman is orgasming by the third pompoir cycle unless she is holding back intentionally. The male beginner will probably experience (very intense) ejaculation orgasm before reaching the second set of five cycles.

During unions without motion, she determines their arousal through her pompoir. During unions with motion, he determines their arousal with his thrusting.

This alternation of giving and taking, or sending and receiving, is one of the secrets to elevating your ecstasy. Each alternation is one more step up the stairway to heaven (see Stairway To Heaven.)

As mentioned earlier, out of ten cycles total, only three involve male thrusting. Meister suggests that a systematic thrusting method in the midst of the madness of intercourse will bring the greatest fulfillment. Echoing the traditional recommendations of the Tao Of Sex masters, Meister advises the following:
(1)   Thrust 10 times after entering, then pull out.
(2)   Stay near the entrance of the vagina on the first 3 thrusts. Don't go deep. This is to stimulate her.
(3)   Follow with 2 fast thrusts into the depths of her vagina to arouse her.
(4)   Follow with 3 more thrusts near the entrance of the vagina to tantalize her.
(5)   Conclude with 2 leisurely thrusts into the depths of her vagina to satisfy her.
(6)   Voluntary orgasm is ideally achieved with a long, leisurely, fully felt thrust that goes all the way to her "North Pole," to her very depths. This is to fulfill ("full-fill") her utterly.

As artificial as Meister's thrusting regimen may seem, it is a valuable aid to ejaculatory control as well as an intensifier of her pleasure. Through the magic of rhythm, the thrusting techniques add elegance and sophistication to the act of lovemaking.

Mastery of such a routine, particularly if it is performed as a team effort, is analagous to learning to dance in a certain style instead of moving on impulse this way and that on the floor. Randomness can be great fun, but the joy of flowing together is usually reserved only for those who first have mastered a routine. The thrill of mutual whole-body coordination enjoyed during a series of fluid position changes provides a similar dance-like delight.

This thrusting sequence works very well with any active lovemaking style. It is a concentrated recipe for ecstasy that takes into account both depth of penetration and speed of penetration. He may want to vary angle of penetration, making straight, slanted, up and down and circular thrusts.

In The Sack With Imsak

The words of wisdom to the male Imsak beginner are "Discretion is the better part of valor."

Success with this method, however, depends as much on female cooperation as it does on male discipline. Her sensitivity to his arousal, e.g., how close he is to genital climax, will determine whether to squeeze or not to squeeze. When a man is near the edge, one little compulsive twist of the waist or clench of the circum-vaginal muscles can put him over.

Keep in mind your ultimate goal as you make love, that acme of erotic arousal in which each touch is like a miniature orgasm. Of course, your goal with this method may differ from time to time. This will motivate cooperation in delaying his ejaculation orgasm.

Keep in mind, too, that transcending ordinary pleasure may be only the beginning. You may find valuable personal insights, soak in an overwhelming sense of oneness, bathe in a peaceful calm of total contentment, swim in a sea of wavelike bliss. These are just some of the possible benefits to you. It is likely that these experiences will occur to you when you are united but not moving.

Should you opt for the traditional orgasm as your grand finale, it will probably be an unforgettable tidal wave straight from paradise. The experience will prove to you that building up the erotic tension far beyond usual tolerance is the best way to guarantee a fabulous climax. Because you have built up such an abundance of energy, mutual orgasm will probably be easier to achieve.

Try to follow Meister's method to the letter, at least at first. There is something uniquely challenging and satisfying about following an effective erotic procedure precisely. This kind of training brings out the sexual artist in you. Any feelings of artificiality will melt away in the fire that engulfs you.

Once you are acquainted with the basics of Imsak, feel free to improvise. Simply use the Imsak secret of repeated coitus interruptus as an erotic elevator to new pinnacles of sexual ecstasy. Each re-entry takes you higher than you were before. Each rest period is yet another peace-filled realm to explore. Ride your Imsak elevator to the penthouse of paradise any way you like.

KABBAZAH SEX (The Tenth Style)

In the old days in the Middle East, a woman who had mastered pompoir (voluntary control of the circumvaginal muscles during sexual intercourse) was known as kabbazah or "holder." If you've ever had the experience, from either side, then you know just how appropriate the label is.

Back then this style was much more widely known and kabbazahs were more numerous. We are convinced that Kabbazah Sex was at one time a stock in trade of many of the more talented prostitutes in India, China, Japan, Persia and other countries in the East. In fact, this tradition is still alive today.

A man taking one of our workshops reported that while he was stationed in Japan during its occupation following World War II, he went to a Japanese prostitute. She bathed him and asked if he wanted to try something new. Without hesitation, he agreed. After he entered her, he was instructed to lie still and fully relax while she did all the work.

The sensations he experienced were incredible and truly

254

exquisite, unlike anything he had ever felt before while inside a woman. Eager, innocent of expectation and starved for the feel of a woman's body, he was the ideal candidate. Because the nature of their relationship was that of leader and follower, or expert and novice, he was not hampered by the obstacle of male pride and followed her suggestions to the letter.

Within half an hour, he reported, they were sharing the ecstasies of the classic TRO experience of energy oneness. It was, he said, to put it mildly, an unforgettable experience.

The ancient institution of sacred prostitution, which was active in Southern India as recently as the 1930's, must have made use of Kabbazah Sex in a similar way. If ever there was a way that a woman could offer a man the ecstasy of the gods, it is with Kabbazah Sex. Her kabbazah ability makes this experience possible, but she enjoys the same ecstasy.

It is difficult for us today to appreciate the training some of the prostitutes, sacred and otherwise, underwent in those days. Some, particularly those destined for temple service, were trained from an early age, much as apple-cheeked cherubs are sent off to their first ballet classes. In some parts of Africa, today girls receive kabbazah training and may even be forbidden to marry unless they display mastery of it.

The practical point in this is that real mastery of pompoir is usually needed to bring off the technique elegantly. If the female partner is struggling and straining to fulfill her part, to "do all the work," Kabbazah Sex can become quite cumbersome. She will not enjoy it and will suffer from performance stress in much the same way that men do when they "do all the work." She will experience fatigue and that will be the end of that lovemaking session, at least in Kabbazah Sex style.

Strategic abstinence is sometimes helpful. If a couple is willing to forego sexual release for three to seven days and yet encourage their sexual feelings for each other, the increased genital sensitivity and cumulative desire intensity may be sufficient to put them over the edge. A good time to try this is when you are reuniting after a physical separation. Still, the best guarantee of satisfactory results using this ancient technique is that she be kabbazah.

For communion this intimate, the quality of the feeling and the depth of the honesty between the man and woman can be decisive. Thoughts and emotions withheld from the consort, though invisible, act as solid barriers to the merging of the currents of your total selves. Well before trying this kind of lovemaking, confess any acts that have separated you from each other if you can.

Kabbazah Sex And Role Reversal

The Kabbazah Sex style follows a very specific format. Like many of the styles already discussed, prolonged motionlessness may be necessary. The woman plays a very specific and dynamic role. In Imsak, application of pompoir is encouraged. In Kabbazah Sex, it is the very heart of the method.

The concept of utter male passivity will strike some people as bizarre, perhaps even offensive. Actually, it is a wonderful experience. It can be a great relief for the man to be completely free of performance demands during lovemaking.

He is also released to focus completely on the not unchallenging process of achieving total relaxation while being sexually stimulated. Finally, if he is a contemplative man, he will find the experience of going into contemplative reverie or some other form of meditation uniquely satisfying in this context.

Kabbazah Sex makes use of an authentic ancient secret, which is the power of kabbazah itself. Most men and women live, make love and die, never suspecting the awesome power of the virtuoso vagina. So great is this power that it could revolutionize current lovemaking if it became popular.

STANDARD SEX	KABBAZAH SEX
man on top	woman on top
man moves penis	woman moves vagina
woman passive	man passive
man in control	woman in control
aggressive male	receptive male
tension-relief orgasm	TRO

Although the Total Relaxation Orgasm can be experienced in other ways, making use of the kabbazah power holder is one of the most logical and reliable methods. Kabbazah Sex successfully restructures the human sex act and achieves an ingenious total reversal of the stereotyped male-dominated sex act.

How To Do Kabbazah Sex

We would like to emphasize staying in the sensory present. Kabbazah Sex is an ancient secret, but fulfillment will not be found by duplicating the past but rather in rediscovering the present.

What is the best way to prepare for Kabbazah Sex?

Elaborate ritualistic procedures have often accompanied this Kabbazah Sex style in the past. Quite a number of books are out now which describe these procedures in great detail. Those who wish to enhance the experience with such techniques will find their way without us.

In Doing It Rite, we describe a simple sexual ritual that can be combined with Kabbazah Sex. Here we spell out the details of the practice. As the experience of the American serviceman with the Japanese prostitute illustrates, you don't have to add a thing. See Basic Boudoir for guidelines on how to enhance your environment.

Physical and mental relaxation, setting aside plenty of time, a woman who is kabbazah and a man who is willing to be blissfully passive are the basic ingredients.

Repetitions of the Root Lock and the Thunderbolt Gesture prior to intercourse are considered helpful by sexual yogis. These, of course, are breath-intensified Kegel exercises so you can do Kegel squeezes instead (see Complete Breath, Sexercises.) There is something to be said for the impromptu union, too.

Now for the essence. Now you will know one of the most powerful techniques for experiencing a blissful alteration of consciousness discovered by mankind.

Here is the key to the Kabbazah Sex:

ONLY SHE MOVES
(WITHIN)

Yes, it really is that simple.

The way she moves is internally. She does not even shuttle back and forth or circle around with her body. She does what no man can do--pompoir.

Allow at least the minimum 30-40 minutes of genital union that is standard for all of the soft styles.

Keep in mind that total relaxation is the secret.

Some positions are definitely better. First there is YabYum and its variations. The classic YabYum is difficult for most people to hold properly. Sometimes sitting on fat pillows or meditation cushions will make holding YabYum easier and more comfortable.

A modified YabYum allows the man to lean back and rest with his back supported. The woman may also be able to lean back, but this will vary from couple to couple. Most positions in which the man is lying down on his back and the woman is on top will do just fine. Though the Scissors makes it harder for the vagina to grasp the penis, its comfort can be sheer luxury.

Kabbazah Sex Step-By-Step

Here is the formula. Even if you don't stick to it, or you don't have the same experience, isn't it reassuring to know that there is a step-by-step way to achieve what may be the ultimate sexual experience?

(1)   Only she moves (pompoir).

(2)   He does not move his hips or pelvis at all (never the entire time--not even once).

(3)   She does not move her hips or pelvis at all. Remember, all the action is internal via pompoir only.

(4)   The couple remains motionless except for the drama of the jewel in the lotus occuring in her womb. This is the classic recommendation. You may find, though, that you can caress and kiss and gaze in each other's eyes without accelerating into the usual arousal, resulting in thrusting and standard orgasm. Basic motionlessness enables maximum focus on the genital sensations. Stillness, not stiffness, is what is being asked here.

(5)   Remember, she, not he, is in control.

(6)   Take your time. Easy does it. The tendency is to rush. Rush where? Ecstasy beyond convenient pleasure takes time.

(7)   You want peace, serenity, calm. Your mood and

every action, every response, is an affirmation of peace. (8)   At the same time, you deeply feel and encourage your desire and arousal.   Your passions are slowly climbing to a white-hot temperature, hotter even than red-hot. You are experiencing genital arousal dialog.   As she stimulates him, his penis throbs.   As his penis throbs, she is further aroused, stimulating him more.   As he gets more stimulated, so does she.   And so it goes on and on in a seemingly never-ending upward spiral.   Remember, she will have to ease up at certain times to avoid stimulating him into genital orgasm.

(9)   After awhile, you reach what can be called the stage of throbbing and pulsating sex organs.   You may feel like you are going out of your mind, the urge for relief will be so great.   Or, you may not experience this stage so intensely.   You may not experience it at all and move right through to the next one.

(10)   After about fifteen (15) minutes of pompoir, you will experience a bioelectrical force field effect.   An aura of peace and benign energy is felt. The best word to describe the feeling is probably sacred.   You may feel that you are on truly holy ground.   You feel startlingly alive and clearheaded.   You feel that the two of you are one.

(11)   You are both now enjoying a wonderful out of this world (meditative) state.   You feel inspired, aglow, rejuvenated.   She stimulates the man as needed.

(12)   Total Relaxation Orgasm takes place for both about thirty (30) minutes from the beginning of the union.   This is fifteen minutes after the force field effect was first felt.

By all means, do not take this outline as gospel. We are all individuals.   Each couple is a unique combination. Listen to your feelings, to your heart.

There is one action the man can take we haven't mentioned.   The man can contract his PC/anal muscles to join in.   It is also possible to develop the muscles that move the penis up and down and side to side to such an extent that the penis can be moved around within the vagina without moving the rest of the body.   The authors of ESO suggest practicing with a full erection in sitting and lying positions to locate the muscles involved.

We have said nothing about visualizations, affirmations and the like.   If you like them, use them.

EPILOGUE

HAPPINESS IS KNOWING YOU ARE SINGLE

happiness is knowing you are single

alone forever
are you

whether your consorts are none, one, few or many
they have but one face

a reflection in the mirror

those who are joined
will eventually part

those who are a part
will eventually be whole

all is a process of
uniting and separating

do not be fooled by appearances

how can relationships be permanent
when life itself is not?

no one can love you
unless you love you

the greatest love, the sweetest love, the best love
stands on ground sanctified
by a love of freedom

without fresh air
even the finest fire
dies

We are advocates of the endless orgasm (climax).

We are advocates of the endlessly orgasmic relationship.

Orgasm is a state of mind-body.

In the sexualove play between man and woman, male and female polarities, the potential exists for endless orgasm.

Orgasm may be experienced while talking, fighting, making love, dancing, eating, touching, listening, looking, laughing.

How paltry, how cheap, how downright self-denying to restrict orgasm to an electric thrill, a spasm of nerves!

When people speak of endless love, of ultimate romantic love, as is sometimes pictured in movies or books, what they are actually referring to is this dynamic condition of endless orgasm.

Something very specific is taking place between the sexes. It is this orgasm without end.

Once it is understood by a man and a woman how to maintain that subtle ongoing sense of orgasm, of thrilling dynamic circulating aliveness, it need never end but only expand and go higher and higher and deeper and deeper.

What is non-stop orgasm?

Endless orgasm is a kind of recycling.

Not that you're always in a state of physical orgasmic spasming. But that your lovemaking never really has to stop. You can make the transition from bed to head and heart and retain the ecstatic glow in daily life. Everything can be foreplay and arousal and orgasm and afterglow all rolled into one resonant bursting forth, for so much of the time that the fundamental tone or quality of your relationship is, somehow, orgasmic.

Endless orgasm is for those who can be responsible for staying in love, for stepping out of the mental trivia trap, out of everyday thinking mind.

Thoughts can kill endless orgasm, just as they can kill ordinary orgasm during ordinary sex.

Desire, left to itself, will end the interaction. Desire wants to achieve the goal, the orgasm, the relief.

Desire is not concerned with what will be after that goal, that relief.

Love, on the other hand, wants never to end. Lovers long for immortality together. The heart is at home in heaven. Endless orgasm is endless giving to and receiving from the lover.

But love, by itself, cannot be enough for lovers. Otherwise, lovers are just friends, mutual benefactors. Desire, an undefinable yet irrefutable magnetic attraction, is needed. Steady desire, stable desire, desire to make love, desire to be with your lover, desire to share joy.

Such desire is fostered by Sexual Energy Ecstasy lovemaking.

Desire is the fuel and the fire. Love is the oven and the temperature control. Life energy is the bread upon which you feast as you exchange essences via your union.

The love, the respect, the esteem between the love partners provides the special space in which this one act play of polar opposites may playfully yet intensely go on and on in endless cycles of expansion and contraction, of rising and falling, of in and out, of for and against, of yes and no, of pain and pleasure, of birth and death of self.

This is possible because the man holds the essence of woman in him, and the woman holds the essence of man in her. What is outside male is inside female. What is outside female is inside male.

Thus men are known to be strong outside and sensitive inside, while women are known to be strong inside sensitive outside. Ideally, of course, strength with sensitivity both inside and outside is present. This ideal of growth is nurtured by a relationship that recognizes the value of the twenty-four hour day after day orgasm, of lovemaking that never ends.

The differences are only in what is on the outside and what is in the inside. The differences provide the track, the circuit, the two poles of positive and negative polarity needed for energy flow to begin and continue. It is the same as with other electromagnetic phenomena.

Our separation from nature that we mourn, our independence from nature that we celebrate are superficial, imaginary, contrary to fact. Immutable laws continue uninterrupted. For there to be energy and ecstasy, there must be polarity. The same polarity is demonstrated at the level of the universe and the atom and man-woman.

Enjoy this polarity. It is a form of balance. In the

game of balance lost, sought and regained three needs are at work: the need to reach for the other, the need to commune and the need to release that union and return to the integrity of self alone.

Authentic action is the key, and it is based on having a deep practical understanding of life's everyday dramas.

For example, anger is utterly orgasmic. Fights, friction, conflicts are inevitable. They are the bites, scratches and screeches of impassioned lovemaking translated to everyday life. A fight can be a feast of life energy. Not only are tensions released and differences worked out, but the sheer aliveness that is felt during anger can be totally shared even as you square off to get into your fight.

What must be understood is the natural cycle, the fundamental reality of rhythm as it applies to a relationship. The ocean tides flow in and out. The sun and the moon share the sky in a rhythm of day and night. Man and woman, as phenomena of nature, are a part of this rhythmic process.

The feeling of closeness will appear and disappear. The feeling of distance will appear and disappear. The feeling of neutralness will appear and disappear.

This cannot be changed. You might as well try to grab the sun out of the sky, or carry the moon in your pocket.

What can be changed is your relationship to it.

It is an impersonal process. In and out, back and forth, together and apart, up and down, like the breath which never ends as long as you are alive. It is quite uncontrollable.

Since you cannot defeat it, join it.

Your feelings of anger and alienation are blessings in disguise. Since we are human beings, we feel these ebbing tides and identify with them. We invest them with personality and emotion. The process itself is utterly impersonal.

Your feelings of indifference and neutrality are a hidden delight. It is the natural time to take a break, to renew the primary relationship, the relationship with yourself. At such times be relieved of the need for others. Glory in your self-sufficiency, revel in supreme aloneness. One eagle soaring through an empty sky.

The key to fulfilling your possibility for endless orgasm in a relationship is to become harmless. Harmlessness is the absence of ill will. It is objective compassion, neutral caring, unqualified good will, high indifference.

Harmlessness is self-esteem in action.

To become even a little bit harmless brings great freedom.

You need inner peace at least a little because the emotional clarity on which harmlessness is based is the by-product of inner peace.

There are no short-cuts.

Become harmless.

There comes a time when it is seen that everything in our world around us, and in our relationships in particular, is a reflection of our relationship with ourselves.

Manhood and womanhood are measured by each other.

To know a man, look at his woman.

To know a woman, look at her man.

On the outside opposites may attract, but inside it is sameness, agreement, that attracts.

Endless orgasm is a celebration of the friction created by the differences between two polarized persons who can remain in emotional agreement with one another. It is not a new standard, a new goal, a new measure of love.

It is a form of fire walking.

It is an invitation to dance, and, in the dancing, to remember why you came to this party in the first place.

GLOSSARY

Body-Mind: Body and mind are, in fact, literally one.

Climax: A peak sexual experience comparable to a sexual orgasm in intensity, pleasure or significance. A climax may take the shape of an experience that is quite out of the ordinary for that person. Climax is frequently used in this book to refer to orgasm-like experiences that are not genital orgasms in the strict biological sense.

Conscious Conflict: Intentional compassionate conflict based on the understanding that conflict between consorts is inevitable and essential.

Consort: A noble companion with whom the art of Sexual Energy Ecstasy is practiced.

Ejac-elation: Ejaculation which is not forced but occurs in harmony with a man's natural rhythm of need for release.

Eduction: The art of drawing forth the sensitivity and vitality of your consort for mutually beneficial intimacy with acts of impassioned kindness.

Everyday Thinking Mind: The conscious thinking mind which is useful for practical matters, such as shopping, planning, working, but must be set aside or somehow left behind for profound lovemaking experiences to take place.

Holistic Lovemaking: Any approach to lovemaking which takes into account the fact that the whole of sexual union is much greater than the sum of its parts. Body, mind and heart make love. The presence of healing life energies is assumed. Holistic lovemaking makes conscious use of the power of sexual energy for healing, growth and harmony. Having or not having genital orgasm is a matter of personal choice and style.

Just Touch: By focusing on the experience of just touching without interpretation or goal pressures, consorts are able to set everyday thinking mind aside and enjoy inspired revitalizing lovemaking (see pages 96-97.)

Life Energy: The life-sustaining force that surrounds and fills and flows through the body-mind. More or less identical to acupuncture energies (chi) and human bioelectromagnetic forces.

Love Spot: Center of deep feeling located in the middle of the breastbone between the nipples. Can be gently stimulated with the open palm, with the tongue, with the mind, etc. The thymus gland, located a few inches above the Love spot, expresses the function of the Love spot at a glandular level. It can be activated by vigorous thumping. Activation of the Love spot occurs spontaneously in deeply fulfilling lovemaking.

Non-Ejaculatory Male Orgasm (NEMO): Male climax without ejaculation.

Peak Of the Peak (POP): The highest point of the genital orgasm when complete loss of ego sense may occur.

Second Penetration: The emotional penetration of the man by the woman. Just as she opens up and yields physically, he can open up and yield emotionally. When he does so, the circuit of energy exchange is completed and the power of lovemaking to stimulate personal growth, joy and understanding of life is multiplied.

Sexual Energy Ecstasy: 1. Holistic approach to lovemaking based on the view that lovemaking is a benign consciousness-raising experience that shows the intrinsic unity of life. It incorporates both hard and soft (yang and yin) practices and insights from around the world. 2. The ultra-ecstasy and ultra-intimacy experiences themselves.

Sexual Energy Recycling: A personal biorhythm of orgasmic discharge is followed. Orgasm is not forced. This biorhythm is arrived at through personal experiments and self-observation. It is subject to change due to external and internal forces. Unnecessary loss of vitality and enthusiasm is prevented, benefiting the relationship as well as the individuals. Dedicated recyclers practice hard and/or soft exercises, especially if a gain in vitality via sexual energization is intended.

Sexual Orgasm: In this book, the terms sexual orgasm, conventional orgasm and genital orgasm refer to the familiar type of orgasm that is accompanied by rapid contractions of the PC muscle. Sexual orgasm is a particular kind of climax (see Climax) or peak experience.

Sexualove: The ideal consort relationship in which desire and loving kindness for each other are powerfully present and effectively balanced.

Soft Style: Soft style lovemaking emphasizes relaxation, emotional intimacy and peaceful interaction. It offers a balance to the athletic goal-orientation tendencies of hard style lovemaking. Soft and hard styles are complementary. Most couples will find that the two approaches enrich each other.

Total Relaxation Orgasm (TRO): A climax that usually requires maximum relaxation. May occur with arousal, as in Kabbazah Sex, or without arousal, as in Extrasensory Sex. It is not the same as conventional genital orgasm. Typical signs of genital orgasm, such as rapid contraction of the PC muscle, may occur, but the chief characteristic of TRO is an experience of blissful fusion. TRO may last a few seconds, several minutes, an hour or longer. TRO can occur without any genital stimulation whatsoever, yet may occur during vigorous hard style lovemaking as well. Sometimes referred to as "Tantric Orgasm" or energy orgasm. Can take place hugging while fully clothed or without any physical contact, e.g., via eye contact alone. There are literally thousands of variations.

Ultra-intimacy: The word intimate comes to us from the Latin intimus meaning "innermost." To enjoy sexual ultra-intimacy means to experience the innermost part or essence of yourself and your consort. Ultra-intimacy is most likely in compassion-based exchanges.

ACKNOWLEDGEMENTS

The authors would like to thank the following persons:

Edmund Chein, M.D., J.D. and Fred Kuyt, M.D. for reviewing selected portions of the text for medical accuracy and for freely sharing their knowledge.

Andrew Lewin, M.D. for his insightful words.

William Schutz, Ph.D. for invaluable advice.

Cheryl Pappas for the use of "Be Love To Have Love."

Dolores Winton for proofreading, editorial comments and enthusiasm.

Robert Howard for comments that improved the cover.

Lee Perry for outstanding editorial services.

Dan Poynter for so generously sharing his knowledge of book publishing and for the format of the Disclaimer.

Morton Maxwell, M.D., Abraham Waks, M.D., Cheryl Gross, R.N., Jerry Schroth, R.N. and Phil Schroth, Ph.D. for their support and kindness.

Steven Koenigsberg, Ph.D., Andrew Lewin, M.D., Jill Casty, Al Abrams, M. Brooks and Bonnie Winton for their comments on the manuscript.

Sage King, Ph.D., Venerable Shinzen Young, Paul Bindrim, Ph.D., Ven. Mettavihari, Jack Rosenberg, Ph.D., Marjorie Rand, Ph.D., Dr. Stephen Chang, Joel Katz, M.A., Al Manning, C.P.A., D.D., Lewis E. Durham, Ed.D., M.Th., Ernest Holden, Lee Perry, Giovanna Bergmann, Cordula Ohman, Carol Shive Churton, Sue Criswell, Steve Gilburne, Steve Swart, Akasa Levi, Jennifer Maglica, Jack Frost, William Miller, Ph.D., Gene Emery, Glenn Bradley, Jeff Labno, Krishna Shah, Rev. Suzanne Hagen, Eldon Snyder, Ph.D., Rev. Juanita White, Swami Sivananda, Swami Satyananda Saraswati, Gry Akones, Paulette Rochelle-Levy, M.F.C.C., Swami Satchidananda, Swami Vivekananda, Swami Janakananda, Elan Neev, Ph.D., Bill Geller, Hollis Cotham, Wendy Mann, Brian Lambert, Dawn, George Caccamise, Michelle Piet, Sabine and M. Brooks for their insights.

Dan Poynter, Alan Gadney, Peggy Glenn, Justin Herold, Jan Nathan, Dick Bye and the rest of PASCAL, Lynda Huey, Jack Pryor, Lee Perry, Irwin Zucker, Brina-Rae Schuchman, Jill Casty, Gene Schwartz, Ed Marcus, Tyrone Huntley, Jane Browne and Zan for sharing their knowledge of book publishing.

Lexisoft technical support, Marsha Lewin, Al Abrams and Charles Ramsdale for sharing their computer expertise.

Leora and Harry Brown-Hiegle, Jocelyn Freid, Chandrika McKay, Burt Dubin, Diana Sacks, Jennifer Burtt, Rosalie Martinez, Daryl Pieta, Ralph Thierry, Steven Lader, Leslie Kaminoff, Linda Huey, Shelley Young, Parvati, Arline Goldberg, David Draper, Tara Realy, Kisha Cohen, Whitfield Reaves, C.A., James Andion, Esq., Sylvia, Carol Hemingway, M.A., Theo Scipio and Kevin, Richard Foulk, Bob Mulhander, Walt and Karen Seubert, Jerry and Maggie Davis, Kevin Noonan and Geneva for inspiration.

The many men and women who so generously shared of themselves at our workshops, seminars and lectures.

Sexual explorers past and present for their wisdom.

Our parents and relatives for sharing our vision.

APPENDIX

Being included in this list of resources does not imply endorsement by the authors or publisher.

Acupressure Techniques:
The G-Jo Institue, Box 8060, Hollywood, Florida 33024.

Astrology & Biorhythms:
A.C.S., P.O. Box 16430, San Diego, CA 92116.
Peak Skill, P.O. Box 5489, Playa Del Rey, CA 90296. (213) 306-6403. Individual and relationship astrology.

Bach Flower Remedies:
Ellon (Bach USA) Inc., P.O. Box 320, Woodmere, NY 11598.

Background Music & Sounds:
Bindu Distr., 1 Penn Plaza, Suite 100, NY, NY 10119.
Narada Distr., 1804 E. North Ave., Milwaukee, WI 53202.
Syntonic Res., Inc., 175 Fifth Avenue, NY, NY 10010
Vital Body Marketing, Box 1067, Manhasset, NY 11030.

Essential Perfume Oils:
The Attar Bazaar, Ltd., Box 99, Sidney, N.Y. 13838.

Floatation Tank Association
Alma Daniel, 300 Central Park N., NY, NY 10024.

Foot Reflexology (Eunice Ingham Method):
Reflexology, P.O. Box 12642, St. Petersburg, FL 33733.

Hatha Tantra Yoga:
Swami Satyananda is a bona fide Hindu Tantric master and gives instruction in the yogic approach to making love.
Bihar School of Yoga, Monghyr 811201, Bihar, India. In USA, Satyananda Ashram, Box 291, Newberry Springs, CA 92365, (619) 257-0913.
Or Swami Janakananda, Scandinavian Yoga and Meditation

School, S-340 13 Hamneda, Sweden.

Herb Suppliers:
Harvest, 1944 Eastern Ave., S.E., Grand Rapids, MI 49507.
Herbalist & Alchemist, Box 63, Franklin Park, NJ 08823.
Herb Prod., 11012 Magnolia Blvd., N. Hollywood, CA 91601.
House of Hezekiah, 4305 Main, Kansas City, MO 64111.

Holistic Health Organizations:
American Holistic Medical Association, 6932 Little River
    Turnpike, Annandale, Virginia 22003, (703) 642-5880.
The Academy of Orthomolecular Psychiatry, 1691 Northern
    Blvd., Manhasset, NY 11030, (516) 627-7260.
The Huxley Institute, 1114 First Avenue, NY, NY 10021.
International Academy of Preventive Medicine, 10409 Town
    and Country Way, Suite 200, Houston, Texas 77024.
National Association of Naturopathic Physicians, 2613 N.
    Stevens, Tacoma, WA 98407, (206) 752-2555.
National Health Federation, 211 W. Foothill Blvd., Mon-
    rovia, CA 91016, (213) 357-2181.
National Women's Health Network, 224 7th St. S.E.,
    Washington, DC 20003, (202) 543-9222.
Society for Clinical Ecology, 109 West Olive Street, Fort
    Collins, Colorado 80524. Allergy help.

Holistic Health Technology:
Duro-Test Corp., 2321 Kennedy Blvd., North Bergen, New
    Jersey 07047. Full spectrum natural lighting.
Flanagan Research Ltd., Box 686, Novato, CA 94948.

Holistic Lovemaking Book Publishers:
ACS Publications, P.O. Box 16430, San Diego, CA 92116.
Ash-Kar, P.O. Box 14547, San Francisco, California 94114.
Aurora Press, 205 Third Ave., 2A, NY, NY 10003.
Chin. Med. Cen., 230 S. Garfield, Monterey Park, CA 91754.
Dawn Horse, Box 3680, Clearlake Highlands, CA 95422.
Gentle Living, 2168 So. Lafayette St., Denver, CO 80210.
Health Research, Box 70, Mokelumne Hill, CA 95245.
Huna Int'l, 30725 Manzano Drive, Malibu, CA 90265.
I.D.H.H.B., Inc., Box 370, Nevada City, CA 95959.
Inner Light Fnd., P.O. Box 761, Novato, California 94948.
Inner Traditions Int'l, 377 Park Ave. So., N.Y., N.Y. 10016.
Llewellyn, P.O. Box 43383, St. Paul, Minnesota 55164.

Mho and Mho Works, Box 33135, San Diego, CA 92103.
Peak Skill, P.O. Box 5489, Playa Del Rey, CA 90296.
Quantum Assoc., 1664 3rd Ave., New York, N.Y. 10028.

Holistic Lovemaking Cassettes, Courses or Seminars:
The Academy of Oriental Heritage, P.O. Box 35057, Station
    "E", Vancouver, B.C., V6M 4G1 Canada.
Margo Anand, P.O. Box 350, Inverness, CA 94937.
Bindrim Ins., 2000 Cantata Dr., Hollywood, CA 90068.
Center for Social & Sensory Learning (See Sex Therapists.)
Dr. Stephen Chang, Tao Academy, 2700 Ocean Ave., San
    Francisco, CA 94132.
Master Mantak Chia, Healing Tao Center, 12 Bowery St.,
    3rd Floor, NY, NY 10013.
Lana Clark, Ph.D., P.O. Box 903, Larkspur, CA 94939.
A. DaPassano, T.E.S., 1020 South La Jolla, L.A., CA 90035.
Concept:Synergy, P.O. Box 159(M), Fairfax, CA 94930.
Helaine Harris, M.A., M.F.C.C., 6506 McLennan Ave., Van
    Nuys, CA 91406.
Inner Light Fnd., P.O. Box 761, Novato, CA 94948
I.D.H.H.B., P.O. Box 370, Nevada City, CA 95959.
Llewellyn, P.O. Box 43383, St. Paul, MN 55164.
The Mystic Trader, 238 West St., Annapolis, MD 21401.
Omega Project, Box 333, Loveland, Colorado 80537.
Peak Skill, P.O. Box 5489, Playa Del Rey, CA 90296.
Source Vacation/Retreats, 1307-E Buena Vista, Pacific
    Grove, CA 93950.
Elliot Jay Tanzer, P.O. Box 2534, Malibu, CA 90265.

Kundalini & Spiritual Crisis Counseling:
Kundalini is primal life force energy.
Stuart Sovatsky, Ph.D., The Kundalini Clinic, Oakland, CA.
    (415) 465-2986.
The Spiritual Emergency Network, c/o C.I.T.P., 250 Oak
    Grove Ave., Menlo Park, CA 94025, (415) 327-2776.

Meditation:
Community Meditation Center, 1041 So. Elden Ave., Los
    Angeles, CA 90006, (213) 384-7817.
Hanuman Tape Library, Box 61498, Santa Cruz, CA 95061.
Insight Meditation Society, Pleasant St., Barre, MA 01005
Justin Stone, P.O. Box 4383, Albuquerque, N.M. 87106.
Vipassana Medit. Ctr., Box 24, Shelburne Falls, MA 01370.

Relaxation & Sexual Self-Improvement Cassettes:
Effective Learning Systems, 6950 France Avenue South, Edina, MN 55435.

Llewellyn Publications, P.O. Box 43383, St. Paul, MN 55164.

Peak Skill Publishing, Box 5489, Playa Del Rey, CA 90296.

Potentials Unlimited, 4808-H Broadmoor, S.E., Grand Rapids, MI 49508.

Valley of the Sun Publishing, Box 2010, Malibu, CA 90265.

Ritual Skills:
E.S.P. Laboratory, Box 216, Edgewood, TX 75117.

Sex Accessories:
Evelyn Rainbird, Ltd., Box 6500, Englewood, NJ 07631.

Eve's Garden, #1406, 119 W. 57th Street, NY, NY 10019. Women's erotic products.

Xandria Collection, Box 31039, San Francisco, CA 94131.

Sex Therapists:
American Association of Sex Educators, Counselors and Therapists (AASECT), 11 Dupont Circle, N.W., Suite 220, Washington, DC 20036, (202) 462-1171.

Bryce Britton, M.S., Certified Sex Therapist, 4111 Lincoln Blvd., #631, Marina Del Rey, CA 90292.

Sexuality Seminars:
Alan Brauer, M.D., 525 University, Palo Alto, CA 94301.

Jack and Melanie Crocker, "Follow Your Heart" Seminar, Route 1, Box 144, Halfway, OR 97834.

Dianne Dunlap, M.A., M.F.C.T., Center For Social & Sensory Learning, P.O. Box 155, Tarzana, CA 91356.

National Sex Forum, 1523 Franklin St., San Francisco, CA 94109, (415) 928-1133.

Singles Networking:
Consort, P.O. Box 5489, Playa Del Rey, CA 90296.

Contact, P.O. Box 9248, Berkeley, CA 94709.

Thymus Gland & Health:
John Diamond, M.D., Institute of Behavioral Kinesiology, P.O. Drawer 37, Valley Cottage, New York 10989.

Jacquelyn McCandless, M.D., Calabasas, CA. Psychiatrist and sex therapist.

SELECTED BIBLIOGRAPHY

Ayres, Alex. "Running and sexuality." Running Times, April, 1984, 12-22.

Bethards, Betty. Sex and Psychic Energy: Beyond the Sexual Revolution. Novato, CA: Inner Light Fnd., 1977.

Bieler, Henry and Sarah Nichols. Dr. Bieler's Natural Way To Sexual Health, Los Angeles: Charles, 1972.

Bindrim, Paul and Helaine Harris. "The Ultimate Sexual Experience." Los Angeles: On-Site Taping, 1982.

Brauer, Alan and Donna. ESO. N.Y.: Warner, 1983.

Britton, Bryce. The Love Muscle. New York: New American Library, 1982.

Burton, Sir Richard, trans. The Kama Sutra of Vatsyayana. New York: E.P. Dutton, 1964.

_____, trans. The Perfumed Garden of the Shaykh Nefzawi. New York: G.P. Putnam's Sons, 1964.

_____ and F.F. Arbuthnot, trans. The Ananga Ranga of Kalyana Malla. New York: G.P. Putnam's Sons, 1964.

Bush, Patricia. Drugs, Alcohol & Sex. New York: Richard Marek, 1980.

Carter, Mildred. Helping Yourself With Foot Reflexology. West Nyack: Parker, 1969.

Castleman, Michael. Sexual Solutions: An Informative Guide. New York: Simon & Schuster, 1980.

Cerney, J.V. Acupuncture Without Needles. West Nyack: Parker, 1974.

Chang, Jolan. The Tao of Love and Sex: The Ancient Chinese Way to Ecstasy. New York: E.P. Dutton, 1977.

_____. The Tao of the Loving Couple. New York: E.P. Dutton, 1983.

Chang, Stephen with Richard Miller. The Book of Internal Exercises. San Francisco: Strawberry Hill Press, 1978.

Chia, Mantak. Awaken Healing Energy Through The Tao. New York: Aurora Press, 1983.

Comfort, Alex, trans. The Koka Shastra. New York: Stein and Day, 1965.

_____, ed. The Joy of Sex. N.Y.: Crown, 1972.

Cook, Keven. "The Brawning of America." Playboy, July, 1982, 146-150, 184-190.

Cutler, Winnifred. "Q&A interview: Researcher leads men and women through the menopause myths." Michael Fink, ed., Los Angeles Her. Exam., Oct. 18, 1983, B7.

Dass, Ravi and Aparna. The Marriage & Family Book: A Spiritual Guide. New York: Schocken, 1978.

Dean, Carole. "Bach Remedies: Secret Power of Plants." Whole Life Times, Jan/Feb, 1982, 49.

Denning, Melita and Osborne Phillips. The Llewellyn Practical Guide to The Magick of Sex. St. Paul: Llewellyn, 1982.

Diamond, John. Your Body Doesn't Lie. New York: Warner Books, 1979.

Douglas, Nik and Penny Slinger. Sexual Secrets: the alchemy of ecstasy. New York: Destiny Books, 1979.

Dunkell, Samuel. Lovelives: How We Make Love. New York: New American Library, 1980.

Ferguson, Marilyn, ed. "Endorphins trigger isolation-tank euphoria." Brain/Mind Bulletin, January 23, 1984, 1.

Flatto, Edwin. Warning: Sex May Be Hazardous to Your Health. New York: Arco, 1976.

Garrison, Omar. Tantra: the Yoga of Sex. New York: A-von Books, 1964/1973.

Gillies, Jerry. Transcendental Sex. New York: Holt, Rinehart and Winston, 1978.

G-Jo Institute. The G-Jo Insitute Sexual Pleasure Enhancement Program, 1980.

Gold, E.J. "Alchemical Sex." Canada: Fourth Way Research Associates, no date. Seven 60 minute audio cassettes.

_____ and Cybele. Beyond Sex. Nevada City, California: I.D.H.H.B. Inc./Hohm Press, 1978.

Gottlieb, Adam. Sex Drugs and Aphrodisiacs. Manhattan Beach: 20th Century Alchemist, 1974.

Gunther, Bernard. Energy Ecstasy and Your Seven Vital Chakras. L.A.: The Guild of Tutors/IC Books, 1978.

Haimes, Leonard and Richard Tyson. How To Triple Your Energy. New York: New American Library, 1977.

Hirsch, Edwin. The Power to Love. New York: Garden City Publishing Co., 1938.

Hollander, Xaviera. Xaviera's Supersex. New York: New American Library, 1978.

Holzer, Hans. Psycho-Ecstasy. New York: Lancer, 1971.

Ishihara, Akira and Howard Levy. The Tao of Sex. An Annotated Translation of the 28th Section of the Essence of Medical Prescription (Ishimpo). Yokohama: Shibundo, 1968.

Kassorla, Irene. Nice Girls Do. Rockville Centre: Playboy Paperbacks, 1982.

Keyes, Laurel Elizabeth. The Mystery of Sex: A Book About Love. Denver: Gentle Living Publications, 1975.

King, Serge. The Secret Science & Sex. Malibu, California: Huna International, 1982.

Kingsland, Kevin and Venika Kingsland. Complete Hatha Yoga. New York: Arco, 1983, Second Edition.

Kline-Graber Georgia and Benjamin Graber. Woman's Orgasm. New York: Popular Library, 1976.

Kuhn, Franz. Jou Pu Tuan. Franz Kuhn's interpretation in German of Li Yu's masterpiece translated by Richard Martin. New York: Grove Press, 1963.

Ladas, Alice, Whipple, Beverly and John Perry. The G Spot and Other Recent Discoveries About Human Sexuality. New York: Holt, Rinehart and Winston, 1982.

Leonard, George. The End of Sex: Erotic Love After the Sexual Revolution. Los Angeles: J.P. Tarcher, 1983.

Levine, Stephen. A Gradual Awakening. Garden City: Anchor Books, 1979.

Lloyd, J. William. The Karezza Method or Magnetation. Hollywood, California: Phoenix House, 1973.

McCary, James Leslie. McCary's Human Sexuality. New York: Van Nostrand Reinhold, 1978, third edition.

Maltz, Maxwell. Psycho-Cybernetics. N.Y.: Pocket, 1969.

Masters, William and Virginia Johnson. Human Sexual Response. Boston: Little, Brown and Co., 1966.

Meister, Robert. "Prolonging Pleasure--An Exotic Technique." Penthouse Forum, November, 1975.

Moffett, Robert. Tantric Sex. New York: Berkley Medallion, 1974.

Moore, Marcia and Mark Douglas. Diet, Sex and Yoga. York, Maine: Arcane, 1970.

Morgenstern, Michael with S. Naifeh and G. Smith. How To Make Love To A Woman. New York: Ballantine, 1983.

Motoyama, Hiroshi. Theories of the Chakras. Wheaton: The Theosophical Publishing House, 1981.

Mumford, Jonn. Psychosomatic Yoga. London: Thorsons, 1962.

_____. Sexual Occultism: The Sorcery of Love In Practice And Theory. Saint Paul: Llewellyn, 1975.

_____. Tantra Sexual Yoga Course. 28 cassette tapes. St. Paul, Minnesota: Llewellyn Publications, no date.

Namikoshi, Tokujiro. Shiatsu: Japanese Finger-Pressure Therapy. Tokyo: Japan, 1972.

Neff, Dio Urmilla. "Tantra: A Tradition Unveiled." Yoga Journal, February, 1983.

_____. "Tantra: A Tradition Unveiled Part II." Yoga Journal, April, 1983.

Nelson, Dee Jay and David Coville. Life Force in the Great Pyramids. Marina del Rey: DeVorss & Co., 1977.

Nobile, Phillip, ed. "Mysteries of Male Multiple Orgasm: Can A Man Learn To Double His Pleasure?" Forum, August, 1983.

_____. "The Forum Interview: Germaine Greer." Forum, April, 1984, 15-17, 70-72.

O'Relly, Edward. Sexercises. New York: Crown, 1967.

Osbourne, Arthur. The Collected Works of Sri Ramana Maharshi. York Beach: Samuel Weiser, 1968?.

Otto, Herbert and Roberta. Total Sex. New York: New American Library, 1972.

Pearson, Durk and Sandy Shaw. Life Extension: A Practical Scientific Approach. New York: Warner Books, 1982.

Penney, Alexandra. How To Make Love To A Man. New York: Dell, 1982.

_____. How To Make Love To Each Other. New York: G.P. Putnam's Sons, 1982.

Rajneesh, Bhagwan Shree. The Book of Secrets-I. Discourses on "Vigyana Bhairava Tantra". New York: Harper Colophon, 1977.

_____. The Book of Secrets-III. Discourses on "Vigyana Bhairava Tantra". New York: Harper Colophon, 1980.

Rama-Andre. Sexual Yoga. New York: Quantum, 1974.

Ramsdale, David A. "Tantra, the Ecstatic Discipline of Love." The L.A. Light Forum, Fall, 1982, 7.

Reagan, Harley Swiftdeer. The Whirlwind-Serpent Fire. Deer Tribe, 1983.

Reuben, Carolyn. "Sex and Your Health." L.A. Weekly, October 1-7, 1982, 34-35.

Reuben, David. Everything You Always Wanted To Know About Sex But Were Afraid To Ask. New York: Bantam, 1971.

Rosenberg, Jack. Total Orgasm. New York/Berkeley: Random House/Bookworks, 1973.

Sannella, Lee. Kundalini--Psychosis or Transcendence? San Francisco: Self-published, 1976.

Saraswati, Swami Janakananda. Yoga, Tantra and Meditation in Your Daily Life. New York: Ballantine, 1976.

Saraswati, Swami Satyananda. Meditations from the Tantras. Monghyr, India: Bihar School of Yoga, 1981.

SAR Guide for a Better Sex Life. San Francisco: National Sex Forum, 1975.

Schultz, William. Shiatsu Japanese Finger Pressure Therapy. New York: Bell, 1976.

Shapescope. "Lean, healthy, but not pregnant." Shape, October, 1982, 115.

Shivanandan, Mary. Natural Sex. New York: Berkley Books, 1981.

Smith, David. The East/West Exercise Book. New York: McGraw-Hill, 1976.

Smith, Howard. The Sensual Explorer. New York: G.P. Putnam's Sons, 1977.

Smith, Manuel. Kicking The Fear Habit. New York: The Dial Press, 1977.

Stockham, Alice B. Karezza: Ethics of Marriage. Mokelumne Hill, California: Health Research, no date.

Tannahill, Reay. Sex In History. New York: Stein and Day, 1980.

Thirleby, Ashley. Tantra: The Key to Sexual Power and Pleasure. New York: Dell, 1978.

Van Lysebeth, Andre. Pranayama: The Yoga of Breathing. London: Unwin, 1979.

von Urban, Rudolf. Sex Perfection & Marital Happiness. New York: Dial Press, 1949.

Walker, Morton and Joan. Sexual Nutrition. New York: Kensington, 1983.

Wander, Zev and David Radell. How Big is Big? New York: Warner Books, 1982.

Watts, Alan. Nature, Man and Woman. N.Y.: Vintage, 1970.

White, John, ed. Kundalini, Evolution and Enlightenment. Garden City: Anchor Books, 1979.

Woods, Margo. Masturbation, Tantra and Self Love. San Diego: Mho and Mho Works, 1981.

Zilbergeld, Bernie. Male Sexuality: A Guide to Sexual Fulfillent. New York: Bantam, 1978.

INDEX

PEAK SKILL

Here are some of the items we offer. Send for our FREE catalog today.

BOOKS

Sexual Energy Ecstasy. Unique, straightforward guide to the higher dimension of erotic love. $9.95.

The Quickest Way To Learn Astrology. Ideal for the beginner in astrology. This book describes an ingenious memory system that will enable you to learn the basics of astrology virtually overnight. Noel Tyl called it a "nifty idea . . . a good and innovative key-word concept." $3.00.

CASSETTE TAPES

All cassette tapes are full-length studio quality recordings.

From Sex To Reality: Explains the Tantric Sexual method for intentionally accelerating personal and spiritual growth. Demystifies the 5 steps beginning with sex and ending with perception of reality. $7.95.

Zen Sex I: Introduction to the approach of Zen Sex. Role of the mind. Beyond goals to the sensory moment. The approach of experiencing sex exactly as it is without thinking or interpretation. The way of the void.

Zen Sex II: Describes how to use the Zen of Sex principles and techniques while making love. The "Just Touch" technique for liberating the mind during lovemaking. Bliss and beyond to the no self.

The Zen Sex I and II tapes are sold only as a set. $15.00.

Your Relationship, Your Mirror: Offers innovative approach to the intimate relationship as a growth and awareness tool. Cycles. Transforming fear, pain, anger. Inner game of romance. Beyond soul mates. $7.95.

EVERYTHING YOU ALWAYS WANTED TO KNOW
ABOUT MYSTICAL SEX
BUT DIDN'T KNOW WHO TO ASK

Here is a unique opportunity to have a confidential and private consultation with an expert in sexual mysticism (co-author of Sexual Energy Ecstasy and Zen Sex workshop leader with 20 years of practice and research). Send your questions with a check or money order for $35. Questions can be personal, practical, technical, philosophical. You will receive your personalized consultation on cassette tape by mail. If possible, please provide specific personal details about your experiences, background and any other information that might be useful. Personal consultations via telephone or in person can be arranged.

ASTROLOGICAL RELATIONSHIP CONSULTATIONS

This is David's specialty as an astrologer. His chief goal is to help you use astrology as a mirror. He is very candid and direct. He will be honest with you about blind spots and inner blocks and tell you exactly what he sees.   Long and short term potential for sexual, emotional, financial and spiritual compatibility are looked at. You receive your birth charts and a chart comparison calculated with computer accuracy and a 60 minute cassette reading. Relationship interpretation: $75 in advance; $50 more for each additional comparison to the same person ordered at the same time. Please supply all the data requested on the order form. Include questions you want answered. Be specific. David also does individual astrological consultations. Individual birth chart with 60 minute reading on cassette: $75 in advance. Order one individual reading with a relationship comparison, the total is $125. Order two individual readings with a relationship comparison and pay only $165.

ASTROLOGY ORDER FORM

Name: _____

Address: _____

_____ ZIP:_____

BIRTH INFORMATION NEEDED FOR EACH CHART:

Name:

Birthplace:

Birth Date (Please give month, day and year):

Birth Time (Please specify a.m. or p.m.):

If you suspect the birth time is not precise, within how many minutes or hours would you say it is accurate?

Background Data (career, education, etc.) For newborn, give data on parents:

PLEASE COMPLETE SAME DATA ON ANOTHER PIECE OF PAPER FOR EACH CHART.

OPTION(S):

_____ Please compare my chart with (give names):

_____ Please prepare a birth chart interpretation for:

FEES: $75 in advance for one comparison; $50 more for each additional comparison to same person ordered now.
$75 in advance per birth chart interpretation.

PAYABLE TO: David A. Ramsdale, Astrology Dept., Peak Skill Publishing, Box 5489-M2, Playa Del Rey, CA 90296.

ORDER FORM (BOOKS & CASSETTES)

PEAK SKILL

Peak Skill Publishing
Post Office Box 5489-M2
Playa Del Rey, CA   90296-5489
Telephone (213) 306-6403

QTY.	DESCRIPTION	PRICE	AMOUNT
____	Sexual Energy Ecstasy	$9.95	_____
____	Learn Astrology Quick	$3.00	_____
____	From Sex To Reality	$7.95	_____
____	Zen Sex I and II	$15.00	_____
____	Relationship = Mirror	$7.95	_____
____	Personal Consultation	$35.00	_____

TOTAL FOR ITEMS IN THIS ORDER _____

CA RESIDENTS ONLY 6% SALES TAX _____

SUBTOTAL _____

SHIPPING CHARGE _____

ORDER TOTAL _____

I understand that I may return any item undamaged within
10 days for a complete refund of the purchase price.

Name: _____

Address: _____

_____ ZIP:_____

SHIPPING & HANDLING: $1.50 for first item. $.50
each additional item.